Neither Plain nor Simple

Neither Plain nor Simple

New Perspectives on the Canterbury Shakers

David R. Starbuck

University Press of New England

Hanover and London

University Press of New England, 37 Lafayette St., Lebanon, NH 03766

5 4 3 2 1

Library of Congress Cataloging-in-Publication Data
Starbuck, David R.
Neither plain nor simple : new perspectives on the Canterbury Shakers /
David R. Starbuck. — 1st ed.
p.   cm.
Includes bibliographical references and index.
ISBN 1–58465–210–1 (pbk. : alk. paper)
1. Shakers — New Hampshire — Canterbury. 2. Canterbury (N.H.) — Religious life and customs.
3. Excavations (Archaeology) — New Hampshire — Canterbury.
4. Canterbury (N.H.) — Antiquities. I. Title.
BX9768.C3S72 2004
289'.8'0974272 — dc22   2003020705

Frontispiece: Sisters Marguerite Frost and Edith Clark with their saxophones. Change
was constant for the Canterbury Shakers, even in their choice of musical instruments.
Courtesy Canterbury Shaker Village Archives, 10-P53.

Contents

Preface   vii

A Shaker Chronology   ix

Part I. History and Material Culture

Introduction. Twenty-Five Years of Shaker Archeology   3
      Sidebar: Archeology at Hancock Shaker Village   6

Chapter 1. A Traditional View of the Shaker Way of Life   13

Chapter 2. The Shaker Mill System   22

Chapter 3. The Shaker Dumps: Unearthing the Unexpected   45

Chapter 4. Blacksmithing and Pipe Smoking   68

Chapter 5. Some Final Thoughts   85

Part II. Surface Archeology: The Shaker Landscape

The Shaker Mapping Project   91

Further Reading   185

Index   189

Preface

This book is dedicated to the memory of the Shakers who made Canterbury Shaker Village their home from 1783 until 1992. I especially wish to acknowledge Eldress Bertha Lindsay, Eldress Gertrude Soule, and Sister Ethel Hudson, New Hampshire's last surviving Shakers when I first visited their community in 1977. I remember them with great fondness for opening up their home to outsiders—my students and me—so that we could document everything that had survived of their community. Eldress Gertrude nicknamed me "digger o' dell" (the undertaker) because she had never met an archeologist before, and she equated me with undertakers because we both like to dig! All three of Canterbury's last Shakers worked hard to make us feel welcome, and so what at first appeared to be a project of a few years' duration has now stretched out to twenty-five years.

I began to direct archeological research at Canterbury in 1978, under the sponsorship of Boston University, and later the project moved with me to the University of New Hampshire (1979–1982) and then to Rensselaer Polytechnic Institute (1982–1989). From 1993 until the present, my work at Shaker Village has been conducted under the auspices of Plymouth State College of the University System of New Hampshire, and Plymouth sponsored archeological field schools at the village in the summers of 1994 and 1996. I am indebted to my colleagues at Plymouth State for their help in continuing this research.

I would like to thank the New Hampshire Division of Historical Resources for encouraging this work from its inception, and especially Linda Ray Wilson, who phoned me at my office in Boston in February of 1977 and invited me to accompany her to Shaker Village so that I could meet the Shakers for the first time. Others in that office who have been immensely helpful over the years include Nancy Dutton, James Garvin, Gary Hume, and Christine Fonda. Julia Fifield, who long headed the State Historical Resources Council that oversees that office, has also been a wonderful source of encouragement.

I am equally indebted to the many staff members at Canterbury Shaker Village, both present and past, who have been extremely helpful in assisting this research. I owe a huge debt to the current staff of the village, especially to Scott T. Swank, director and president; Sheryl Hack, chief curator; Darryl Thompson, interpreter; Karen Redd, office manager; Glenda Yeaton, receptionist; Donavan Freeman, property manager; and Renee Fox, archivist. To this list I should add several former staff who have now moved on to other endeavors, and these include Mary Boswell, Charles "Bud" Thompson, Galen Beale, Sharon Rask, Roger Gibbs, Sarah Kinter, and the late Jack Auchmoody.

Between 1978 and 1982, I directed a series of summer field projects at Shaker Village that were funded by seven National Park Service Grants-in-Aid administered through the New Hampshire Division of Historical Resources. I would like to thank the project staff during that period, including my 1978 codirector, Margaret Supplee Smith, along with Penny Watson, Richard Borges, Ellen Savulis, Terry Kidder, Charles Harbage, Peer Kraft-Lund, Brian Powell, Emily Van Hazinga, George Van Hazinga, Elizabeth Solomon, Gina Campoli, Linda Trowbridge, Christopher Whalley, Bruce Fernald, Lynn Whitney, Robert Brown, Tom Keegan, Joan Lilly, Ann Marie Wagner, Anouk Markovits, and Jonathan Schechtman. It was Peer Kraft-Lund who completed the mapping of the surface of Shaker Village and Alec Nicholas, then with the New Hampshire Department of Resources and Economic Development, who drafted nearly all of the surface maps and archeological drawings that appear in this volume.

Since 1982, the archeological projects conducted at Canterbury Shaker Village have not been continuous, but we have tried to undertake archeology whenever possible. I would like to thank the participants and staff in the 1994 and 1996 field schools, including Merle Parsons, Elizabeth Hall, Gordon DeAngelo, Barbara DeAngelo, Paula Dennis, Gini Miettunen, Maureen Kennedy, Roland Smith, June Talley, Sherry Mahady, Louise Luchini, Cara Medyssey, Linda Fuerderer, Walter Ryan, Herman Brown, Bruce Batten, Joseph Champlin, Robert Clark, Silas Holmes, Marily Wilson, John Cerami, Steve Bradbury, and Herbert Swift.

In more recent years, Elizabeth Hall, Judy Balyeat, Roland Smith, and Linda Fuerderer helped in salvaging the Church Family blacksmith shop in 2000, and the Church Family cow barn ramp in 1998 and 2000. From 1996 until the present, Elizabeth Hall of Plymouth State College has spent an immense amount of time in the laboratory, processing and analyzing the artifacts from these most recent excavations. Assistance in identifying artifacts from the blacksmith shops, the cow barn ramp, and the site known as "Hog Heaven" was also given by William C. Ketchum, an expert in American material culture. Most of the photographs that appear in this volume were printed by Ed O'Dell of Lake George, New York.

I wish to thank Canterbury Shaker Village for giving me the opportunity to direct this research, and I also wish to thank Tim Meeh, Jill McCullough, Greg Meeh, and Hillary Nelson, owners of the land that once encompassed the Shaker North Family and West Family; and David Curtis, David Wyman, Midge Wyman, Dudley Laufman, and Jacqueline Laufman, owners of the land that formerly made up the Shaker Second Family. All of these property owners have been most generous in allowing us to map and/or excavate on their properties, and they have done much to make this a very pleasant experience.

September 2002   D.R.S.

A Shaker Chronology

1736	(February 29) Ann Lee is born in Toad Lane, Manchester, England.
1747	James and Jane Wardley leave the Quakers and form the Shaker faith.
1758	Ann Lee joins the Wardleys in their new society.
1762	Ann Lee marries Abraham Standerin, a blacksmith.
1770	Ann Lee becomes the leader of the Shakers and assumes the title of "Mother Ann."
1774	Mother Ann and a small group of followers travel to America.
1776	The first Shaker Village is formed in Niskeyuna (Watervliet), New York.
1784	Mother Ann dies in New York State and is succeeded by Father James Whittaker, who becomes head of the Shaker Society.
1787	New Lebanon Shaker Village is gathered and becomes the site of the Lead Ministry for the Shaker faith.
1792	The Church Family is gathered at Canterbury Shaker Village.
	Moses Johnson erects the first meetinghouse in Canterbury.
1793	The first dwelling house is erected in Canterbury.
	Enfield Shaker Village is gathered and joins with Canterbury to form the New Hampshire bishopric.
1797	Benjamin Whitcher, Israel Sanborn, and Chase Wiggin deed their farms to the Canterbury Shakers.
1800	The Second (Middle) Family is founded in Canterbury.
	Construction begins on Canterbury's mill system.
1801	The North Family is founded in Canterbury.
1806	The West Family is founded in Canterbury (a branch of the North Family).
1819	The West Family closes in Canterbury.
1821	The Shaker Central Ministry passes rules that become known as the Millennial Laws; these govern every aspect of the Shakers' lives.
1829	The garden seed industry begins in Canterbury.
1831	Nathaniel Hawthorne visits Canterbury.
1843	The first book is printed in Canterbury, the *Sacred Roll*.
1845	The Central Ministry passes additional Millennial Laws.
1846	The garden seed industry comes to an end in Canterbury.
1863	President Abraham Lincoln exempts the Shakers from fighting in the Civil War after a meeting with Canterbury trustee David Parker.
1882–1899	The monthly *Shaker Manifesto* is edited and printed in Canterbury.
1894	The North Family closes in Canterbury, and the surviving members move to the Second Family, which becomes known as the "Branch Family."
1916	The Second (or "Branch") Family closes in Canterbury.
1919	Elder Arthur Bruce of Canterbury is appointed lead minister of the Shaker faith.

1920	Canterbury sells its extensive herds of cattle.
1934	The Canterbury Shakers close their school.
1939	Irving Greenwood, the last New Hampshire brother, dies in Canterbury.
1957	The Lead Ministry of the Shakers moves to Canterbury.
1961	Elder Delmer Wilson, the last male Shaker, dies in Sabbathday Lake, Maine.
1965	The Lead Ministry votes not to accept any additional members (the Shaker covenant is closed).
1969	Canterbury becomes a nonprofit museum, "Canterbury Shaker Village, Inc."
1977	Canterbury Shaker Village hires its first professional museum director.
1978	Archeological research begins at Canterbury Shaker Village.
1988	Eldress Gertrude Soule dies in Canterbury.
1990	Eldress Bertha Lindsay, the last Shaker eldress, dies in Canterbury.
1992	Sister Ethel Hudson, the last New Hampshire Shaker, dies in Canterbury.
1993	Canterbury Shaker Village becomes a National Historic Landmark.

PART I

History and Material Culture

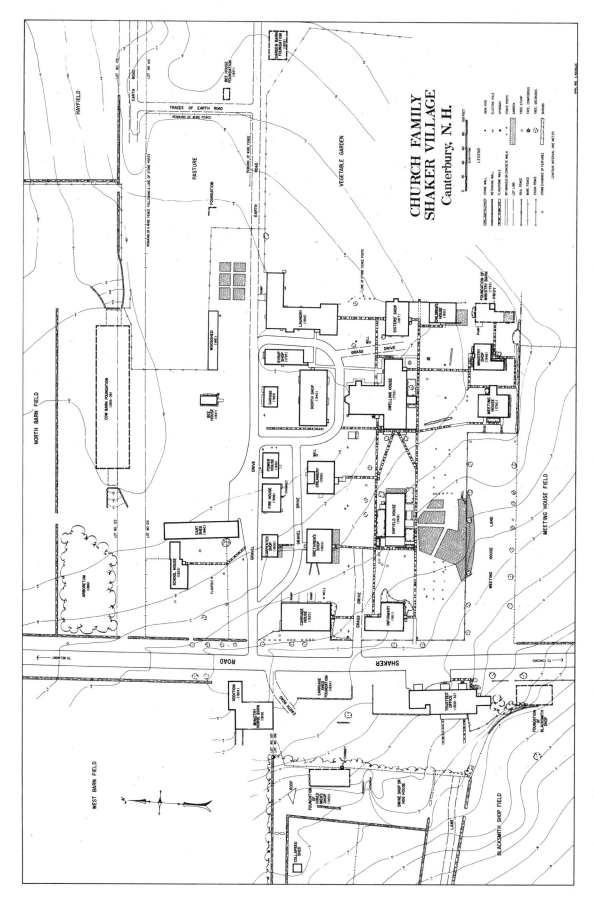

I-1. A plan view of the center of the Canterbury Church Family, drawn by Alec Nicholas in 1983.

Introduction:
Twenty-five Years of Shaker Archeology

Beginnings

I grew up in the Adirondack Mountains of New York State about seventy miles north of Watervliet, where Mother Ann Lee founded the first Shaker community in 1776. While I knew that Shakers had once lived in the Albany area, and that part of their village was now covered by the Albany Airport, I cannot claim to have known until 1977 that there were any other Shaker communities elsewhere in America. Before that time, my work as an archeologist had included research in central Mexico, at Native American sites in the northeastern United States, and at sites of early American industry. In the last case, I had just finished excavating Eli Whitney's gun factory in Hamden, Connecticut, and was in the process of digging the site of a 1780 glass factory in Temple, New Hampshire.

It was in early 1977 that I first learned of the existence of Canterbury Shaker Village, sited in an idyllic setting about twenty minutes northeast of Concord, New Hampshire (figure I-1). On a cold February day, I was asked to drive to Canterbury to meet Jack Auchmoody, whom the trustees of the village had just hired to become their first professional director. Jack had previously been a vice president at Old Sturbridge Village, and it had been arranged that Jack would escort a group of us from Boston University through the various Shaker buildings in order to view firsthand some of the conservation problems that had resulted from years of deferred maintenance. Our visit had been organized by Linda Ray Wilson, then the director of the New Hampshire State Historic Preservation Office. Linda was eager to see a systematic inventory prepared of all that survived at Shaker Village, both above- and belowground, and she wanted to make it easier for the village to apply for preservation-related grants. Our visit might also help to begin the process of long-term planning for the future of the community.

Our small group represented several departments and programs at Boston University, and collectively we worked with several different aspects of the historic preservation field. It was no doubt Linda's hope that we would see and want to assist with the standing water and ice in the cellars, the "rising damp" that was rotting many of the foundations, and the lack of professional staff that made it hard to effect some of the necessary changes from within. While the community was already termed a "museum," and offered some tours to visitors, it lacked the money to change quickly, and Linda hoped that we outsiders—and our students—might become a catalyst for much-needed change.

Bundled in our winter clothing, we toured the halls and cellars of several rather sad-looking buildings, asking questions and making a few suggestions about things we might do if ever given permission to conduct a field project. I will never forget how, in the frigid hallway of the first floor of the brethren's shop, Jack suddenly erupted and began shouting, "We can't afford to do any of these things! And you even want to do archeology here. What a waste!" The five of us all looked sheepishly at Linda, who calmly began to explain that we were not going to cost Shaker Village a cent, that grant money and students would enable us to do the historic structure reports, the archival research, the archeology, the mapping, the interviewing, and whatever else might be needed. Still, I'll admit to being nervous because it was *my* specialty, archeology, that had just been attacked!

We then crossed Shaker Road and entered the trust-

I-2. The Canterbury eldresses pose with the Boston University team in front of the Church Family trustees' office in 1978.

ees' office, where we were warmly greeted by Eldress Bertha Lindsay and Eldress Gertrude Soule, the last leaders of the entire Shaker faith (figure I-2). In many ways this was the high point of our visit because we knew that we couldn't proceed without their approval. Yet we belonged to the "World's People," outsiders from Boston who wanted to be granted access to every document, to every building, and to wander freely through the remains of 185 years of Shaker otherworldliness. Our very presence might permanently disrupt the lives of the last three Shakers who lived in Canterbury, including the third Shaker, Sister Ethel Hudson, who lived by herself in the 1793 dwelling house. But the Shakers would perhaps alter our lives just as profoundly, as we representatives of two quite different cultures sought to understand each other. I will admit that I have never so

wanted to be on my "best behavior" as we explained, cautiously, what we hoped to accomplish at the Shakers' home. Would we say something inadvertently that would be taken as rude, insensitive, or pushy, and would we forever be blocked from this exciting research opportunity? Would the Shakers accept us in spite of our secular ways and welcome us into their home?

The beginning of anthropological fieldwork can often be traumatic, and I am reminded of Napoleon Chagnon's description in *Yanomamo: The Fierce People* of what it was like to conduct research among the Yanomamo Indians of Brazil and Venezuela. On his very first day in the field Chagnon mused, "Would they like me? This was important to me; I wanted them to be so fond of me that they would adopt me into their kinship system and way of life." We may have felt a little bit like Chagnon, but our fears were unfounded, for the Shaker eldresses were unbelievably gracious and patient. True, on a superficial level their clothes were different from ours—they wore the traditional Shaker bonnets and long, modest, flower-print dresses—and their speech was often sprinkled with "yeas" and "nays." But at a more meaningful level, the eldresses conveyed the most profound sense of calm and dignity. It could have been rather unnerving to be in the presence of individuals who were so deeply spiritual. After all, I did not want to offend them and did not know whether it was acceptable to joke or banter in the same way that I might with other strangers at a first meeting. Needless to say, the Canterbury Shakers proved to be far more wonderful, and kindhearted, than I ever could have hoped for. It was their willingness to accept us into their midst that prompted what has now become twenty-five years of scholarship at Canterbury Shaker Village.

Archeological Approaches to the Shakers

Most of the archeological projects conducted at other Shaker Villages have been the result of cultural resource management surveys, typically to mitigate the impact of utility lines that have threatened the integrity of archeological sites. Studies of this type have been conducted at the Shaker Villages located in Watervliet, New York, New Lebanon, New York, Hancock, Massachusetts, Enfield, Connecticut, Sabbathday Lake, Maine, North Union, Ohio, South Union, Kentucky, and elsewhere. These projects are becoming more frequent because most of the Shaker Villages are now faced with modern development, or "progress," and many communities are losing their rural character.

However, the first intensive, research-driven excavation at a Shaker Village commenced in 1975 with the work of Donald Janzen of Centre College of Kentucky at Shakertown at Pleasant Hill, Kentucky. Over the next several years, Janzen excavated the gristmill on Shawnee Run, with an eye to the eventual rebuilding of the original 1805 Shaker settlement on that stream. More recently, Kim McBride of the Kentucky Archaeological Survey has excavated numerous sites at Pleasant Hill with summer field schools, and she discovered the outdoor worship area at that village in 1997.

Soon after Janzen began his excavation in Kentucky, I commenced my own survey at Canterbury Shaker Village in New Hampshire, where work has continued until the present day. I also spent 1983 and 1984 digging at Hancock Shaker Village in western Massachusetts, where some of my graduate students from Rensselaer Polytechnic Institute (RPI) excavated the North Family mill system and the Church Family slaughterhouse (see the sidebar). This work had been requested by Hancock's departing director, John Ott, and the sites selected tied in well with the industrial archeology focus at RPI.

Other research projects have included periodic fieldwork since 1985 at Mount Lebanon Shaker Village in eastern New York, both by Ernest Wiegand of Norwalk Community College and Michael Coe of Yale University. The Mount Lebanon effort has included excavations at foundations and dump sites, but perhaps the most interesting accomplishment by Coe and Wiegand has been to record the Shaker graffiti on the walls of some of the buildings. Just as important has been the work by Leon Cranmer and crews from the Maine Historic Preservation Commission at sites created by all three Shaker families in Sabbathday Lake, Maine, where two of the families survive today only as archeological sites.

Each of these projects has been descriptive, and none has sought to use archeology to challenge existing paradigms about the nature of Shaker society. Perhaps the only different approach has been that of Mark Leone, who visited Shakertown at Pleasant Hill in 1980 and subsequently recorded his perceptions as an anthropologist. For Leone, "Once an archaeologist, who was a materialist, looked through the fragmentary picture of Shaker life presented today and realized the absence of a subsistence base, he would excavate the remains of the means of production." Leone raised interesting questions about how the Shakers responded to the rise of industrialization, but his view of the Shakers was quite traditional, essentially frozen somewhere in the nineteenth century. Without actually conducting archeology, it was impossible for him to judge the degree to which the Shakers have constantly changed over two-hundred-plus years and become increasingly like the rest of American society. Yet archeology is uniquely suited to examining the processes of change, and what Shaker research has taught me is that no one can dig at a Shaker Village and ever again accept the myth of a static, idealized way of life that was immune to worldly pressures.

The Canterbury Shakers: The Early Research

Canterbury Shaker Village has seen more archeological research than any other Shaker community. The Canter-

Hancock Shaker Village stretches along both sides of Route 20 just west of Pittsfield, Massachusetts. Set in the beautiful Berkshires, Hancock was home to a community of Shakers from 1790 until the community's final closing in 1960. Today it operates as a nonprofit museum village with about twenty buildings and numerous special events throughout the year. Although no Shakers live there today, the setting at Hancock continues to be one of warmth and tranquillity.

In 1983, when I was a professor at Rensselaer Polytechnic Institute (RPI), I directed excavations at several house and mill foundations at Hancock's North Family. Throughout much of the nineteenth century a series of mills were located there along-side a stream, and two dams controlled the flow of water into turbines inside the mills. Eventually all of the North Family buildings either burned or were taken down by the Shakers, and few histori-cal records have survived. The staff of the modern museum were eager to see this industrial complex mapped and interpreted, and they asked me and several of my RPI graduate students to excavate the remains of a North Family sawmill, a carding (woolen) mill, and a large dwelling house. At the same time, we mapped the entire mill system in order to understand how the system had been modified and improved over time.

While we were exploring Hancock's industrial component, we also excavated inside the founda-tion from a garden seed shop in the Church Fam-ily, on the northern edge of Route 20. The struc-ture had been removed in 1905, and we found that its foundation contained practically a solid mass of domestic refuse. It appeared that bushel baskets had been filled with glass bottles, highly decorated ceramics of many types (chiefly whiteware), bones, nails, kitchen utensils, and more. These definitely had the appearance of having been stacked up inside the foundation. Clearly in Hancock, as in Canterbury, large-scale communal dumping into cellar holes was commonplace after buildings had been removed.

We also found many fragments from dolls,

The excavation of the fireplace base inside the North Family dwelling house at Hancock Shaker Village.

which had probably been kept for the amusement of the children who were being raised by the Shak-ers. While popular belief holds that the Shakers were a spartan, otherworldly group, their bright and decorative ceramics at Hancock began to sug-gest to us that the Shakers were fully able to ap-preciate the products of the outside world.

During the following summer, in 1984, another one of my graduate students at RPI, Jeffrey Owen Keatley, conducted an excavation at the site of a slaughterhouse located in the Church Family next to Hancock's famous round barn. Evidence of slaughtering animals was uncovered in the sheet refuse, along with insights into the methodology of Shaker slaughtering practices. Keatley chiefly found cow bones, although there were bones from at least two sheep, and all of the bones were from the nonmeaty parts of the body—mandibles, teeth, a hyoid bone, carpals and tarsals, metacarpals and metatarsals, phalanges, and sesamoid bones. The majority of the cows had been at least 1.5 to 2.5 years of age when they were slaughtered. Not un-expectedly, no pig bones were discovered. It was curious that the Shakers had made no effort to bury these butchered bones in pits out of sight—the bones had been left on the surface of the ground and were now just slightly below the surface.

bury project began in 1978 with a thorough assessment of the Shaker-built environment, and this resulted in the mapping of about 600 acres of the surface of Canterbury Shaker Village between 1978 and 1982 (figures I-3, I-4). We drew sixty-one base maps, each representing an area of 200 × 200 meters, and we also prepared dozens of measured drawings of foundations and mill features (chapter 2). To accompany the maps, we wrote several hundred archeological site reports describing the history and present condition of every field, dump, foundation, wall, path, and orchard within the community. These maps, drawings, and site reports became the first really comprehensive look at both the built and natural environment of any Shaker Village, and this aboveground study—with much updating—forms part II of *Neither Plain nor Simple*. Other students prepared historic structure reports for the twenty-four still-standing Shaker buildings in the Church Family, together with measured drawings tracing the historical development of each building. We also prepared drawings to the standards of the Historic American Buildings Survey (HABS) for the meetinghouse, schoolhouse (figure I-5), and dwelling house.

Our research in the Shaker archives allowed us to inventory hundreds of documents and thousands of photographs, and I was fortunate to be able to conduct many interviews with Eldress Bertha Lindsay, Eldress Gertrude Soule, and Sister Ethel Hudson. The interviewing did not go exactly as planned, however, even though the Shakers had agreed in advance to be interviewed. A graduate student had been hired for that purpose, but when we arrived in 1978 to commence our research, we discovered that a staff member at Shaker Village had convinced the Shakers to "interview themselves"; they had been told not to allow outsiders to do this. All interviews thus had to be less formal and usually consisted of me chatting with the Shakers and then running for my notepad as soon as each conversation was over.

Our graduate student, Emily Van Hazinga, instead undertook the equally-important task of preparing a comprehensive card file for every Shaker who had ever lived in Canterbury. This eventually grew into the Ph.D. dissertation of Richard Borges, who was in the History Department at the University of New Hampshire. Borges successfully completed an exhaustive computer analysis of dates of birth and death, admission and departure, offices held, prior religion, town of origin, Shaker family resided in, occupations, and more for every Canterbury Shaker.

Our grant funding was available chiefly for aboveground recording and rarely for excavations, except when a site was threatened or when architectural details needed to be exposed to complete a map. Still, from the beginning there was endless speculation as to what types of unexpected artifacts or "contraband" might be found if excavations were conducted in the Shaker dumps or in the nicely manicured lawns behind the village's communal dwellings. Unfortunately, as the years went on, this line of inquiry received little attention, partially because of lack of funding for "pure" research but also because we were frequently reminded by promoters of the Shaker experience that it would not be good to portray the Shakers in a less than positive light. In addition, it had become difficult to be fully objective or critical about Canterbury Shaker Village, because some of its members were still alive, and we archeologists did not want to take advantage of the trust we had been given.

The last Canterbury Shakers were kindly and generous, told jokes and other amusing stories, often treated me and other visitors and staff to lunch, and did everything possible to make us feel at home with them. It would prove nearly impossible to repay their kindness by using archeology to show that the Shaker world was not always perfect! Every scholar who knew the New Hampshire Shakers wanted to protect them, not to criticize them, and no one wanted to be the first to question Shaker behavior in print or to examine the possible contradictions between the Shakers' laws and their actual behavior. The humanity of the last Canterbury Shakers was a delight to watch, and I will never forget the day when Eldress Gertrude told me that *Wall Street Week in Review* was her favorite television show because Louis Rukeyser was "so handsome!"

A New Paradigm Takes Shape

With the passing of Sister Ethel Hudson in 1992, it became increasingly clear that archeology was one of the few ways to add some new insights to the story of the Canterbury Shakers. More important, it was obvious that Canterbury Shaker Village represented an unparalleled opportunity to use archeology as a cross-check on surviving nineteenth-century historical records and visitors' accounts. The Canterbury Shakers constitute one of the very best test cases for historical archeology precisely because they were a society that tightly controlled their internal descriptions of themselves, suggesting that

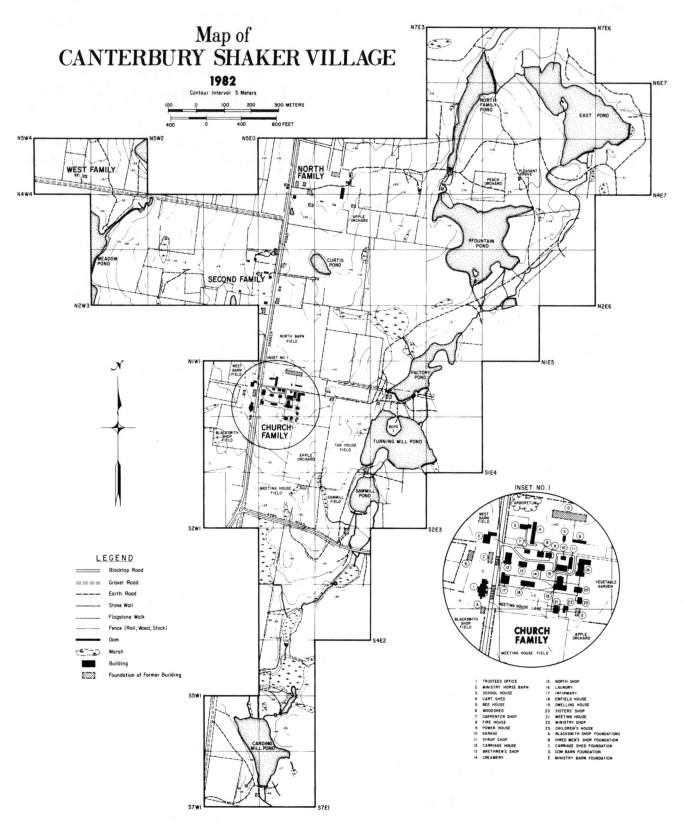

Map of CANTERBURY SHAKER VILLAGE
1982
Contour Interval 5 Meters

INSET NO. 1

1. TRUSTEES OFFICE
2. MINISTRY HORSE BARN
3. SCHOOL HOUSE
4. CART SHED
5. BEE HOUSE
6. WOODSHED
7. CARPENTER SHOP
8. FIRE HOUSE
9. POWER HOUSE
10. GARAGE
11. SYRUP SHOP
12. CARRIAGE HOUSE
13. BRETHREN'S SHOP
14. CREAMERY
15. NORTH SHOP
16. LAUNDRY
17. INFIRMARY
18. ENFIELD HOUSE
19. DWELLING HOUSE
20. SISTERS' SHOP
21. MEETING HOUSE
22. MINISTRY SHOP
23. CHILDREN'S HOUSE
A. BLACKSMITH SHOP FOUNDATIONS
B. HIRED MEN'S SHOP FOUNDATION
C. CARRIAGE SHED FOUNDATION
D. COW BARN FOUNDATION
E. MINISTRY BARN FOUNDATION

LEGEND

Blacktop Road
Gravel Road
Earth Road
Stone Wall
Flagstone Walk
Fence (Rail, Wood, Stock)
Dam
Marsh
Building
Foundation of Former Building

I-3. The final Canterbury map, prepared by combining 61 individual base maps, each representing a block of 200 × 200 meters. This shows the present (1982) surface of Canterbury Shaker Village and includes the locations of the Church, Second, North, and West Families. (The center of the Church Family has been enlarged so as to show the Shaker buildings that still stand today.) The Shaker mill system runs from northeast to southwest along the east side of the village. Not shown is the "Long Ditch," which began about 2 miles to the north and supplied water into the northern end of North Family Pond.

historical documents might be less than forthcoming. Personal diaries were all destroyed by the Shakers, and the more official records that have survived describe such practical matters as repairs to buildings, journeys taken, deaths, purchases, and the names of visitors. The Church Family records do not describe individual preferences or feelings, nor do they contain value judgments about fellow Shakers—even those who had left the community—nor about the World's People. Also, the more recent literature that has been created about the Shakers, idealizing their way of life, and the many Shaker laws describing *exactly* what they were not allowed to do or consume absolutely invite scholarly investigation. This, of course, is patterning that archeologists can easily investigate using the Shakers' extensive material culture. Because we know what the Shakers expected of themselves, we can use excavations to determine whether they actually lived up to their own ideals, certainly a difficult challenge within *any* culture.

When work began on the Canterbury Shakers in the 1970s, the scale of our digging was quite small, so we found very little evidence of contradictions between Shaker law and actual practice. We did find the stems from two red clay tobacco pipes in a cellar hole at the West Family in 1979 (figures I-6, I-7), but that was a part of the community that had been abandoned by 1819, when tobacco was still popular and acceptable. It was not until 1994, when we excavated a garden barn foundation that had been filled in during the first half of the twentieth century, that we better understood how archeology might alter our perceptions of the Shakers. The findings included a whiskey bottle, perfume bottles, a wealth of manufactured items that had all come from the outside world, and even a can of Welch's grape juice concentrate.

We have excavated several other dumps since then (chapter 3), discovering that very little was manufactured by the Canterbury Shakers after the early 1900s, other than "fancywork" (containers, boxes, and needlework) that was sold by the thousands to the World's People. Instead, archeology is demonstrating unambiguously that the Shakers were long part of the world economy: The contents of their dumps suggest that the Shakers' garbage was little different from anyone else's garbage.

Much larger excavations into dumps began in 1996, when an Intermodal Surface Transportation Enhancement Act (ISTEA) grant was awarded to Shaker Village that allowed us to dig several previously untouched

I-4. A member of the survey team, Elizabeth Solomon, mapping a penstock as it runs through the North Family turning mill foundation in 1980.

foundations and dumps. One example was the blacksmith shop foundation at the Canterbury Second Family, where we discovered thousands of pipe wasters (chapter 4). This was the very first evidence that the Canterbury Shakers had been manufacturing red earthenware tobacco pipes for sale to the World's People, a fact that had never been mentioned in the village's historical journals.

Another foundation discovered in 1996 was the Shakers' hog house, filled with tens of thousands of artifacts dating to the late 1800s and finally abandoned and filled circa 1905 (chapter 3). I gave the site a somewhat irreverent name, Hog Heaven, partially because it had been a hog house but also because it was discovered at a religious community that was intended to be heaven on earth. It also contained a "heavenly" assortment of ceramics and glass bottles, two categories of artifacts that had not been well represented in the collections of the museum village.

Next, in 1998 and 2000, we excavated a dump at the east end of the Church Family cow barn, discovering nearly one hundred stoneware bottles for beer or ginger beer, as well as whiskey flasks, perfume bottles, and even false teeth. We excavated only a tiny portion of the dump, and it appears that the entire barn ramp is composed of artifact-laden fill (chapter 3).

Most recently, in the summer of 2000, I directed an intensive salvage effort at the foundation and dump of the 1811 Church Family blacksmith shop, the largest of the Canterbury blacksmith shops. The shop building had been removed in 1952, and its foundation still contains the base of the original 1811–1849 brick forge. However, its adjacent dump contains immense quantities of industrial and domestic artifacts that date principally to the years between 1820 and 1860. These include plain and transfer-printed whitewares, stoneware beer or ginger beer bottles, wine or cider bottles, nine "TD" pipe

bowls, and dozens of other redware and white clay pipes (chapter 4).

Contradictions and Interpretations

The artifact record presented in part I of *Neither Plain nor Simple* is beginning to tell a story about the Canterbury Shakers that is more complex than I had previously imagined. During the early years of our research, my students and I documented the Shaker-modified landscape in a value-neutral way, even as we admired the care and craftsmanship that the Shakers had put into their natural and built environments. But as our mapping has been replaced by excavations, we have increasingly been sur-

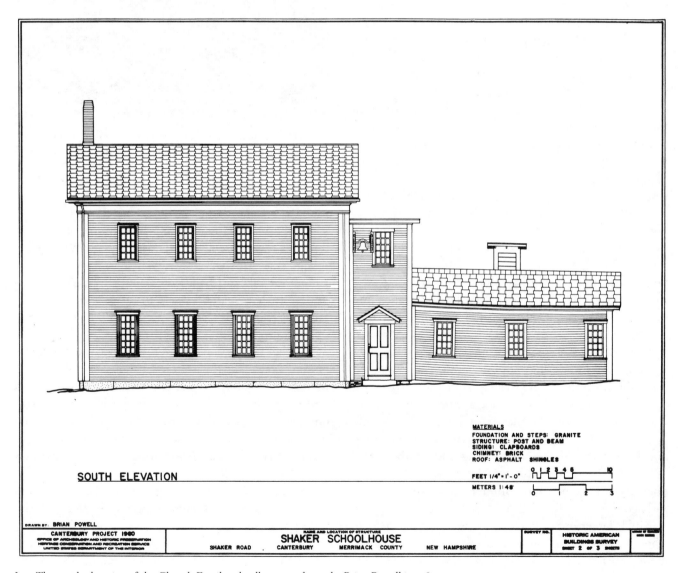

I-5. The south elevation of the Church Family schoolhouse as drawn by Brian Powell in 1980.

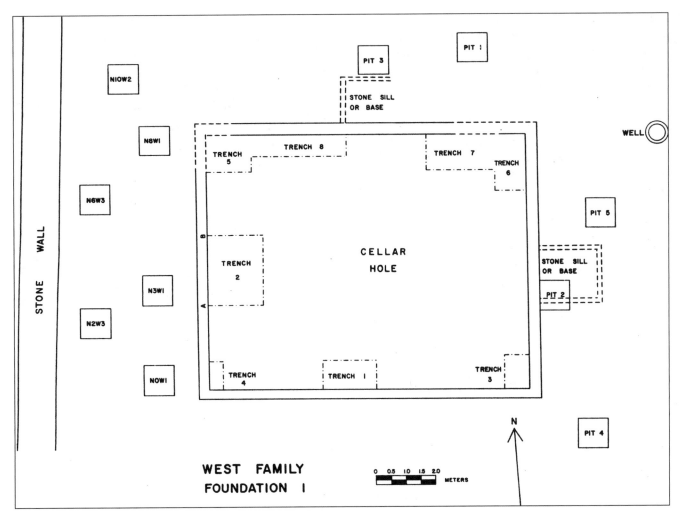

I-6. A plan view of a cellar hole excavated at the Canterbury West Family in 1979.

prised, even astonished, by the many types of material culture that were accepted into the Canterbury Shaker community after the middle of the nineteenth century. In fact, for roughly two-thirds of their existence the Shakers embraced, and could afford, the same consumer items that were enjoyed by the World's People.

It is always exciting to find something that is unexpected, and I believe that this new image of the Canterbury Shakers as consumers of mass culture is a far more accurate picture than has been portrayed by many of the popularizers and interpreters of Shaker life. The degree to which we have been shocked, amused, and ultimately satisfied with our archeological findings may reflect the extent to which we had been overwhelmed with too many stories of hundreds of Shaker inventions, otherworldliness, and the pursuit of perfection. These are certainly admirable goals within any community, but

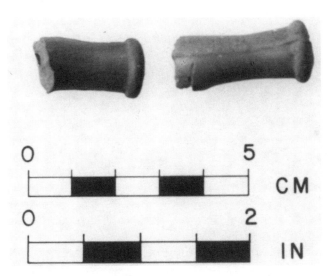

I-7. Fragments of two red earthenware tobacco pipes excavated at the West Family in 1979.

archeology suggests that we might just as easily want to emphasize the similarities between the Shakers and ourselves; after all, it appears that the Shakers often shopped and consumed just like the rest of us. Hopefully, in demonstrating this paradox within a religious community, *Neither Plain nor Simple* will help to reveal some of the contradictions and conflictedness that existed within the Shaker way of life. Archeological findings suggest a society that was more technologically sophisticated and aware of the world around them than many writers would lead us to believe. I would suggest that this is a much-needed counter to those authors who are unwilling to examine the Shakers with the same critical eye that we automatically use when studying other types of communities. But while the Canterbury Shakers were often very much like the outside world, they were able to combine an appreciation of the "good things" in life with their more fundamental desire to serve God. I believe that their overall success in integrating spiritual with material needs was one of the key factors that enabled the Canterbury Shakers to live a long and prosperous existence as an alternative style of community.

Chapter One

A Traditional View of the Shaker Way of Life

The Shaker Faith

In 1747 the Shaker faith began as a Christian religious movement in Manchester, England, under the leadership of two Quakers, James and Jane Wardley. While the name Shakers is said to be a contraction of "shaking Quakers," reflecting the ecstatic dancing or "laboring" of members during worship, the complete and proper name for this communal society has always been The United Society of Believers in Christ's Second Appearing (figure 1-1). Shaker religious beliefs included the controversial tenet that Ann Lee, the young Manchester woman who became their charismatic leader and prophetess in 1770, was in fact the second appearing of the Christ spirit and the firstborn of the new creation. Thus for the Shakers, Christ appeared first in the person of Jesus, representing the male, and later in the person of Ann Lee, representing the female element in God. Mother Ann, as she came to be known, experienced a series of revelations and visions she believed came from God, and she became a symbol and model for the humble and chaste style of life that was expected of all other Shakers.

While the Shakers did not accept the doctrine of the Trinity, and did not worship either Jesus or Ann Lee, they nevertheless saw the establishment of their church as marking the beginning of Christ's kingdom on earth. The Shakers viewed themselves, the "Inner" or "Gospel Order," as representing the true Church, characterized by the common ownership of property, celibacy, a policy of nonresistance, and separate government. By eliminating sex and natal ties, the Shakers sought to move ever closer to a state of grace and purity, arguing that only he who leads a sinless life is a true servant of God.

Just seven Shaker believers, led by Mother Ann, emigrated from England to America in 1774, and they formed their first communal village in Niskeyuna (Watervliet), New York, in 1776. Although Mother Ann died in September of 1784, her followers went on to establish a total of nineteen small, utopian communities in the states of New York, Massachusetts, New Hampshire, Maine, Connecticut, Ohio, Indiana, Kentucky, Georgia, and Florida. Some of these villages were extremely short-lived, yet seventeen of them lasted into the twentieth century. Shakerism initially took root during a period when waves of religious fervor often swept the American colonies, plucking members from more traditional church congregations. As converts established new Shaker Villages, they came from a variety of urban and rural settings, reflecting a diversity of religious and ethnic backgrounds. Shakerism attempted an equality between men and women, and the tasks performed by the sisters or brothers were not defined as interchangeable. Each sex typically ate at separate tables, worked in separate buildings, were not allowed to touch members of the other sex or give them gifts or speak with them in private, and men and women even entered rooms through separate doorways. While individualism was thus reduced, life in a Shaker community provided a measure of protection during sickness, infirmity, and old age.

In order to achieve an idealized society, the Shakers lived communally in relative isolation from the outside world, and as Shaker believers sought to achieve Mother Ann's level of holiness, they practiced celibacy so as not to be distracted by worldly concerns. After all, for the Shakers, marriage represented a lower order of society. One's primary devotion was thus to God, rather than to family, and outsiders were referred to as "the World's

1-1. Shaker sisters gathered in front of the Church Family trustees' office, which also functioned as the "E. Canterbury, N.H., Post Office," ca. 1914. Courtesy of Canterbury Shaker Village Archives.

People." The requirement of celibacy necessitated that new members had to be received from the outside world and then educated in appropriate Shaker behavior. After the initial years of village formation in the late eighteenth century, when whole families often joined at once, most later recruits typically arrived as orphans and subsequently chose to become members when they reached adulthood at the age of twenty-one (figure 1-2). Children who lived with the Shakers were provided with clothing, food, and formal education, and each received training in the manual occupation or business that seemed best suited to that particular child. Not all decided to remain, however, and the Shakers were remarkably flexible in allowing individuals to leave if they decided that the Shaker way of life was not for them.

As the Shakers organized themselves into relatively self-sufficient villages, each of these, in turn, was subdivided into "families" that consisted of a well-defined hierarchy of brothers and sisters, more powerful deacons and deaconesses, trustees (responsible for business deal-

ings with the outside world), and elders and eldresses, who were the ultimate religious and secular authorities. While brothers and sisters were the most numerous and performed most of the work in a Shaker community, they were assisted by dozens of boys and girls who were not yet old enough to have become Shakers. Each Shaker family averaged between 50 and 100 members, and each Shaker Village had between 200 and 1,000 occupants.

At their peak in the early and mid–nineteenth century, all of the Shaker Villages combined never had more than about 5,000 members, and a slow decline set in after about 1850. It is sometimes said that it may have become harder to maintain the religious zeal that had marked the early years, and the growing industrialization of America was certainly providing more work opportunities for women. Most of the Shaker communities closed in the early twentieth century, and after that it became impossible for the few that remained open to obtain orphans as state governments established their own orphanages. In 1965 the Lead Ministry of the Shaker Society, composed of the final three Shaker eldresses, voted to accept no more converts into their faith, a difficult decision necessitated by several factors: the passing of the last Shaker brother, Delmer Wilson, in 1961, such that it was no longer possible for a mature Shaker male to teach new male converts; the creation of a sizable trust fund that the Shakers' lawyers sought to protect from new converts who might have a mercenary interest in becoming Shakers; and the fear that new members with alternative lifestyles might change the Shaker legacy in ways that would be detrimental to two hundred years of Shaker tradition.

Of the three Shaker Villages that survived into the late twentieth century, Hancock Shaker Village in western Massachusetts became a museum in 1960, Canterbury Shaker Village in central New Hampshire saw the passing of its last Shaker sister in 1992, and now only Sabbathday Lake in New Gloucester, Maine, still has an active Shaker community. While the end of Shakerism thus appears to be near, there are numerous daybooks, church and historical records, maps, school records, and so forth that have survived at many of the Shaker Villages; there are a great many Shaker archeological sites and standing buildings; and there is a vast literature prepared by hundreds of non-Shakers who wrote down their observations as they visited Shaker Villages. There is, however, one type of historical record that typically has not survived: the diaries of individual Shakers.

1-2. Canterbury Sisters Marguerite Frost (1892–1971, *left rear*) and Bertha Lindsay (1897–1990, *right rear*) supervising a group of girls. Courtesy of Canterbury Shaker Village Archives.

Diaries were systematically destroyed when each Shaker died because those who lived after them considered diaries to be too personal for others to read (Eldress Bertha Lindsay, personal communication, 1984). And, perhaps, there was the risk that diaries might have revealed individual beliefs or opinions.

While the Shakers have chosen to live apart from America's mainstream culture, there is no denying that they have been generally well tolerated and often admired by the World's People, who have come to accept them as what is now considered to have been America's most successful experiment in communal living. Unlike other communal societies and such alternative societies as the Amish and the Mennonites, the Shakers have been extremely progressive in their attitudes toward technology. Given their music, crafts, literature, beliefs, and inventions, the impact of the Shakers upon American life has been considerable. After all, even though the Shakers have espoused a set of religious beliefs somewhat different from those of other Christian sects, they are nevertheless very much a product of British/American culture, and they have given back to that culture in countless ways.

While the beliefs and practices of the Shakers are

well documented, it may be argued that the nature of scholarship over the course of the twentieth century sometimes made it difficult to develop an objective understanding of the Shakers. This is because a host of observers and Shaker authors increasingly dictated exactly how they wanted the world to view the Shakers. This began with the pioneering books of Edward and Faith Andrews, who wrote about Shaker furniture, crafts, and religion from the 1930s through the 1970s. Most modern authors have repeated the conclusions drawn by the Andrewses, presenting an idealized look at Shaker life without themselves delving very deeply into the primary literature. All too often this has resulted in what is now a vast body of platonic imagery, nostalgia, and craft reproductions that have become the basis for modern interpretations of Shaker life.

Promoting Shakerism as an ideal way of life has, in some cases, become a twentieth-century industry shaped by authors who yearn for a simpler, golden age when everyone was deeply spiritual and creative, shunning materialism, and when a communal existence assured that everyone would be well taken care of. This model of reality may be compared to the efforts by early explorers and anthropologists to discover simpler cultures that had not yet been corrupted by the modern Western world. Contributing to the image of Shaker plainness and morality are the craftspeople who sell Shaker reproduction boxes, baskets, chairs, and tables; the collectors and investors who sell their original Shaker antiques for many thousands of dollars at auction; and the Shaker museum villages that greet many thousands of visitors each summer, presenting them with a warm and inviting look at an earlier rural America, occupied by a people who had no vices, where everyone worked well together, and where there was no alcohol, no tobacco, and no sex.

Anyone who has listened to a tour guide at a Shaker museum village knows the familiar litany—the Shakers made everything they needed themselves (unless they could purchase comparable items more cheaply from the outside world); they never turned anyone away from the door; they had schools that were the envy of their neighbors; and they made the very finest boxes, chairs, buildings, et cetera. This inspirational message further states that the Shakers were the brilliant inventors of the flat broom, the circular saw, and a hundred other inventions, and that the Shakers also raised the finest cattle

and maintained the best orchards. In other words, the Shakers had achieved a level of perfection that the outside world could only dream about, but which may now be witnessed by visiting one or more of the restored Shaker communities. It might be said that this image of Shakerism, now largely controlled by non-Shakers, has become a marketing phenomenon.

The Canterbury Shakers

Although some of the early Shaker communities closed after just a few months, Canterbury Shaker Village (figure 1-3) became one of the most long-lived and ultimately one of the most influential Shaker Villages of the twentieth century. Its origins, though, date to 1782, when the first Shaker missionaries to visit New Hampshire, Israel Chauncey and Ebenezer Cooley, began preaching in the nearby town of Loudon. Ten years later, one of their converts, Benjamin Whitcher, invited believers to join him in communal living on his 100-acre farm in Canterbury. In February of 1792 Whitcher, who had

1-3. A woodcut of the Church and North Families in Canterbury (*left to right*),
facing northeast. From *Harper's New Monthly Magazine* (July 1857, p. 15).

1-4. The 3-story Church Family meetinghouse was designed and constructed by Shaker master builder Moses Johnson in 1792 with double entrances on the west facade.

been a Freewill Baptist, "gathered" forty-three converts into a Shaker community, and a "Church Family" for senior members came to reside in his farm buildings. Converts dissolved their own families and turned over their possessions to the new community. Other Shaker families subsequently took root, consisting of a Second (or Middle) Family for those who had never been married (formed in 1800), a North Family for novitiates (formed in 1801), and a short-lived West Family (formed in 1806).

Because the small cluster of Whitcher farm buildings was inadequate for their needs, the Canterbury Shakers promptly added a meetinghouse for worship services in the summer of 1792 (figures 1-4, 1-5), and a large, three-storied dwelling house in 1793 (figure 1-6). They subse-

quently added workshops, farm buildings, an infirmary (1811) to house the sick, a laundry building (1816), a schoolhouse (1823) where Shaker children and orphans were educated, and a trustees' office (1830–1832) that managed external business affairs (figure 1-7). Ultimately the village expanded to about 3,000 acres, with an economy based on agriculture, extensive orchards, dairy cattle, crafts, and light manufactures. Among the more important activities were woodworking, weaving, maple sugaring, beekeeping (figure 1-8), the "fancywork" industry (the manufacture of boxes from poplar wood or straw), and the production of patent medicines. Canterbury also achieved special prominence by virtue of its seed industry, selling thousands of packets of seeds to the World's People. The processing of raw materials was

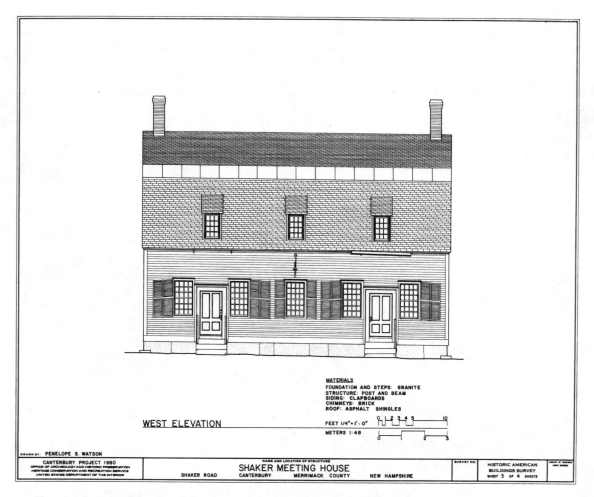

WEST ELEVATION

MATERIALS
FOUNDATION AND STEPS: GRANITE
STRUCTURE: POST AND BEAM
SIDING: CLAPBOARDS
CHIMNEYS: BRICK
ROOF: ASPHALT SHINGLES

FEET 1/4"=1'-0"

METERS 1:48

1-5. The west elevation of the Church Family meetinghouse as drawn by Penelope Watson in 1980.

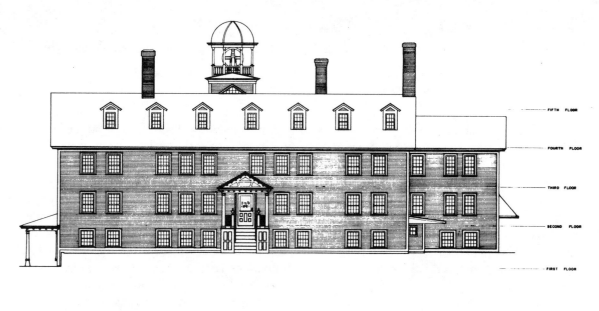

SOUTH ELEVATION

FEET 3/16"=1'-0"

METERS 1:64

FIFTH FLOOR

FOURTH FLOOR

THIRD FLOOR

SECOND FLOOR

FIRST FLOOR

1-6. The Church Family dwelling house, built in 1793, reached its final form in 1837 with 56 rooms, 3½ stories, 13 bays, and a gable roof. South elevation drawn by Richard M. Monahon, Architects, in 1980.

1-7. The Church Family office building was constructed of pressed bricks manufactured by the Shakers and was raised between 1830 and 1832. It was the first building in the community to have a roof of slate, rather than shingles. Courtesy of Canterbury Shaker Village Archives.

1-8. Elder Henry Blinn (1824–1905) tending his bees. In the rear is the Church Family cow barn. Courtesy of Canterbury Shaker Village Archives.

1-9. Elder Arthur Bruce (1858–1938) was, at various times, the Church Family trustee, an elder, and a lead minister in the Parent Ministry. He managed most of Canterbury's business affairs in the early twentieth century. Courtesy of Canterbury Shaker Village Archives.

1-10. Irving Greenwood (1876–1939) was Canterbury's last Shaker brother. With his parting, virtually all of the field and mill chores were taken over by hired men. Courtesy of Canterbury Shaker Village Archives.

also important, and a highly efficient but low-power mill system was developed, consisting of eight artificial ponds and eighteen mill buildings, all linked by ditching. The Shakers manufactured everything from clothespins to wooden pails to washing machines, and the publishing center for all of Shakerism was established in Canterbury under the leadership of Elder Henry Blinn; most notably, the *Shaker Manifesto* was published in Canterbury between 1882 and 1899. Canterbury produced more music than any other Shaker society, and one of the Canterbury eldresses, Dorothy Durgin, is recognized as having been the foremost composer of Shaker music. The distinctive style of Shaker cloak known as the "Dorothy Shaker Cloak" was named after her.

All together, the Canterbury Shakers constructed over one hundred dwellings, craft shops, mills, and farm buildings, but declining membership rendered many of these unnecessary. Some structures burned, others were taken down when no longer needed, and in the 1950s still more were removed to save money on taxes

and maintenance. The remaining Shaker buildings are surrounded by farmland, woodlands, millponds, and pasture, but the much greater extent of the original community is evidenced by the many cellar holes, mill foundations, old roadways, fences, dumps, and even by weathered fruit trees from orchards that were abandoned years ago. Just twenty-four Shaker buildings survive at the Church Family, which is operated as a non-profit museum village; another building, a barn, remains at the Second Family; and another, a trustees' office, stands at the North Family and is currently used as a residence. Many lots were sold in the 1930s and 1940s, reducing the size of the remaining museum village to about 617 acres.

Mother Ann Lee never visited Canterbury Shaker Village, but the community nevertheless grew to a peak of 233 members in 1843. Many of the early New Hampshire Shakers had been Freewill Baptists prior to moving to Canterbury. Later, after the Civil War, there was a long period of decline, and a great many of the children who had been left as orphans with the Shakers chose to return to the outside world. The West Family closed very promptly, in 1818, while the North Family lasted until 1894, and the buildings of the Second Family remained standing until 1915 or 1916. Also, by the twentieth century fewer men were joining the Canterbury Society, and the village was increasingly dominated by women. Consequently, the death knell for the community was sounded in 1938 and 1939 with the passing of the last Shaker brothers, Arthur Bruce and Irving Greenwood (figures 1-9, 1-10). Even so, in 1957 the village saw a resurgence in importance when the Lead Ministry of the entire Shaker Society moved to Canterbury. However, this did not prevent the ministry from voting in 1965 to close the society to any additional members, and steps were later initiated to allow Canterbury to become a museum village.

Since that time, Canterbury Shaker Village has been transformed into a nonprofit educational corporation, professional museum staff and guides have increased to nearly a hundred each summer, and a wide range of exhibits interpret Shaker life to about seventy thousand visitors each year. Much of this transition was guided by Eldresses Bertha Lindsay (1897–1990) and Gertrude Soule (1895–1988) (figure 1-11), ensuring that the beliefs of the twentieth-century Canterbury Shakers are well represented in what is now a very professional museum setting.

1-11. Eldresses Gertrude Soule (1895–1988, *left*) and Bertha Lindsay (1897–1990). Courtesy of Canterbury Shaker Village Archives.

Chapter Two

The Shaker Mill System

The Big Picture

I learned of the existence of an extensive and technologically sophisticated Shaker mill system during my
very first visit to Canterbury Shaker Village in 1977
(figures 2-1, 2-2). The last Canterbury Shakers revealed
to me that the woods on the eastern side of their village
concealed well-preserved remains of millponds, dams,
ditches, and mill foundations that spanned a distance of
about two miles. During the following year, as my team
began a major effort to document, physically and historically, these industrial sites, it became clear that many of
the Shaker land acquisitions in the nineteenth century
had been for the purpose of creating and expanding this
water-powered mill system. I was stunned to discover
that the Shakers had invested so much time and capital
in an industrial enterprise that was forward-looking, took
advantage of the very latest technology, and was built
so as to last for many lifetimes. The Canterbury Shakers
were unquestionably far ahead of what I would have
expected in a contemplative, otherworldly community.
But looking back now, I should not have been surprised
by their ability to conceptualize industry on such a grand
scale, because nearly all Shaker Villages were largely
self-sufficient in the processing of raw materials. Since
we conducted our own survey, fieldwork conducted at
nearly every other Shaker Village has now revealed one
or more water-powered sawmills, gristmills, turning
mills, carding mills, and other processing and manufacturing establishments.

The industries in Canterbury are described in considerable detail in surviving journals from the nineteenth
and early twentieth centuries. Included in them are
daily summaries of the Shakers' business dealings,
including everything from the costs for purchasing land

to the names of the vendors who sold Hercules turbines
to the Shakers. The journals even give the annual levels
of production for blocks of ice, for dairy products, and
for manufactured goods. There also are a handful of
accounts written by outsiders who visited Canterbury at
the height of its industrial expansion. In 1840 Isaac Hill
gave what was easily the most complete early description of industry in Canterbury as he described "The
Novel Artificial Water Power":

Our next object of attention was the artificial water power created by the first family at an almost incredible amount of labor
and expense. . . . Here, where no natural stream ever ran, they
have created a more permanent and durable water power than
can be found within the distance of ten miles. To make this
water power effective in the dry as well as in wet seasons, no
less than eight artificial ponds covering from five to thirty acres
each have been created, one rising above the other, and each
furnishing a stream large enough to carry different mills and
factories. . . .

A still-earlier Shaker account described how in 1800 a
canal or ditch (sometimes referred to in Canterbury literature as the "Long Ditch") was dug to bring water from
Lyford Pond (a naturally occurring body of water) south
to East Pond (a Shaker-made pond). Next, in 1816 the
ditch was extended to the "road east of Huckins—a
costly job," and between 1839 and 1840 the ditch was
widened, straightened, and deepened for a stretch of
two miles. Nine stone bridges were built across the ditch
at that time so a neighbor of the Shakers named "Ham"
could reach his pastures on the eastern side of the ditch
(figure 2-3).

With the passage of time the principal water source
for the system, Lyford Pond, proved inadequate, and in

2-1. The Church Family turning mill (the largest building in the right center), sometime before its removal in 1916 (facing southeast). Turning Mill Pond is on the left, and the smaller Sawmill Pond is on the right. The smaller buildings near the turning mill are probably associated lumber sheds. Courtesy of Canterbury Shaker Village Archives.

2-2. Turning Mill Pond at the start of the mapping project in 1978 (facing north). Due to lack of maintenance, the dam gave way in 1980, and the pond lost its water. However, a new dam was constructed in 1988, and years of brush clearing have now given the pond a much more open appearance.

2-3. A small stone bridge, ca. 1839, crossing the "Long Ditch" (facing north).

off brush from Chestnut and Runaway dams. Also cut bushes on ditch from Runaway to Wood mill ponds." And then on Monday, November 16, 1936, "Oscar and Harvey come down ditch taking out leaves." As the Shakers and their hired men tore down the mills in the twentieth century, the water was no longer needed. Both Lyford Pond and New Pond were sold, and the ditch was allowed to fall into disrepair.

The "Long Ditch" is now dry, and it would require major expense to return it to service. All but one of the millponds still retain some water, obtained through rainfall, but most of their present volume comes from many small streams that were rechanneled by the Shakers so as to flow into the ponds. Isaac Hill commented upon this practice of altering the local watershed in 1840:

Several small streams running from springs weeping and oozing from the ground have been turned from time to time into the artificial stream; the right to turn these the Shakers have purchased whenever they could not obtain the full assent from their neighbors to the change.

None of the streams provides sufficient water to put a mill into operation today, and clearly the water that came through the "Long Ditch" was essential to the continuous and predictable operation of the system.

The Shakers described these ponds and mills in detail (tables 2-1 and 2-2), and they clearly were proud of the scope and boldness of their creation. Isaac Hill noted that the Shakers had had no ponds and no large, naturally occurring streams prior to the commencement of the "Long Ditch" and its associated mills in 1800. Henry Blinn's "Historical Record" did describe, however, how

1885 another pond, named "New Pond," was constructed at a cost of about $5,000. The Shakers dug a ditch containing a 12-inch cast-iron pipe to connect the two, thereby assuring a much larger water supply for the "Long Ditch" than before. The Shakers no doubt cleaned the ditch and repaired its banks on an annual basis, although I could find explicit journal references to this maintenance process only for the years 1908, 1911, and 1936. For example, the Shakers wrote on Thursday, September 24, 1936, "Men finish cutting and cleaning

Table 2-1
The Canterbury Shaker Millponds

Pond	Date of construction	Surface area, 1982 (acres)	Depth of water at dam, 1982 (meters)	Elevation of water's surface, 1982, relative to N0E0 (meters)
North Family Pond	1814	4.62	1.44	+7.35
East Pond	1836	16.45	0.82	−1.2
Fountain Pond	unknown	12.57	2.00	−0.2
Factory Pond	1802	4.52	1.80	−9.6
Turning Mill Pond	1817	8.39	1.41	−14.4
Sawmill Pond	1800	2.28	0.45	−19.9
unnamed pond	unknown	lacks water	0.17	−41.1
Carding Mill Pond	1811	5.55	0.91	−44.4

Table 2-2
Chronology of the Canterbury Shaker Mills

Mill	Dates	Location
Church Family saw- and gristmill (horse-drawn)	1797–c1800	west side of Shaker Road
North Family sawmill (wood mill)	1814–1912	North Family Pond
North Family turning mill	1814–c1891	North Family Pond
West Family sawmill	1805–1850	Meadow Brook
Second Family sawmill	1850–?	Meadow Brook
Church Family fulling mill	1804–?	Factory Pond
Church Family tannery	1815–?	Factory Pond
Church Family clothiers' mill	1828–1905	Factory Pond
Church Family pump mill	1905–c1951	Factory Pond
Church Family wood mill	1812–c1886	Factory Pond
Church Family wood mill	1886–c1915	Factory Pond
Church Family wood mill	1915–1952	Factory Pond
Church Family threshing mill and icehouse	1876–1952	Factory Pond
Church Family turning mill	1818–1916	Turning Mill Pond
Church Family saw- and gristmill	1800–1832	Sawmill Pond
Church Family saw- and gristmill	1832/34–1915	Sawmill Pond
Church Family sawmill	1915–1954	Sawmill Pond
Church Family sawmill	pre-1824–?	unnamed pond
Church Family carding mill	1812–1896	Carding Mill Pond

they had a single saw- and gristmill that had been constructed in the vicinity of the Church Family buildings in 1797:

a building 36 × 36 was raised on the west side of the highway and designed for a mill in which to saw wood, grind corn and grain and for wood turning. Four horses were used on this circular sweep.

The capacity of this horse-powered mill was limited, and it appears to have been taken out of service in 1800 when the first grist- and sawmill was built south of Sawmill Pond (table 2–2).

I am not surprised that the Shakers chose to convert their processing activities from horse to water power, but in the total absence of naturally occurring bodies of water, the scale at which they launched their new mill system was bold and farsighted. Their extensive system of reservoirs, linked by ditching, enabled water to flow downhill slowly, following a slight declination from north to south. As the water traveled through the successive ponds, it was alternately held and then released through sluiceways so as to power waterwheels in the mills that were located on several of the ponds. Earthen dams, ranging up to 4.5 meters in height and 13.0 meters in thickness, were faced with fieldstones (figure 2-4) and

occasionally with cut stones, and stone-lined spillways were built into the dams to permit water to run out safely during spring freshets (figures 2-5, 2-6). Most ponds or headraces also contained wood or metal trash racks that filtered out floating debris before it could enter the penstocks of the various mills (figures 2-7, 2-8).

The Shaker mill system generated power that was chiefly intended to process wood products, and the Shakers were doing this at a large enough scale that they could meet all of their own needs and those of their non-Shaker neighbors as well. Quite late in the history of this system (1910), the Shakers added to their ability to generate power by erecting a powerhouse with storage batteries, a gasoline engine, and a direct-current generator, and this powered the residences of the Church Family. Soon after, in 1925, an alternating-current line was run to the village, and power was purchased from the New Hampshire Power Co. From that time on, electricity was available to the mills as a "backup" power source at times of low water.

However, while Shaker journal accounts give many of the dates of construction, some building dimensions, and some listings of products for individual mills, they are by no means adequate for locating mill components such as dams, trash racks, wheel pits, tailraces, and

2-4. The crumbling earth and stone dam on Carding Mill Pond (facing north).

2-5. The smaller of the two spillways on Turning Mill Pond (facing north). The scale board is 1 m long.

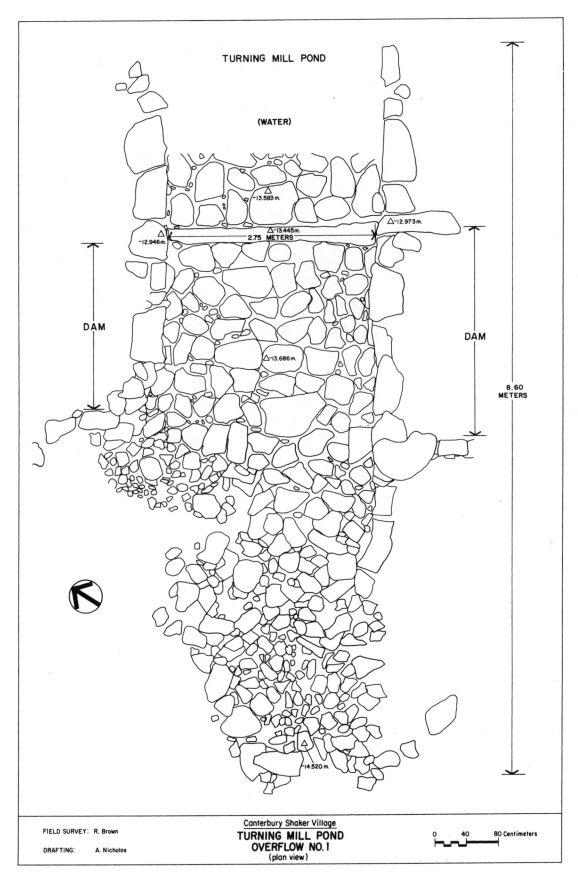

TURNING MILL POND

(WATER)

△
-13.583 m.

△-13.445 m.
2.75 METERS

△-12.973 m.

-12.946 m.

DAM

DAM

8.60
METERS

△-13.686 m.

△
-14.520 m.

FIELD SURVEY: R. Brown

DRAFTING: A. Nicholas

Canterbury Shaker Village
TURNING MILL POND
OVERFLOW NO. 1
(plan view)

0   40   80 Centimeters

2-6. A plan view of the spillway in fig. 2-5.

2-7. A wood trash rack and sluice gate associated with the last wood mill (1915–1952) built on Factory Pond. The trash rack consisted of vertical wood members anchored in the floor of the millpond and ringing the entrance to the penstock. The wood sluice gate was positioned against the open mouth of the iron penstock in the face of the dam. This photograph was taken in 1978, when the water level in the pond was low, but both the sluice gate and trash rack were destroyed in 1984 when the pond regained its water.

spillways. This became a powerful incentive for using surface recording to document thoroughly what the Shakers had accomplished here. Consequently I decided to map the mill areas at the same scale as the rest of the village (see part II). However, because many features could not be adequately represented at a scale of 1:500, we subsequently cleared and mapped some of the industrial components at the larger scale of 1:20 (both plan views and elevations). We prepared these more detailed drawings for a total of four wheel pits, six dam profiles, four spillways, two bridges, and one trash rack. We also combined sections of the sixty-one present-day base maps (part II) so as to create detailed plan views of each of the eight millponds (figures 2-9, 2-10). We then summarized the history, physical dimensions, and present condition of every industrial feature, and we assessed each in terms of what its potential might be to reveal further information.

Our final stage in mapping the mill system was to prepare comprehensive maps showing exactly how water flowed through the ditches, mills, and ponds. We accomplished this by drafting a series of plans and corresponding cross-sectional views, beginning at the northernmost point where water from the "Long Ditch" entered North Family Pond, and then continuing downhill through each successive pond until water finally exited from Carding Mill Pond, nearly 3,300 meters to the south (figures 2-11, 2-12, 2-13). Over this distance of nearly two miles, the water dropped 51.75 meters from north to south, equivalent to an average slope of just 1.57 percent over the entire length of the system. The ditching that connected the millponds was rarely more

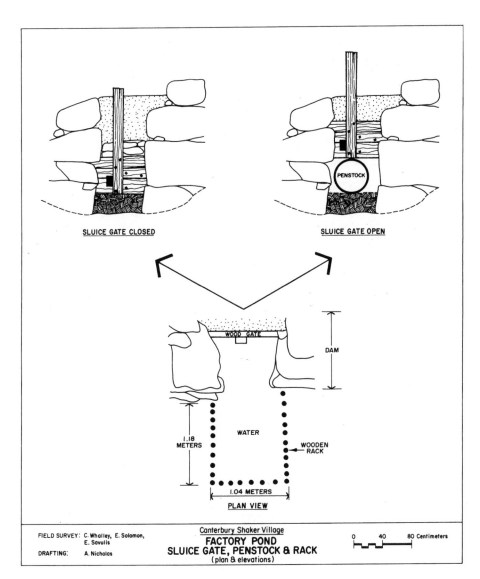

SLUICE GATE CLOSED   SLUICE GATE OPEN

PENSTOCK

DAM

WOOD GATE

WATER

1.18 METERS

WOODEN RACK

1.04 METERS

PLAN VIEW

FIELD SURVEY: C. Wholley, E. Solomon, E. Sovulis

DRAFTING: A. Nicholas

Canterbury Shaker Village
FACTORY POND
SLUICE GATE, PENSTOCK & RACK
(plan & elevations)

0   40   80 Centimeters

2-8. A plan view and elevations of the trash rack and sluice gate in fig. 2-7. When the sluice gate was lowered (*upper left*), it prohibited the flow of water, but when raised (*upper right*) it permitted water to flow into the penstock and on to the turbine inside the wheel pit.

than 1 meter deep as it snaked across the fields, carrying water from Lyford Pond and New Pond to the more southerly Shaker ponds and mills. While the cross section of the mill system represents the year 1982, rather than a time when the system was still operational and filled with water, this should not affect the accuracy of the drawings. The Shakers designed their ditches and their millponds so as to take advantage of natural contours and depressions, and these have not changed from the time of abandonment up to the time when the features were mapped.

Tracing the history of these features was somewhat more complicated than we had expected because historical sources were often ambiguous, and there were discrepancies between history and the oral accounts of the surviving Shakers. Many of the Shakers' own documents

differed in the names they applied to ponds and fields, and the same pond might have had a half-dozen different names, depending upon the mill that was located there at the moment. One of the most intensively utilized ponds had the successive names of "Tan House Pond," "Wood Mill Pond," "Bark Mill Pond," "Factory Pond," and "Ice Mill Pond." Another difficulty was that the Shakers had multiple turning mills, sawmills, and wood mills (see table 2-2), sometimes successively in the same spot and sometimes simultaneously in several locations. Thus when a journal referred to one of these mills, it was oftentimes impossible to distinguish which one was the subject of discussion. Nowhere did the Shakers define why they identified some mills as "sawmills," some as "turning mills," and some as "wood mills." However, based upon their usage of these terms,

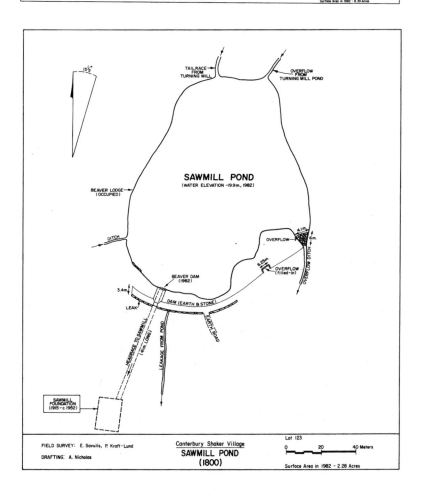

TURNING MILL POND
(WATER ELEVATION ~14.4m, MAY 1982)

BOYS' ISLAND

FIELD SURVEY: E. Savulis, P. Kraft-Lund
DRAFTING: A. Nicholas
Canterbury Shaker Village
TURNING MILL POND
(1817)
Lot 123
0   20   40 Meters
Surface Area in 1982 - 8.39 Acres

2-9. A plan view of Turning Mill Pond. Maps of this type were prepared for each of the eight Shaker millponds in order to show inlets, spillways, leakage, dams, and associated mill foundations.

SAWMILL POND
(WATER ELEVATION ~19.9m, 1982)

BEAVER LODGE
(OCCUPIED)

FIELD SURVEY: E. Savulis, P. Kraft-Lund
DRAFTING: A. Nicholas
Canterbury Shaker Village
SAWMILL POND
(1800)
Lot 123
0   20   40 Meters
Surface Area in 1982 - 2.28 Acres

2-10. A plan view of Sawmill Pond, the earliest of the Shaker millponds.

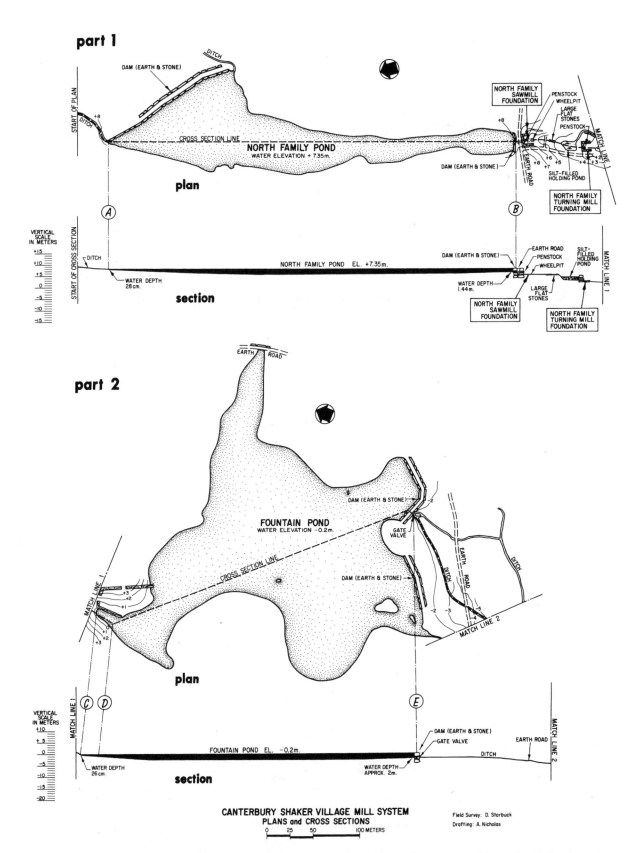

part 1

DITCH

DAM (EARTH & STONE)

START OF PLAN

DITCH

+8

CROSS SECTION LINE

NORTH FAMILY POND
WATER ELEVATION + 7.35 m.

plan

NORTH FAMILY SAWMILL FOUNDATION

PENSTOCK
WHEELPIT
LARGE FLAT STONES
PENSTOCK

MATCH LINE 1

+8

EARTH ROAD

DAM (EARTH & STONE)

+8 +7 +6 +5

+4 +3 +2

SILT-FILLED HOLDING POND

NORTH FAMILY TURNING MILL FOUNDATION

Ⓐ

Ⓑ

VERTICAL SCALE IN METERS
+15
+10
+5
0
-5
-10
-15

START OF CROSS SECTION

DITCH

WATER DEPTH 28 cm.

NORTH FAMILY POND EL. +7.35 m.

DAM (EARTH & STONE)
EARTH ROAD
PENSTOCK
WHEELPIT

WATER DEPTH 1.44 m.

LARGE FLAT STONES

NORTH FAMILY SAWMILL FOUNDATION

SILT-FILLED HOLDING POND

MATCH LINE 1

NORTH FAMILY TURNING MILL FOUNDATION

section

part 2

EARTH ROAD

DAM (EARTH & STONE)

-2

FOUNTAIN POND
WATER ELEVATION -0.2 m.

CROSS SECTION LINE

GATE VALVE

DAM (EARTH & STONE)

EARTH ROAD

DITCH

MATCH LINE 1

+3
+2
+1

+1
+2
+3

-2 -3

-5

MATCH LINE 2

plan

VERTICAL SCALE IN METERS
+10
+5
0
-5
-10
-15
-20

MATCH LINE 1

Ⓒ Ⓓ

WATER DEPTH 26 cm.

FOUNTAIN POND EL. -0.2 m.

Ⓔ

DAM (EARTH & STONE)
GATE VALVE
EARTH ROAD

DITCH

WATER DEPTH APPROX. 2 m.

MATCH LINE 2

section

CANTERBURY SHAKER VILLAGE MILL SYSTEM
PLANS and CROSS SECTIONS

0   25   50   100 METERS

Field Survey: D. Starbuck
Drafting: A. Nicholas

2-11. Plans and cross-sectional views demonstrating how water flowed through the Shaker mill system from north to south. Elevations are all expressed in meters relative to Datum N0E0. Parts 1 and 2 show water from the "Long Ditch" entering the northwest corner of North Family Pond, passing through the North Family sawmill and turning mill, and then continuing on through Fountain Pond. Figs. 2-12 and 2-13 show the system as it continued south.

part 3

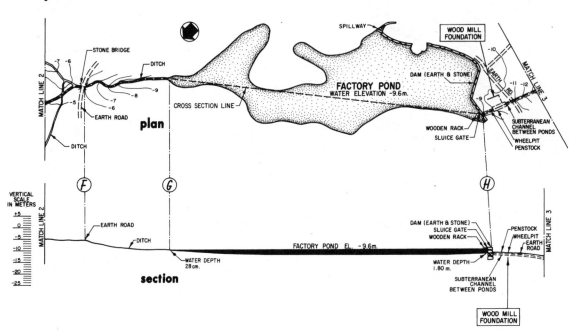

part 4

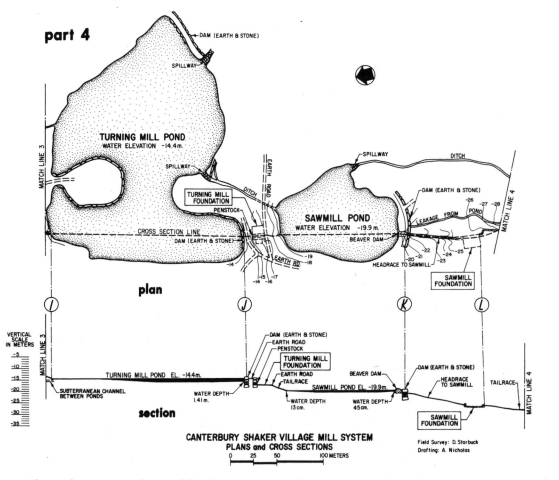

CANTERBURY SHAKER VILLAGE MILL SYSTEM
PLANS and CROSS SECTIONS

0   25   50   100 METERS

Field Survey: D. Starbuck
Drafting: A. Nicholas

2-12. Plans and cross-sectional views of the mill system (parts 3 and 4) as the water continued south through Factory Pond, Turning Mill Pond, and Sawmill Pond.

Elevations are expressed in meters relative to Datum NoEo. Fig. 2-13 shows the system as it continued south.

part 5

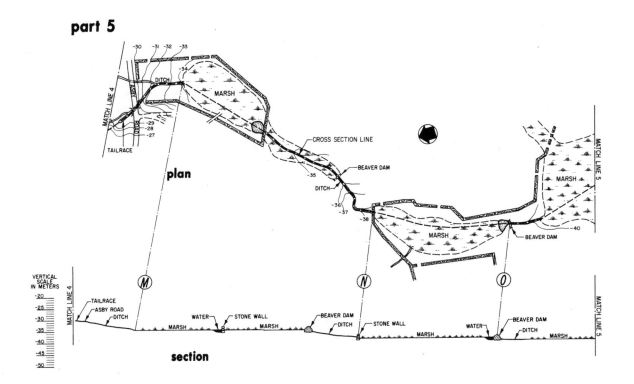

plan

section

VERTICAL
SCALE
IN METERS

part 6

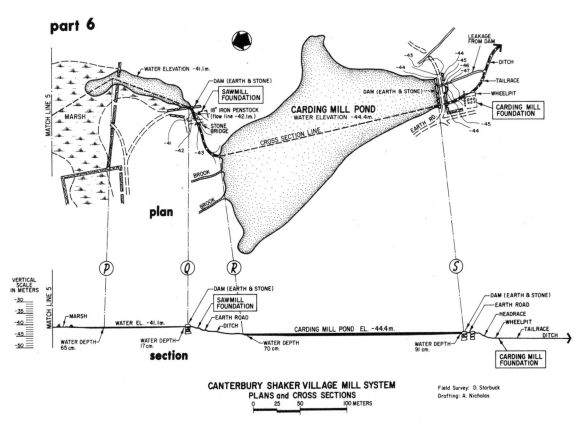

plan

section

VERTICAL
SCALE
IN METERS

CANTERBURY SHAKER VILLAGE MILL SYSTEM
PLANS and CROSS SECTIONS

Field Survey: D. Starbuck
Drafting: A. Nicholas

2-13. Plans and cross-sectional views of the mill system (parts 5 and 6) as the water continued south through an unnamed pond (now a marsh) and through Carding Mill Pond. Elevations are expressed in meters relative to Datum NoEo. After exiting from Carding Mill Pond, the water flowed off Shaker land and out of Shaker control.

quite clearly turning mills were used for wood-turning functions, producing brooms and chair and table legs, while sawmills were used for sawing boards from logs, and wood mills were used for cutting up firewood.

The ambiguity in referring to mill buildings was further compounded by the Shaker practice of literally moving buildings around the village whenever they had outlived their usefulness. The Shakers also changed the functions of their mills when new technology was introduced or when manufacturing priorities changed. Even though most of these industries were conducted on a small scale, modernization and upgrading were continual.

The History and Operation of the Mills

A synthesis of available historical records reveals that the Canterbury Shakers began their milling activities quite modestly with the already-mentioned horse-drawn saw- and gristmill in 1797. They built their first water-powered sawmill in 1800 on the side of a newly formed millpond and then rapidly expanded their ponds and ditching so that they had nine water-powered mills in operation by 1850 (figure 2-14). As the village's population and industrial needs declined in the latter part of the century, they slowly dropped to six water-powered mills by 1900 and to just four mill buildings by 1950, all of which had ceased operation some years before (see table 2-2). Most of the mills were built and operated by the Church Family, but each of the other Shaker families had at least one mill as well.

The northernmost Shaker Family, the North Family, was established in 1801, and shortly afterward (1814) the Shakers created a pond just east of this family, which, appropriately, was named "North Family Pond." They constructed two North Family mills in 1814 below the dam on the southern perimeter of the pond, one for

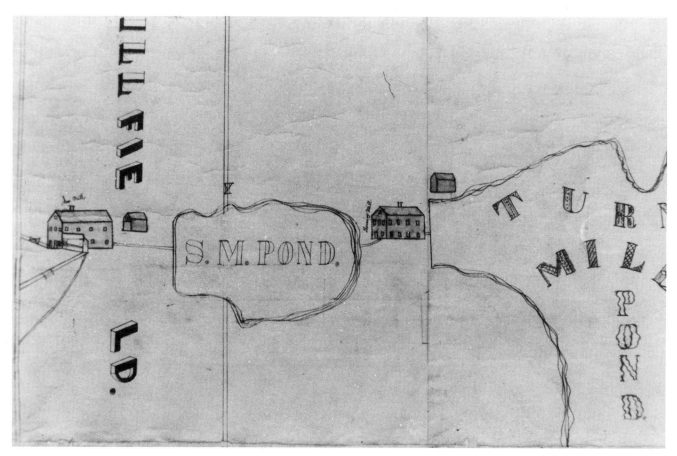

2-14. Detail from a watercolor of Canterbury Shaker Village drawn by Elder Henry C. Blinn in 1848. Shown here (*left to right*) are the Church Family sawmill (1832/34–1915), Sawmill Pond, the Church Family turning mill (1818–1916), and Turning Mill Pond. North is on the right. Courtesy of Canterbury Shaker Village Archives.

2-15. Foundation of the North Family turning mill in 1979.

sawing firewood and the other for turning furniture. The Shakers wrote very little about the sawmill (or wood mill) during its early years, except that a dining room had been added to the mill in 1824. In 1894, the same year that the North Family officially closed and combined with the Second Family, the Shakers removed the sawmill's flat roof, and a pitched roof was put on. Between 1902 and 1905 they made numerous improvements at both the dam and the mill, including the installation of a new penstock (1902), the purchase of six lumber rolls (1902), the installation of two drag saws (1903), and the addition of a new slide gate (1903). These alterations notwithstanding, the Shakers tore down the remains of the old mill in 1912 and burned them. The sawmill foundation and its wheel pit now stand open, but no artifacts or equipment are visible within the wheel pit. The dam at the southern end of the pond has been well main-

tained, and there is an open spillway channel (1 meter in width) at the eastern end of the dam, which—at times of high water—carried water south from North Family Pond, around the two mill sites, and into Fountain Pond.

The North Family turning mill lasted nearly as long as the sawmill, but it was finally taken down prior to 1891 because it was in poor repair. In 1840 Isaac Hill described this as a "mechanics' shop with water power for various machinery," and he noted that an addition was attached to it "with the apparatus and machinery requisite for the ready construction of common family water tubs." Years later, Brother Irving Greenwood described the turning mill as used for making "tables, chairs, beds & tubs & pails." The 15-inch penstock that brought water into the mill is still intact, and water continues to flow through it into the foundation (figure 2-15). The wheel pit stands open, but no equipment is visible.

2-16. The breached dam at the West Family with Meadow Brook pouring through (facing north).

Nearly 500 meters to the west of the North Family are the remains of what was termed the "West Family," a short-lived branch of the North that erected buildings between 1801 and 1805 and then was formally "gathered" in 1806. Because a stream, named "Meadow Brook," ran along the western edge of the village, the Shakers were able to dam it and to raise a combined sawmill and turning mill in 1805. This sawmill contained two turning lathes, and it apparently continued in use until the West Family was abandoned, a drawn-out process that lasted from 1808 until 1819. There is no record of further activity here until 1850 (at which time the dam was repaired), and the sawmill ceased to be used, although it may have

survived until as recently as 1916, when the "Branch" Family (composed of remnants of the Second and North Families) finally closed. The dam was subsequently breached, and stones from the sawmill and dam are now scattered along the bottom of Meadow Brook (figure 2-16). A massive, stone-lined spillway (some 5.1 meters in width) is still intact at the westernmost end of the dam (figures 2-17, 2-18), but the pond that was once held back by the dam is gone.

The milling that was conducted by the North, West, and Second Families was on a small scale when compared with that of the senior Church Family. The Church Family had by far the most members (typically

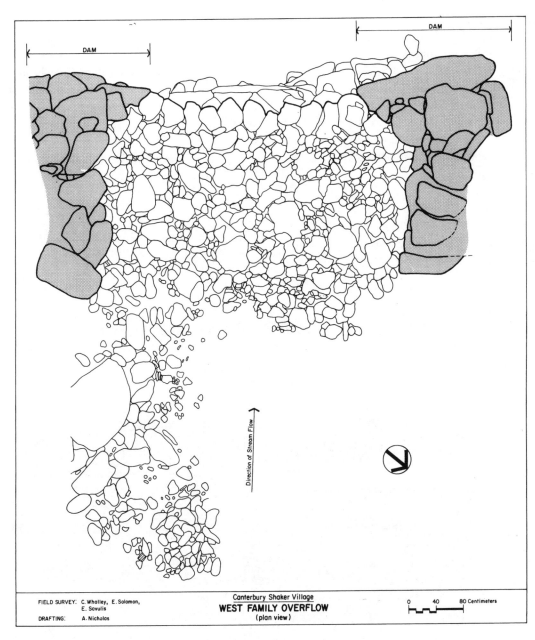

2-17. A plan view of the spillway atop the West Family dam.

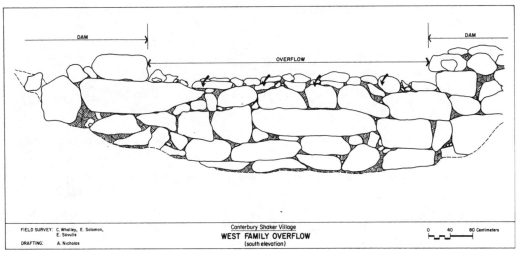

2-18. The south elevation of the spillway in fig. 2-17.

over 100, whereas each of the other families rarely contained more than 50); it had the most capital available for investment purposes; and it usually had the best-developed sales network for its manufactures. The construction of the extensive Shaker mill system appears to have been carried out chiefly for the benefit of the Church Family (table 2-2), and they placed mills on five of the ponds, while deriving water from the three ponds located north of them. East Pond and Fountain Pond served solely as reservoirs for the Church Family, and the same water was used over and over as it passed through the mills. I cannot mention Fountain Pond without chuckling, because in 1978 I was taking a prominent historian of technology, Theodore Penn, on a tour of the millponds when he suddenly stripped off his clothes and, buck-naked, jumped from the dam into the pond. Later, he explained quite matter-of-factly that on every consulting project, he always made it a point to have a swim in the old millponds!

The most intensively utilized millpond was "Factory Pond," and the Shakers created this in 1802 about 300 meters east of the Church Family buildings. They built a fulling mill, 25 × 25 feet, on this pond in 1804 and moved a tannery there in 1815. No surface evidence has survived from either of these mills.

The Shakers built the first of several wood mills on Factory Pond in 1812, followed by other mills in 1886 and 1915. The best account of the earliest wood mill was written by Isaac Hill in 1840 and reads:

building . . . covered a tannery and bark-mill in the basement story, and a mill for the manufacture of shingles and a thrashing machine room. The last machine was an invention of the Shakers and had been used by them for thrashing their grain for more than twenty years. . . . The head and fall at this mill is fifteen feet. . . .

The 1886 wood mill had a 24-inch Tyler turbine, whereas the 1915 wood mill had a penstock built of 4-inch chestnut and a 15-inch Hercules turbine. This last mill was built at a cost of $800.00, and it operated a circular saw

2-19. The wheel pit of the Church Family wood mill on Factory Pond in 1980 (facing north). The metal rods that line the sides of the wheel pit are all that is left of the turbine box it once contained. Note the 24-in.-diameter iron penstock as it comes through the face of the dam.

2-20. The 1905 pump mill as it appears today with a new roof. The pump mill was built
south of Factory Pond in order to pump water to cisterns in the North Orchard.

purchased from the Lane Manufacturing Company of Montpelier, Vermont. The turbine box for the last wood mill presently contains many burnt timbers and fallen stones from the associated dam, but no machinery survives (figure 2-19).

Just east of the wood mill, the Shakers erected a building in 1876, measuring 40 × 50 feet, that was used as both a threshing mill (until 1914) and an icehouse (until 1929). It was subsequently used chiefly for storage after 1929, and then the building was sold and removed from the site in 1952. None of the foundation stones presently visible clearly pertain to this building, but about 25 meters to the southwest stands the well-preserved stone foundation of a "pump mill" that the Shakers built in 1905. This was recently restored by the museum, and it now has a roof once again but none of its original machinery (figures 2-20, 2-21). This, in turn, was on the same site as an earlier "clothiers' mill" that the Shakers had built here in 1828. Isaac Hill described how this was

where the beautiful woollen cloths and flannels manufactured by the sisters are fulled and dressed. Here were samples of all wool, mixed worsted and cotton cloths. . . .

The preservation of industrial features has been unusually good on Factory Pond, for not only is there an intact spillway (varying from 2.9 to 4.0 meters in width) on the eastern side of Factory Pond, channeling excess water to Turning Mill Pond, but two trash racks survived until recently, along with a sluice gate. (All of these were destroyed in 1983 or 1984.) One of these was an iron trash rack located within the headrace that ran to the pump mill (figure 2-22), and the other was a wood trash rack located within Factory Pond, protecting the entrance to the penstock that ran in to the wood mill (figures 2–7, 2–8). After the water exited from the mills (or through the spillway) on Factory Pond, it then traveled into Turning Mill Pond, which was created in 1817 and which was named after a turning mill constructed there in 1818 (figures 2-1, 2-2).

2-21. An overshot water wheel of oak inside the 1905 pump mill. This wheel replaced an earlier cast-iron wheel that had rusted too much. Courtesy of Canterbury Shaker Village Archives.

The turning mill was always accompanied by several subsidiary mill buildings south and southwest of the pond. In 1840 Isaac Hill described the dimensions of the main building as 40 × 30 feet and said that it was used for various purposes:

Here the Shakers have made the improved pails . . . The water power of this building is also used for various other economical purposes; among them was a cannon ball in a mortar turned for the purpose of pulverizing barks and medical roots—a machine for polishing metals, and machines for turning and boring.

The Shakers added machinery for making brooms to the turning mill in 1861 and made hoops there for a few years beginning in 1885. In 1913 a direct-current electrical line was run to the mill, but in the following year it was abandoned, and the mill was taken down in 1916. In the years that followed, Turning Mill Pond often lost its water for lack of maintenance on its dam, although beavers occasionally plugged the leaks and thus restored the water

level. Mildred Wells, a longtime resident of Shaker Village, liked to describe how she enjoyed walking across the muddy floor of the pond on snowshoes whenever it went dry!

The foundation of the turning mill is currently filled with recent farm trash, and an excavation of the wheel pit in 1980 failed to reveal any of the original machinery. The dam that the turning mill once sat upon collapsed in 1980, and the museum constructed a modern dam just north of it in 1988. This pond is rather unusual in that it has two spillways, a smaller one (2.9 meters in width) that probably dates to the original construction of the pond, and a larger one (5.75 meters in width) that was constructed in 1915. A swan is the current occupant of the pond, and it typically swims up to visitors, hoping for a handout.

The next pond to the south was known as "Saw-mill Pond," and this was the earliest (1800) of all the Shaker ponds. It supplied water to a long succession of grist- and sawmills, even though it appears to have been the smallest of the ponds in the mill system (see table 2-1). The first mills erected south of the dam dated to 1800. Brother Francis Winkley described them as, "The grist Mill 24 by 30—Saw Mill 16 feet by 42." Both mills were in one building. These were both torn down in 1832 and replaced by a new grist- and sawmill just north of the old building, which Isaac Hill described in 1840:

an extensive building eighty feet by forty and three stories high—a building framed of stouter timber than is often found in the largest structures. This building covers a grist mill with four runs of stones, of which is one set of burrs for the manufacture of flour. This mill is visited by customers ten, fifteen and twenty miles distant, who are unable to find another so good. . . . Under the same roof and moved by the same wheel is a mill for sawing common boards from logs—a circular saw for slitting—a machine for sawing pail staves—a mill for grinding malt—also, a shop for manufacturing measures, as half bushels, pecks &c. The great wheel which moves the machinery . . . exceeded ten thousand dollars. . . .

Elder Henry Blinn described this same mill in 1855:

A large circular saw for the cutting of timber logs took the place of the old upright saw, and was used for several years, but finally this was taken away and the old upright saw again brought into use as being less expensive. An overshot wheel, 33 ft. in diameter was used when the mill was first built. This gave place after a few years to three Russell wheels and these, in turn gave place to four Tyler wheels.

Blinn did not note in this listing of turbines that two Parker wheels were also used. The sawmill's power system thus shows an evolution over the years from an overshot wheel to two Parker wheels to three Russell wheels to four Tyler wheels. The principal type of saw being used also underwent a progression, from an up-and-down saw, to a circular saw, to another up-and-down saw, to a "Muley" saw (another up-and-down type), and finally to a 54-inch Lane circular saw in 1893. The Shakers finally took down this sawmill in 1915 to make way for yet another sawmill.

2-22. A vertical iron trash rack that filtered water that ran to the 1905 pump mill. The scale board is marked in 10-cm units. This feature collapsed in 1983 or 1984 because of the action of large tree roots and because of cows walking alongside it.

2-23. The final Church Family sawmill (1915–1954) south of Sawmill Pond.

Foundation remains are currently visible for the 1915 sawmill, which remained standing as recently as 1954 and which was, in fact, the last operative mill at Shaker Village. This final sawmill was one story high, measured 54 × 40 feet, and had a roof and siding of galvanized iron (figure 2-23). The Shakers purchased for it a 6-inch Register Gate wheel that developed 25 horsepower with a 54-foot head. Because this far exceeded the head at any of the Shaker dams, they ceased using Sawmill Pond at this time and ran a 25-inch cast-iron pipe to the sawmill from Turning Mill Pond. After the mill building was sold and removed in 1954, a farm manager sold the penstock for scrap and contracted with the Town of Canterbury to have the mill foundation filled with recent, non-Shaker trash. Fortunately, this was cleaned out in 1995, and the foundation walls of the mill are again visible. At the eastern end of the dam on Sawmill Pond there is a stone-lined spillway (4.1 meters in width), allowing some water to escape from the pond.

After leaving the sawmill complex, the Shaker "Long Ditch" carried water for another 650 or 700 meters before arriving at the seventh millpond, for which there is no surviving name. This pond is now chiefly a marsh, and even in 1879, when Shaker Village was surveyed by John McClintock, the pond was already gone. Little is known about the mill that was constructed below it, except that it was a sawmill. In 1840 Isaac Hill described it as "A building with a machine for sawing wood. At this place, being near an extensive and beautiful woodlot, the fuel used by the family is prepared." The wheel pit now stands open within the foundation of the sawmill, and it is generally free of debris except for large stones that have fallen in from the sides. Water still flows rapidly through an iron penstock into the wheel pit and on into the tailrace.

The Shakers named the last of their ponds "Carding Mill Pond," and it was created in 1811 to supply water to a carding mill that was constructed there in 1812. In 1840 Isaac Hill described the carding mill as "A building 35 by 50 feet and two stories, containing apparatus and machinery for carding wool." Elder Henry Blinn also noted that there was

An overshot waterwheel . . . at the east end and outside of the building, and the water was conveyed from the pond in an open trough. The carding machinery were manufactured at the Society [by the Shakers] of New Lebanon. . . .

The mill housed two carding machines and a wool picker and a shearing machine, and it also contained a trip-hammer and a furnace for casting stoves. The Shakers installed new waterwheels in 1840 and 1860, and in 1861 they sold the carding machines and purchased new ones. Finally, they sold off the carding machinery in 1881 but continued to make brooms here.

The mill burned in 1896, and its foundation, together with the remains of two smaller buildings, is presently littered with foundation stones. No machinery is visible in any of them. The associated dam on Carding Mill Pond is one of the highest of the Shaker dams (4.3 meters), but it has slumped badly at its eastern end and will soon be totally breached (figure 2-4). The remains of two filled-in spillways are located at the southeastern corner of the pond, and from here—the southernmost point in the mill system—the water was allowed to flow south without further ditching. The Shakers had used the same water repeatedly to power their mills, but the distance by road was now nearly a mile from the nearest Church Family buildings, making further mill construction in this direction impractical.

Comments and Interpretations

Throughout the nineteenth and early twentieth centuries, the energy requirements of the Canterbury Shakers demanded that they develop an unusually elaborate system of water transfer and power generation. When the Shakers founded their community, the lack of expandable sources of power was an intolerable situation, and this could have posed a permanent barrier to the long-term growth of the community. They needed mills to process the products of their lumbering and farming; they needed to manufacture goods for use within the village; and they needed to make cash sales to the outside world so that they could then buy items that they could not manufacture themselves. Without the autonomy and added income that adequate power sources would give them, their desire for "purity" and isolation from the vices of the world would have come to nothing.

The Shakers clearly had a significant organizational advantage over surrounding communities in that their common ownership of property generally ensured that they had sufficient capital with which to make large, immediate acquisitions of technology, and they could initiate new industries or rehabilitate older industries with relative ease. All risks were shared, and new male recruits to the society (other than young orphans) typically brought some financial resources with them and much practical knowledge of construction methods and milling techniques. Also, in the mid–nineteenth century the Shakers actively subscribed to journals like *Scientific American*, and the archives at Canterbury Shaker Village contain various of the product catalogs and manuals that the Shakers acquired while shopping for new turbines and related equipment. The costs of building new mills were sometimes listed in the Shakers' records, and a few examples—ranging from $800 to over $10,000—have already been mentioned. It would be false to imply that such expenses were easily met, but economic cooperation among Shaker families and among the various Shaker Societies was definitely the rule. The close cooperation brought about by a centralized village leadership must also have led to a more efficient, less divisive scheduling of water usage than the usage on a more typical river or stream, where conflicts would develop among the various millers dependent on the same water. No references could be found in Shaker journals to conflicts over water among the Shaker millers, and so it appears that water sharing was well regulated.

Regrettably, the Shakers wrote relatively little about the numbers of men who worked in the mills at any given time, although it appears that the numbers were always low. Some of the Shaker millers had distinguished reputations, as in the case of the miller who was in charge of the 1832/34 sawmill, one Levi Stevens: "a man of about sixty years, . . . known for some ten or fifteen miles round as probably the best miller in the county of Merrimack." Most workers were required to specialize in several different skills, chiefly because a process could be lost completely if an experienced brother were to die or otherwise leave the village. In the twentieth century the last few Shaker brothers hired and then supervised workers from the outside world who joined them in the mills and in the fields. A wood mill on Factory Pond and a sawmill on Sawmill Pond became the last operative mills, but when the last brother, Irving Greenwood, died in 1939, the mill operation died as well.

The technology with which the Shakers addressed their problems of power generation was quite straightforward, and nothing that was utilized within the mill system was radically different from what was available in the outside world. Still, the Shakers had no prohibitions (or inhibitions) about "borrowing" technology, especially if it had the desired result of ensuring their society's security and longevity. What was different, though, was that the Shakers were located in an area that had no natural power sources, and any amount of damming of small, local streams would not have stored up water sufficient to power more than one or two seasonal mills. They had no swiftly flowing rivers or large ponds, and yet just eight years after they gathered, the Shakers had created their first millpond; in another two years they began digging the "Long Ditch"; and in another fourteen years the system was essentially complete.

Journal accounts do not indicate who first conceived of this system of reservoirs, or whether outside expertise was required to undertake the actual surveying and engineering of the ditches and dams. They clearly followed natural contours very closely so as to have a very gradual descent of the water along its entire course, and millponds were placed within natural depressions so that the amount of earth removal would be minimized as basins were dug. The fall of the water, or its "head," is difficult to measure today because dams have slumped,

the waterwheels have been removed, and wheel pits and tailraces have been at least partially filled in. As already noted, the Shakers' journals referred to head only two times, the first being at the 1812 wood mill on Factory Pond, which had a head of 15 feet, and the other being the 1915 sawmill on Sawmill Pond, where the head was 54 feet. Based upon the height of the various mill dams (and mills were quite predictably located where dams were the highest), 15 feet appears to be much the more typical figure. This was clearly a low-head system and was not well suited to powering fast-turning machinery.

One of the unfortunate aspects of this type of system was that its maintenance requirements were continual, and little was done between 1939 (the time of Irving Greenwood's death) and 1988 (when the fire protection system was created) to plug leaks in dams, to remove silt from ponds, or to remove trees from atop dams and mill foundations. This sort of rural mill system was clearly fragile, and while our mapping and historical research have helped to bring about an understanding of what used to be there, even today the system requires annual maintenance to help preserve the parts that are left. Fortunately, in recent years a walking tour has been developed through that part of the mill system that is closest to the Church Family, and visitors are now able to walk past the many sites on Sawmill, Turning Mill, and Factory Ponds.

Chapter Three

The Shaker Dumps:
Unearthing the Unexpected

Potential Sources of Conflict

The communalism of the Shakers was clearly not for everyone, and the Shakers freely acknowledged that fact by expecting new arrivals to enter first into a novitiate family, after which those who accepted the Shaker way of life would spend a lifetime gradually maturing in their faith. Sources of stress no doubt included tension over sex, over group ownership of property and the powerful hierarchical structure that controlled the daily lives of brothers and sisters, and over the appropriateness of behaviors and consumption patterns that were allowed for outsiders but not for Shakers. Potential problems involving sex were somewhat reduced by maintaining a rigid separation of the sexes, such that separate doorways, stairways, and working and living quarters were mandatory, and brothers and sisters were not allowed to speak with each other unless more-senior Shakers were present. Still, brothers and sisters sometimes chose to leave the confines of the community forever when sexual urges became too great. Sister Ethel Hudson mischievously enjoyed telling stories about brothers and sisters "running away together" (personal communication, 1987), even though this brought stern disapproval from Eldress Gertrude.

What constituted appropriate behavior periodically changed, often reflecting trends in the outside world, and Millennial Laws were passed in 1821 and 1845, in effect banning various types of inappropriate behavior. The laws approved in 1845 were especially significant because they banned the consumption of coffee, tea, alcohol, cider, tobacco, and pork. This type of proscribed behavior provides an excellent opportunity to determine, through use of the archeological record, whether the Shakers actually observed their own laws. The fact that

the Shakers were passing these laws does not, of course, necessarily mean that a majority of members were engaged in inappropriate behavior or that the Shakers were then able to eradicate all types of improper behavior. Rather, the laws were being passed because more uniformity in behavior was desired, and it was necessary to clarify, especially for newer arrivals, what would not be tolerated.

The consumption of alcohol was perhaps most controversial. In 1828 the Canterbury *Historical Record* stated:

A temperance wave seems to have passed over the Society this year which must have made a deep impression on the minds of all who were accustomed to the use of alcoholic drink or of cider. It had been a universal custom for all who chose so to do, to take a glass of spirits every morning before breakfast, as an appetizer, and then more or less through the day as circumstances favored. . . . For dinner each brother had two gills & each Sister two thirds of one gill. Besides this quantity furnished at the meals, the Brethren were allowed one quart, a day. The above custom was continued till the fall of 1841 when another change was made demanding greater abstinence.

In the 1840s, much tighter prohibitions were enacted on food and drink, and the Canterbury *Church Record* recorded:

The drinking of drams has also passed away, as a custom forever. Alcoholic drinks if taken at all, is in the form of medicine & must come from the physician. No cider is made & of course no alcohol is distilled. . . .

Attitudes toward alcohol changed periodically, usually reflecting the progress of the temperance movement elsewhere in America. As the above passage indicates, the Shakers increasingly disapproved of spirits and then banned them altogether.

However, in the late twentieth century the last of the Canterbury Shakers acknowledged having had wine with their meals when they were younger. Eldress Bertha Lindsay described in her cookbook, *Seasoned with Grace*, how

the Shakers made a good deal of wine and many varieties. Some of the best wines are homemade, I think. These were kept under the care of the Eldresses, who stored them in a three-cornered cupboard in the Sisters' Shop cellar. They were given to individuals as needed, especially if the Brothers or Sisters had been out in the cold and needed something to warm them up. . . . I think one of the best was the dandelion wine. . . . We also made elderberry wine. Raspberry wine was sometimes made. . . ."

Eldress Bertha also noted that the Canterbury Shakers made a hop beer that was "widely used by our haymakers."

The use of tobacco went in and out of acceptance, and Julia Neal collected the following statements from South Union, Kentucky: "July 1, 1818 We (Molly and Mercy) went out to the flaxfield and gave all the sisters a drink of wine—lit our pipes and took a union smoke," but after 1828, "The members were asked to refrain from the use of tobacco as well as alcohol. As one Shaker wrote, they were to use 'their mouths for glad and heavenly songs instead of smoke.'" Before tobacco was finally banned for good, Shakers at the Niskeyuna and New Lebanon communities in New York manufactured thousands of tobacco pipe bowls and stems, of both red and white clay. Edward Deming Andrews, in his classic *Community Industries of the Shakers*, noted that these were sold to the World's People between at least 1809 and 1853. Earlier entries in Shaker historical journals contain many references to smoking tobacco, and in later times, older Shakers were usually still allowed to smoke.

During the early years of the Shaker faith, believers sometimes received the gift from God of a "smoking meeting"—they would gather together and smoke to the point of nausea. Stephen Stein, in *The Shaker Experience in America*, wrote:

The "smoking meeting," observed by the Believers in 1826 . . . celebrated in several villages in honor of Ann Lee's arrival in America, united brethren, sisters, and children in billowing smoke as all puffed on their pipes. . . . The clouds of smoke rose quickly, but the hour passed slowly. When adjournment came . . . "we rushed for the doors, glad to breathe again in the pure air."

In the Canterbury, New Hampshire, community, tobacco was initially popular, and the Canterbury *Church Record* circa 1800 recorded,

it was almost the universal custom for the Brethren and Sisters to smoke tobacco, and quite a number of the pipes were taken into the social gatherings & the tobacco smoke, no doubt, filled the room. This was, however, soon discontinued, as already some were to be found who could not endure the nauseating fumes of tobacco, and on this account would leave the company.

Later, in 1848, the Canterbury Shakers had turned against tobacco, and the *Church Record* now stated that

its use has been reduced extremely low. We occasionally find a person who uses a pipe, but the cases are rare. The fumes of tobacco are not to be found in any of our buildings. It has proved to be a decided blessing to us that its use was not recommended by Believers. . . . our prayer is that the Believers may not be forced to go back and adopt these useless indulgences.

Another theme that suggests values and preferences were changing among the Canterbury Shakers was the growing materialism of the late nineteenth and twentieth centuries. While most of the Shaker communities had little money during the earlier years, especially as the construction of communal-style buildings drained their resources, the Shakers of the early twentieth century often had considerably improved finances and tended to be more acquisitive. Canterbury journals and photographs record the impressive automobiles purchased by the community (figure 3-1) (table 3-1), as well as sizable motorboats that the Shakers used at their summer camp, "Point Comfort," on Lake Winnisquam beginning in 1926. And even after automobiles had taken over as the preferred mode of transportation, Elder Arthur Bruce enjoyed acquiring horses from local racetracks.

Hobbies and pets flourished, and many of the Shaker sisters purchased Brownie and Eastman Kodak cameras, even as Brother Irving Greenwood purchased for himself a large-format Ideal camera (manufactured by the Rochester Optical Co.), as well as a Westinghouse radio outfit with accessories for $234.50 (figure 3-2). While the Shakers were certainly entitled to enjoy themselves, their latter-day buying habits nevertheless raise serious questions about whether the austere simplicity and near poverty of the early years—requisite to a God-centered existence—had been replaced by consumer habits more like those of the outside world.

Table 3-1
Automobiles Purchased by Canterbury Shaker Village (1907–1933)

Year purchased	Model	Purchase price
1907	Reo Touring Car	$1,400.00
1908	Atlas Touring Car	$2,750.00
1912	Stoddard Dayton Touring Car	$2,500.00
1913	Model 30 Buick	$1,125.00
1916	Hudson Sedan	$2,061.76
1916	Hudson Roadster	$1,475.00
1916	Hudson Cab	$1,490.00
1917	Pierce-Arrow Touring Car	$5,000.00
1917	Hudson Sedan	$2,300.00
1918	Pierce-Arrow Coupe	$5,829.23
1919	57 Cadillac Sedan	$4,800.00
1920	59 Cadillac	$5,636.04
1920	61 Cadillac	$5,761.04
1921	Reo Speed Wagon	$1,544.00
1923	Pierce-Arrow Sedan	$7,154.24
1925	Reo Speed Wagon	$1,800.00
1925	74 Marmon	$3,850.00
1927	75 Marmon	$3,200.00
1928	443 Packard Sedan	$4,848.00
1928	(second hand) Marmon Coupe	$800.00
1929	640 Packard Coupe	$3,680.00
1929	640 Packard Sedan	$4,213.00
1930	845 Packard Sedan	$4,543.00
1930	833 Packard Club Sedan	$2,918.00
1931	845 Packard Sedan	$3,000.00
1933	Model 90 Buick Sedan	$2,276.00

3-1. The Shakers' Pierce-Arrow touring car. This was purchased by the village in 1917 for $5,000 and then sold in 1919 for $4,065. Courtesy of Canterbury Shaker Village Archives.

3-2. Brother Irving Greenwood and his dog Dewey listening to his "Westinghouse Type R.C. Radio Outfit with a Magnavox Loud Speaker, Storage Battery and Antenna of the Lewis Electrical Supply Co. Boston" in February 1923. Courtesy of Canterbury Shaker Village Archives.

The changing nature of Shaker life was also accompanied by less "separateness" from the rest of the world, occasioned by the decreasing numbers of Shaker brothers, especially after about 1900. Whereas all tasks had long been defined as either "male" or "female," the loss of male members meant that increasing numbers of hired men came to reside within the community. Without the efforts of paid male labor in the fields and mills, the community would not have taken in enough income to survive. Shaker scholars have rarely dealt with this subject, although Scott Swank in *Shaker Life, Art, and Architecture* has noted that "as the number of brothers dwindled through deaths and defections, and the boys' order was closed, the old boys' house was moved to the

west side of Shaker Road where it became the hired men's house," and by the early twentieth century, "construction was done exclusively by outside non-Shaker contractors and workmen, and the buildings had little in common with earlier Shaker style and design."

The creation of the formal hired men's house on the west side of Shaker Road came in 1902, replacing an earlier lodge for the men that had burned in 1901. Small numbers of hired men had previously arrived as day laborers in the nineteenth century, but their presence was always controversial. The Canterbury *Historical Record* recorded in 1842:

all the hired help is dismissed from the family, this year, and the Brethren did all the work on the farm. . . . This dismissal of hired men, however, did not continue very long. In a few years from this date, the Societies began to hire again and have so increased, that in many of the Shaker families the number of rough and vulgar hired men have become ruinously large. At this date [1892], all the farm work in the N.H. Societies is performed by the aid of hired help.

The hired men worked under the supervision of the last few Shaker brothers, and after about 1900, many historical photographs show hired men working in the fields and mills (figure 3-3).

What had begun as economic necessity must have had a disheartening effect on the Shakers as they invited individuals with non-Shaker values to live among them. A communal society that had chosen to separate itself from the world to maintain its spiritual purity, the Shakers had now brought the world into the heart of their community. This was exemplified in a fascinating journal account in which the Shakers tried to decide whether to brew beer for the hired men, perhaps in the hope that somehow this would help them to control the drinking that was already occurring among their employees. In effect, the orderly Shaker system was undergoing stress, and some of the vices they had preached against, such as the consumption of alcohol, were being practiced within the borders of their ideal society.

The Shakers' primary records do not make it clear whether this exposure to worldly influences was altering their own behavior, but it must have been difficult for the Shakers to balance their economic needs against worldly influences. Increasingly, they needed to decide whether to tolerate a wider range of behaviors because they needed the skills of newly arrived individuals who might believe differently from the older members. For the historical archeologist, this provides an ideal envi-

3-3. Hired men working in the North Barn Field, ca. 1924. They were being supervised by Brother Irving Greenwood, who took this photograph. Courtesy of Canterbury Shaker Village Archives.

ronment in which to conduct archeological research, a chance to use material culture to find out whether Shaker consumption patterns and values changed after some of the religious fervor cooled. Over the course of several excavations, described below, it has been possible to gather some answers to this question.

The Garden Barn (1828) and the Bee House (1837)

In the summer of 1994 I directed an archeological field school at two sites within the Church Family at Canterbury Shaker Village, and this work was sponsored by the Department of Social Science at Plymouth State College. The first of these sites was the filled-in cellar hole from an 1828 garden barn that had later been torn down in the 1950s (figure 3-4). The second was the original site of the 1837 bee house that had subsequently been moved in 1940 (figure 3-5).

The garden barn was raised on June 6, 1828, at the northeast corner of the Church Family vegetable garden (originally the Shaker seed garden). It measured 30 × 40 feet and had two stories with an attic and a full cellar.

Historical records provide little specific information about the structure, other than noting that it was "arranged very conveniently for the use of the gardeners," and Brother Irving Greenwood indicated that it was "Reshingled in 1905, old clapboards taken off and 'Novelty' siding put on. This siding is machined to resemble clapboards." There are no historical references to when the building was removed.

About 17 meters to the northwest stood the Church Family bee house, on the other side of an earth road running east and downhill to the Shaker millponds. This was constructed in 1837 as a drying house (first for drying apples and later for drying lumber), and it later became a bee house in 1865, under the supervision of Elder Henry Blinn. The bee house was moved from this site in 1940 and now rests south of the Church Family cow barn and west of the 1814 cart shed. It measures just 12 × 25 feet, and historical records provide little information other than that it was shingled in 1906 and again in 1926.

During our field project in 1994, the objective at each building site was to locate and expose the complete outline of each foundation, excavating just enough test pits

3-4. The foundation of the 1828 garden barn during excavation in 1994 (facing east).

3-5. The foundation of the 1837 bee house during excavation in 1994 (facing north).

to determine the depth and integrity of artifacts and to establish when dumping had occurred inside the ruins of each structure. The garden barn foundation was the primary focus of our work because of the likelihood that it would eventually undergo reconstruction. Prior to excavation, all four foundation walls were well defined on the surface of the ground, although there were short stretches—chiefly on the east side—where the foundation stones were partially buried. A grid of 1 × 1–meter test pits was laid out over the surface of the foundation, and these were taken down to sterile soil, or until large stones were encountered that blocked further excavation. Toward the end of the project, to save time, linear trenches were placed atop the western and northern walls of the foundation, following the alignment of each wall so as to quickly expose all of the stonework. The trench atop the western wall was 7 meters long, and that atop the northern wall was 9 meters long.

Whereas the garden barn was clearly demarcated on the ground surface, the bee house was more thoroughly buried, and it was necessary to employ a backhoe to locate the foundation and to follow the walls until corners could be reached. The backhoe quickly located the southwest corner, but backhoe trenching to the north and east failed to discover either the northwest or the southeast corner. This foundation clearly had been seriously disturbed at some time in the past, and it was

difficult, if not impossible, to determine its dimensions using the power equipment. However, shoveling by hand later exposed the northwest and southeast corners. This revealed a foundation that measured exactly 12 feet (north-south) by 25 feet (east-west), the known dimensions of the bee house. After the corners were located, four test pits were then excavated in and around the foundation.

Within the cellar hole of the garden barn foundation, the surface was covered with a layer of topsoil, stones, and recent garbage, below which were thousands of fieldstones that had been thrown into the open cellar after the building was removed. A mixture of stones and artifacts (chiefly tin cans) extended all the way down to sterile subsoil, and artifacts usually occurred in "clumps" within the larger matrix of earth and stones—suggesting that trash had been thrown in from baskets or wheelbarrows as the overall filling of the foundation was occurring.

In many of the garden barn pits it was impossible to go all the way down to sterile soil because large stones filled the bottoms of the pits. Many of these were sizable, quarried stones (as opposed to fieldstones), and in general they appear to have been the upper courses of the garden barn's foundation, pushed into the cellar at the time of abandonment in order to level off the ground surface. We hoisted out a few of these using the museum's tractor. There also were large, burned, wood beams lying within the cellar. At the bottom of the debris, underneath the stones, timbers, and artifacts, the sterile "floor" of the cellar consisted of gray clay, with no sign of floorboards or of a stone floor. However, there were some pockets of coarse yellow sand that had definitely been deposited here atop the floor.

Literally thousands of twentieth-century artifacts were recovered from the garden barn foundation, including hundreds of whiteware sherds, butchered bones, nails, and tin cans. One of the few intact labels was from a can of Welch's grape juice concentrate (figure 3-6)! There also were Atlas and Ball canning jars, redware flowerpots, fuses, a glass whiskey flask, and a beer bottle (figure 3-7), a perfume bottle (figure 3-8), bits of newspaper, a Clorox glass bottle, a trowel, tin foil, clumps of rusted barbed wire, and lots of asphalt roofing material.

At the site of the bee house, the artifacts were generally similar in time period to those of the garden barn, and they included many pottery sherds, fragments of glass and complete bottles, tin cans, nails, and butchered animal bones. There also were fragments from Shaker medicine bottles. Distinctive artifacts included a small pitchfork, Styrofoam fragments, a metal twist cap, a spoon, bits of plastic, a plow blade, a muffler pipe,

numerous metal tools, a bottle of Vicks, a Canada Dry bottle, and a glass jar labeled "Dr. Hubbard's Vegetable Disinfectant Deodorizer & Germicide Nashua N.H. U.S.A." Generally speaking, the bee house foundation did contain more diverse and interesting artifacts than the garden barn. The artifacts from both the garden barn and the bee house are still being processed in the laboratory, and that is why no totals appear in table 3-2.

About 25 square meters were dug within the garden barn and only 4 square meters within the Bee House. Both foundations contained artifacts that indicated backfilling in either the 1940s or 1950s, and both would

3-6. An empty can of Welch's grape juice concentrate found in the garden barn foundation. Its height is 4 in.

3-7. A whiskey bottle and a beer bottle found in the Garden Barn foundation.

3-8. A perfume bottle found in the garden barn foundation.

Table 3-2
Selected Artifacts from the Principal Canterbury Shaker Village Dumps

	Cow barn east ramp (1998, 2000)	Hog Heaven (1996, 1998)	Total
Ceramic sherds			
whiteware	14,175	2,577	16,752
creamware	231	255	486
pearlware	88	114	202
tin-glazed	5	30	35
yellowware	3,289	29	3,318
Rockingham-decorated	576	126	702
porcelain	401	474	875
unrefined stoneware	1,130	405	1,535
beer/ginger beer bottles	366	6	372
redware	644	122	766
Glass (whole & fragments)			
medicine bottles	335	220	555
vials	28	34	62
wine bottles	61	45	106
whiskey flasks	—	5	5
beer bottles	2	16	18
Saratoga Congress Water	—	1	1
perfume bottles	9	3	12
Tobacco-related			
tobacco pipes	1	2	3
tobacco tins	1	—	1
Entertainment			
harmonica parts	3	—	3
doll parts	2	3	5
Personal			
buttons	37	202	239
buckles	23	6	29
cuff links	8	1	9
earrings	6	—	6
hair combs	16	9	25
false teeth/dentures	3	—	3
ivory toothbrushes	1	13	14
napkin rings	—	3	3
Tools/utensils			
knives	5	4	9
spoons	11	7	18
forks	1	2	3
files	5	—	5
hoe blades	2	—	2
wedges	1	—	1
worked soapstone	4	3	7
drills/drill bits	1	—	1
hinges	1	2	3
pail bails	—	2	2
knitting machine needles	14	—	14

no doubt have revealed many thousands of artifacts if they had been completely excavated. Perhaps the most significant finding was that there were no clearly Shaker-made artifacts in the cellar of the garden barn, where the most recent artifacts dated to the 1950s and the very last stages of the Shaker experience in Canterbury. However, the bee house, removed slightly earlier, did contain Shaker medicine bottles. Presumably hired men did much or most of the backfilling and dumping into these foundations, so there is little way to determine which artifacts had been used by the Shakers and which by their employees. This does not reduce their significance, since all items were consumed within the confines of Shaker Village, but it does raise questions about how best to interpret these recent remains. These two modest-size excavations in 1994 also caused me to want to examine the contents of other, earlier dumps, hoping to trace Shaker consumption patterns over the life of the community.

3-9. The interior of Hog Heaven as exposed by the backhoe trench in 1996.

Hog Heaven

During the spring of 1996, a crew that was installing a culvert behind the trustees' office building in the Church Family discovered a deep, trash-filled cellar. Their backhoe had just torn into the center of a foundation, and literally hundreds of bottles, shoes, roof slates, and bricks now lay scattered on the adjacent piles of backdirt (figure 3-9). They could see an interior wall of brick within the foundation, and at the bottom of the backhoe trench, a well-built brick floor was now exposed at a depth of approximately 2.3 meters. Not disturbed was the base of a brick chimney that was positioned in the southeast corner of the foundation (figure 3-10).

Recognizing that this dump site might provide a windfall of information about Shaker life and material culture, the museum left the cellar open so that my team from Plymouth State could excavate it during the summer of 1996. I reviewed historical sources, and it became apparent that several buildings had once stood here behind the trustees' office. The earliest of these was the very first of the Shaker mills, a combination saw-, grist-, and turning mill (built in 1797), powered by horses pulling in a circular sweep. This probably ceased to be used soon after 1800, because the village's water-powered mill system was created at that time.

The village's swine or hog house, constructed in 1817, had been next to the horse mill. This hog house had ini-

tially measured 32 × 15 feet and was probably used until the Shaker prohibition of pork in the 1840s. Isaac Hill, writing in 1840, described it as "a one-story building eighty feet long by forty feet in width," adding: "The pens for the hogs are apartments of some twelve by twenty feet on either side of an alley running the length of that end of the building. . . ." It was during the week that ended on April 5, 1902, that the hog house was finally demolished. The "Historical Record of the Church Family" described "The demolition of the old slaughter house, N.W. of Office—an eyesore for years," and, from a notation on March 28, 1902: "Tear down the old buildings [west] back of Office to make room for Men's Shop."

We know that at the north end of the hog house there was a root cellar, also built circa 1817, because Isaac Hill observed:

At one end is a well and pump, a chimney with kettle and apparatus for boiling potatoes and other roots, a machine for mashing them when boiled, a meal room with lock and key, and a cellar underneath in which potatoes and other articles that will not bear frost shall be preserved.

This description appeared to match the foundation that was hit by the backhoe in 1996, and we concluded that installation of the culvert had just torn into the root cellar for the hog house. Given the function of the hog house and its associated cellar, and acknowledging the

3-10. Hog Heaven near the completion of excavation in 1996 (looking due west). The brick chimney base (*lower left*) has been exposed, as well as the brick floor along the south foundation wall (*left*). The hog house would have been to the left. The scale boards are marked in 10-cm increments.

richness of the artifacts, we naturally concluded that we were "digging in Hog Heaven!" and this name stuck for the remainder of our project.

We also learned from historical sources that the area behind the trustees' office had once contained a small brick bacon house, built in 1828 for the curing of ham. And north of this there formerly was a workmen's lodge (built in 1813) that housed the village's hired men, a shoemaker's shop, a workshop for trustees, and storage. Fire destroyed the workmen's lodge in 1901, and a hired

men's shop later replaced it. This final building, raised in 1902, was also used to house hired men, and the "Historical Record of the Church Family" recorded:

the rest of lower story being used as a Shoemaker's Shop, Carriage room, Workshop and storage by Office Sisters. Second story used for Bed-rooms and Store-rooms. Attic for Storage.

The hired men's shop stood here until 1959, at which time it was sold and removed. The foundation outline is still clearly visible, as is the front doorsill.

During the early years at Canterbury Shaker Village, the raising of hogs was a major industry, and some production figures have survived. For example, Elder Henry Blinn wrote that the Shakers slaughtered 5,616 pounds of pork in 1811 and 11,416 pounds in 1817. While pork production was quite successful, Shaker Millennial Laws passed in 1845 banned the consumption of pork, at which time their several hog-related buildings fell into disuse, probably including the root cellar. Interestingly, though, small numbers of pigs were again being raised at the village later in the century, in apparent defiance of the earlier Millennial Laws. Because the hog house was demolished in 1902, we can probably assume that the Shakers filled in the root cellar at about the same time.

Still, trash may have been deposited there any time after the 1840s, and the process of filling may have continued well after 1902.

The backhoe left a few thousand artifacts lying scattered on the surface of Hog Heaven. Most of these were common nineteenth-century types, including sherds of whiteware and yellowware, wine and medicine bottles, fragments of pressed glass, tin cans, enamelware, and even the bowls from two tobacco pipes. After erecting a large wood frame with a pulley system to hoist dirt out of the bottom of the root cellar, we proceeded to remove the layers of fill from Hog Heaven and to expose the floor and walls for mapping (figure 3-11). As museum visitors strolled past our excavation, they often were treated to

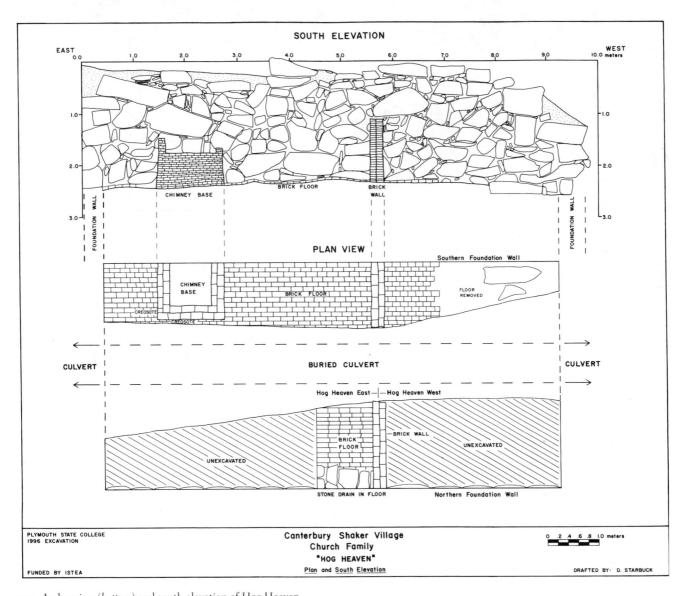

3-11. A plan view (*bottom*) and south elevation of Hog Heaven.

3-12. The 1996 excavation inside Hog Heaven (looking southeast), showing the interior brick wall (*left*), the hoist built to lift buckets out of the cellar, and the trustees' office in the background.

3-13. The chimney base discovered inside Hog Heaven (facing south). The scale board is marked in 10-cm increments.

the sight of stoneware jugs, medicine bottles, and old shoes emerging from the cellar. But they were not as prepared for my irrepressible assistant, Roland Smith, who cheerily told all who would listen that we were "convicts from a work release program at the New Hampshire State Prison Farm" (figure 3-12). Everyone would nervously look from Roland to me and back again, not quite sure if convicts were allowed to do archeology!

We discovered that the Shakers had deposited pockets of trash inside a matrix of building material: bricks, stones, charcoal, and plaster, and everywhere there were dense clusters of gray roof slates. The foundation or cellar measured 89 inches deep by 30.5 feet (east-west) by just over 14 feet (north-south). Bisecting the foundation into eastern and western portions was an interior brick wall that ran north-south across the cellar, and this was poorly built and clearly a later (ca. 1880s) addition, constructed of old, reused bricks. Curiously, much of the dirt west of this wall positively stank, suggesting that this interior

wall may have been installed in order to create a late, and short-lived, privy at the west end of the root cellar.

We exposed a brick floor at the bottom of the cellar that was slightly uneven because of frost heaves or tree roots, but it nevertheless was unusually well constructed for a cellar floor. A stone- and brick-lined drain was discovered in the floor, running along the edge of the northern foundation wall. In the southeast corner of the cellar —flush against the face of the south foundation wall— was the brick base from the previously mentioned chimney, probably the same one used in preparing mash for the hogs (figure 3-13). It may also have been part of a heating system for keeping the hogs warm. Inside, the chimney interior was full of loose sand and gravel fill, containing bricks and roof slate fragments. There also were artifacts inside, including bottle fragments and a handblown, incandescent lightbulb with a patent date of November 8, 1904 (figure 3-14). The walls of the chimney were relatively thin, and all around the base of the chimney were encrustations of hardened creosote. Just north of the chimney, lying embedded in creosote, was the blade of a shovel, probably used for cleaning out the chimney.

From within the root cellar we recovered literally hundreds of patent medicine, ink, and food container bottles; dozens of stoneware bottles, jars, and crocks; and ivory (bone) toothbrushes (figure 3-15). There were

3-15. Examples of ivory toothbrushes found in Hog Heaven, each of which is 5½ in. long. All were missing their bristles.

3-14. An incandescent lightbulb found inside the chimney base in Hog Heaven. The base of the bulb reads "PAT. NOV. 8, 1904," and its location at the very base of the foundation strongly suggests that the cellar was filled in no earlier than 1904.

3-16. Fragments of leather shoes discovered inside Hog Heaven.

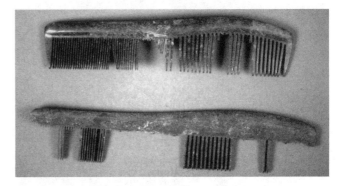

3-17. Examples of combs found inside Hog Heaven.

even dozens of fragments of Shaker shoes (figure 3-16), probably discarded from the Shaker shoemaker's operation that once functioned next door in the hired men's house. Most of these small, personal, and craft-related objects have heretofore been only marginally represented within the collections of Canterbury Shaker Village. Some of the more interesting artifact types found within Hog Heaven are many small brick-size pieces of soapstone that were probably used as bed warmers; beauty aids, specifically shoe blacking and hair medications such as "Mrs. A. Allen's Hair Restorer"; clay marbles; several combs (figure 3-17); bathroom fixtures; buttons; dry cell batteries; two pins shaped like intertwined hearts (figure 3-18); and a toothbrush holder of whiteware. (Many of these artifacts are summarized in table 3-2, although thousands of other artifacts from Hog Heaven are still being processed and could not be included here.)

The ceramic artifacts from Hog Heaven are among the most interesting because, while we may have expected all Shaker ceramics to be white and plain (figure 3-19), that was decidedly not the case. Most of the pottery was highly decorative, including Rockingham nappies (figure 3-20), several hand-painted, tin-glazed fireplace tiles (figure 3-21), and brightly colored transfer

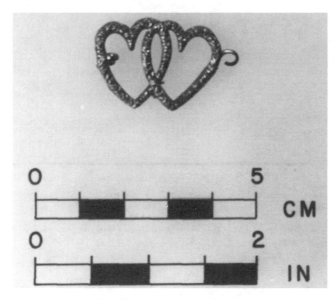

3-18. One of the pins shaped like intertwined hearts found inside Hog Heaven.

3-19. Sets of dishes are visible in this dining room scene inside the Church Family dwelling house. Eldresses are seated at the table in the foreground and sisters at the three tables in the rear. Courtesy of Canterbury Shaker Village Archives.

prints on whiteware (figure 3-22) that really were no different from the mass-produced prints that every non-Shaker was using a century ago. Many of the ceramics were Meakin ironstone china that easily could have been ordered from a Sears Roebuck catalog of that time (figure 3-23). Vessels included several intact stoneware jars, jugs, and crocks, as well as English stoneware bottles for beer or ginger beer (figure 3-24). Most common, though, were the sherds from dozens of earthenware plates, saucers, cups, and pitchers, chiefly manufactured of whiteware. (See table 3-3 for a list of some of

3-20. A yellowware nappy (baking dish) with Rockingham decoration found in Hog Heaven in 1996. This measures 12¼ in. in diameter.

3-21. A tin-glazed tile with polychrome decoration, probably from a fireplace surround. This was found in Hog Heaven in 1996.

the more common makers' marks that appeared on the whiteware.) There also were very small quantities of the ceramic types known as yellowware, porcelain, semi-porcelain, and redware. We did not recover any ceramics that definitively date from the eighteenth century, and none clearly postdate 1910. Perhaps the most distinctive ceramic vessel was the base of a transfer-printed "Father Matthew" whiteware plate, portraying the mid-nine-teenth-century Irish temperance leader surrounded by members of his flock (figure 3-25). The plate bears the words "ADMINISTERING THE TOTAL ABSTINENCE PLEDGE."

The cellar also contained an extraordinarily broad representation of glass bottles, but there were only a small number of half-pint whiskey hip flasks, beer bottles, or pictorial flasks (figure 3-26). American household

3-24. English stoneware bottles found in Hog Heaven that would have contained beer or ginger beer. These have a brown ferruginous glaze combined with a white Bristol glaze. The heights are either 8 in. or 10¾ in.

3-22. A transfer-printed whiteware plate discovered in Hog Heaven in 1996.

3-23. The base of a platter of ironstone china, with the maker's mark indicating it was manufactured by "J. & G. MEAKIN HANLEY ENGLAND."

3-25. The base of a temperance plate showing Father Matthew "ADMINISTERING THE TOTAL ABSTINENCE PLEDGE" to his followers. This was discovered in Hog Heaven in 1996.

Table 3-3
Makers' Marks on Whiteware in Hog Heaven Dump

Manufacturer	Mark
D. E. McNicol Pottery Co. East Liverpool, Ohio 1892–1950s	PRINCESS within a globe
Prospect Hill Pottery Dale & Davis Trenton, New Jersey 1879–1894	British coat of arms
New England Pottery Co. East Boston, Massachusetts 1875–ca. 1914	flower w. GNEPC
Warwick China Company Wheeling, West Virginia 1887–1951	Warwick over China
Dresden Pottery East Liverpool, Ohio 1876–ca. 1920	DRESDEN within a globe; Naomi within a banner; PERFECT within a banner; DRESDEN over globe with WARRANTED within globe; DRESDEN within shield, 1885 on shield's exterior, EAST LIVERPOOL on banner under shield
J W Pankhust & Co. Hanley, Staffordshire Potteries 1850–1882	British crest
J & G Meakin Hanley, Staffordshire Potteries post-1890	Ironstone China over British crest; Crown over circle w. bar, Autumn Time
Alfred Meakin Tunstall, Staffordshire Potteries 1875–	ALFRED MEAKIN above crown; WINDERMERE
Charles Meakin	ROYAL IRONSTONE CHINA above British crest
Diamond Pottery Co. Hanley, Staffordshire Potteries 1908–1935	PEARL STONE over WARE over D. P. & CO.
Anthony Shaw & Son Tunstall (ca. 1851–1856) and Burslem (ca. 1860–ca. 1900)	OPAQUE STONE CHINA, SHAW WARRANTED
John Meir & Son Tunstall, Staffordshire Potteries 1837–1897	British crest over JOHN MEIR & SON over ENGLAND
Johnson Brothers Hanley (1883–) and Tunstall (ca. 1899–1913), Staffordshire Potteries	WAVERLY over crown over JOHNSON BROS. ENGLAND over PAT. NOV 7 '99
John Edwards Fenton, Staffordshire Potteries 1847–1900	WARRANTED IRONSTONE CHINA, plumes over TRADE MARK

Table 3-3 (*continued*)

Manufacturer	Mark
T. & R. Boote Ltd. Burslem, Staffordshire Potteries 1842– (printed marks: 1890–1906)	PREMIUM T & R BOOTE ENGLAND YOSEMITE IV 13 17RK
G. W. Turner & Sons Tunstall, Staffordshire Potteries 1873–1895	G.W.T. over BRAZIL over TUNSTALL
John Alcock England	JOHN ALCOCK over TRENT SHAPE
Burslem Pottery Co. Ltd. Scotia Works, Burslem 1894–1933	BURSLEM, ENGLAND, HARROW
John Maddock & Sons Burslem, Staffordshire Potteries 1855–	MADDOCK & CO.
Ridgways Hanley, Staffordshire Potteries 1879–1920 (printed marks: ca. 1905–1920)	RIDGWAYS STOKE ON TRENT
Unknown	MADE IN GERMANY in a circle within a circle

dumps from the nineteenth century often have larger numbers of whiskey bottles, yet here they were relatively rare. However, several nineteenth-century wine bottles were present that suggest the Shakers were most likely drinking wine. It is unlikely that these were thrown out by hired men, who typically consumed much stronger drinks! There also were dozens of fragments of pressed glass, from small glass pitchers, relish dishes, and candy dishes.

Most impressive were the great numbers of glass patent medicine bottles. Some of the medicines had been purchased from the outside world and some bottled by the Shakers, but nearly all contained alcohol as the primary ingredient. This is to be expected at any American community of this time period and size. Essentially everyone in the nineteenth century used patent medicines to excess, including the Shakers. However, as many as two-thirds of the bottles discarded into Hog Heaven were medicine bottles, and this is an unusually high proportion. Most likely they had been brought here from the Shakers' infirmary building, located on the east side of Shaker Road about 500 feet away. Perhaps the Shakers had done a cleaning-out of the infirmary at

about the time this foundation was filled in. Most of the medicines found in Hog Heaven derived from the outside world, purchased by the Shakers for their own consumption. These included "Red Star Cough Cure" by the Charles A. Vogeler Co.; various styles of bitters bottles, including "Atwood's Jaundice Bitters"; "Eastman & Fitch Pharmacists Concord, N.H."; "Dr. Kennedy's Rheumatic Linament"; "Dr. B. J. Kendall's Blackberry Balsam"; "Volatiti, Aromatic and Headache Snuff"; "Ayer's Cherry Pectoral Syrup"; "Dr. Killner's Swamproot Kidney Liver and Bladder Cure"; "Bromo-Seltzer"; "Hagee's Cordial Cod Liver Oil Compound"; "Pisco's Cure for Consumption"; "Healy & Bigelow's Kickapoo Indian Cure"; "Schenick's Pulmonic Syrup"; and others.

The only well-represented Shaker medicine—bottled by and sold by the Shakers—is "SHAKER CHERRY PECTORAL SYRUP CANTERBURY, N.H. NO. 1." Nine bottles that once contained cherry pectoral syrup were unearthed by the backhoe trench in early 1996, and two whole bottles and fragments of five or six more were recovered in the summer of 1996 (figure 3-27). But the backhoe trench also revealed bottles embossed with "Doctor Corbett's Renovating Bitters," "Shakers, Enfield

3-26. An assortment of bottles discovered in Hog Heaven, including (*clockwise from upper left*) a beer bottle, a bottle of "WORLD'S HAIR RESTORER," a bottle of "SARATOGA CONGRESS WATER," a whiskey flask, a perfume bottle, and a second whiskey flask.

3-27. Shaker medicine bottles found in Hog Heaven, embossed with the words "SHAKER CHERRY PECTORAL SYRUP CANTERBURY, N.H. NO. 1."

3-28. Bottles of "HOOD'S TOOTH POWDER C.I. HOOD & CO. LOWELL, MASS." found in Hog Heaven. The height of each is 3⅜ in.

New Hampshire, Witcher Anodyne," and "Shaker Syrup #1." The Shakers' patent medicines had probably been produced in the Church Family syrup shop, which contained a still for the production of alcoholic medicines until it was closed down by Prohibition.

The bottles in the root cellar also included many food containers, flavoring extracts, ink bottles, Hood's Tooth Powder bottles (figure 3-28), glass vials of all sizes, Atlas and Mason canning jars, and mucilage bottles. In smaller quantities, there were specialty bottles such as piccalilli (relish) bottles (figure 3-29), "Pepto Mangan Gude" (figure 3-30), bottled water (including Saratoga "Congress Water" [figure 3-26]), vanilla extract ("Grand Union Tea Co."), sewing machine oil, Armour's food bottles of milk glass, "Listerine" bottles, "Vicks" bottles, a musterole jar, a bottle of "Humphre Homeopath" (a horse liniment), the glass bases from oil lamps, and even a bottle of Hoyt's German Cologne, made in Lowell, Massachusetts.

Metal artifacts were just as common, including thousands of nails, a great deal of tinware and enamelware, barrel hoops, sections of metal stovepipe, a coal shovel, a metal ashes' grate from a stove, a large pitchfork, hundreds of tin cans, tin roofing, and much more. Oftentimes, the *smallest* metal artifacts were the most interesting, though, including pins, a tiny lead pestle, thimbles, cuff links, hundreds of brass grommets employed

in shoemaking, and a small sterling silver spoon, probably used for sugar or salt (figure 3-31).

Food remains were represented by only a small number of pig bones, but it was not expected that pig bones would be common here, since the pork industry had ended as much as sixty years before the root cellar was filled in. Still, there were many implements made from bone, notably the ivory toothbrushes and several ivory napkin rings (figure 3-32).

3-30. A bottle of "PEPTO MANGAN GUDE" (liquid food) discovered in Hog Heaven.

3-31. A sterling silver spoon discovered in Hog Heaven.

3-29. Four piccalilli (relish) bottles discovered in Hog Heaven. Each is 10 in. tall and 2 in. in diameter.

3-32. One of the ivory napkin rings discovered in Hog Heaven.

3-33. Miniature brass scallop shells found in Hog Heaven.

These artifacts and craft remnants can be used to establish a chronology for the deposits in Hog Heaven: It appears that most of the trash was thrown inside the stone foundation soon after the turn of the twentieth century. Most definitive for dating purposes was the presence of lightbulbs and fuses. However, while it appears that the root cellar may have been filled in all at once, the dating of the artifacts ranges from a few late-eighteenth-century bottles, to early-nineteenth-century delft tiles, to great quantities of ceramics and glass from the last quarter of the nineteenth century, up through the early-twentieth-century fuses and lightbulbs.

What is most apparent about this wealth of material culture is that the objects found in this Shaker dump are *not* significantly different from those in anyone else's dump during that time period. There is little here that is distinctively "Shaker-like" in appearance, little that was actually produced here. Canterbury Shaker Village was clearly dependent upon the outside world for any number of manufactured products. In fact, some of the artifacts appear quite *unlike* what might be expected at a Shaker site. The presence of remarkably ornate objects (including the pins with intertwined hearts, the small sterling silver spoon, miniature brass scallop shells [figure 3-33], etc.), perfume bottles, and several whiskey and beer bottles (figure 3-26) was quite surprising given the austere reputation of the Shakers. Given the location of this cellar alongside the hired men's house, it is possible that some of the artifacts were used and discarded here by hired men and not by the Shakers. But regardless of who actually used these products, the point

is that some very worldly goods were being consumed within this Shaker community, and mass-produced wares were everywhere. The easiest interpretation may be that the Shakers had evolved into middle-class consumers. This is not to disparage the Shakers but to suggest that they were becoming more like the World's People and less like the Shakers of old.

Another inevitable conclusion from archeological evidence is that the material possessions of the Canterbury Shakers from one hundred years ago do not suggest that the Shakers were particularly self-sufficient. This slice of Shaker life at the turn of the century reveals that the Shakers generally ate off white earthenware dishes with gilded edges and from plates decorated with any number of bright, transfer-printed designs. The Canterbury Shakers had vast sets of dishes, just like other Americans of their day, and their dumps reveal material culture that is at times gaudy, colorful, attractive, and attention-getting. They also consumed the same highly alcoholic patent medicines that the World's People enjoyed and were quite attentive to their own personal appearance. This last point may seem strange when it is considered that the Shakers were usually carefully covered from head to toe to ensure that no one would look provocative to members of the opposite sex.

The Cow Barn Ramp

In the fall of 1998 and again in 2000, we excavated a dump within the east ramp of the massive 1858 Church Family cow barn (figure 3-34). Before a vandal burned down the barn in 1973, this had been the largest wood structure in the state of New Hampshire, some 200 feet long. When I first arrived in Canterbury in 1977, I heard from the Shakers themselves that a bottle collector had been digging at the end of the cow barn. Still, I did not check this out for myself, because my research at that time was focused more on recording the remains of Shaker architecture than interpreting material culture. However, over the years there was a continuing problem with museum visitors wandering over to the barn ramp and digging out artifacts, so I was finally asked by the museum's curator, Shery Hack, to do a small salvage excavation in 1998.

With a small team of volunteers, and working within a relatively small area, we found nearly one hundred complete stoneware bottles for beer or ginger beer, plus sherds from many others (figure 3-35), as well as wine

3-34. The east ramp of the Church Family cow barn (facing north).

3-35. Some of the stoneware bottles for beer or ginger beer that were discovered inside the east ramp of the Church Family cow barn in 1998.

3-36. Examples of wine bottle fragments discovered inside the east ramp of the Church Family cow barn.

3-37. Examples of perfume bottles (the left has an atomizer) discovered inside the east ramp of the Church Family cow barn in 1998.

3-38. One of the sets of false teeth (dentures) found inside the east ramp of the Church Family cow barn in 1998.

bottles (figure 3-36) and perfume bottles (figure 3-37) (see table 3-2). Because the stoneware bottles were so close to the hay barn, one interpretation is that these may have contained the "hop drink" that Eldress Bertha described as having been brewed for the hay makers. There even were false teeth, which had most likely been manufactured by the Shakers themselves (figure 3-38). A journal reference from March 7, 1863, described how it was done:

A young man comes from Enfield, N.H. to learn of Elder H. C. Blinn how to make vulcanite plates for artificial teeth. We have purchased the right of vulcanizing for the Society and have bought the apparatus.

Our excavation covered only a tiny proportion of the barn ramp, but we definitely concluded that this may have been the richest of all the known dumps in Canterbury. In the end, the only way to protect this site was to bury it, so when we finished our excavation, the museum covered the dump with a thick layer of fill. Visitors can no longer enjoy the guilty pleasure of digging for Shaker artifacts, but at least future generations of archeologists will know where to obtain a truly spectacular variety of Shaker ceramics and glassware.

Alternative Explanations

Because some of the findings in the Shaker dumps were unexpected, they have provoked negative responses from those who prefer the popular image of Shaker society as wholly self-sacrificing and otherworldly. When *Discover* magazine carried the story "Shakers Behaving Badly," and *National Geographic* magazine published its "New Window on Shaker Life," and *The Boston Sunday Globe* ran "Shaking Up Shaker Myths at N.H.'s Canterbury Village," the result was letters to the editor, caustic letters to the archeologist, and a host of rationalizations about how the Shakers could not possibly have consumed any of those products. It is extremely unfortunate that sometimes a highly sanitized image of the Shakers has been allowed to replace reality, and some of the Shakers' more fervent supporters have shown a remarkable resistance to new perspectives.

Some of the responses stated that the Shakers must have recycled empty liquor bottles from the outside world, putting other beverages into them; that everything in the dumps must have been given to the Shakers, each item a "gift" that they promptly threw away; that all "contraband" goods had been brought to the village by new converts, who had immediately thrown them out; and that anything remotely "improper" must have been thrown into the dumps by the hired men. The last point contains the most peculiar reasoning, in that hired men were seen throwing garbage into the dumps in the 1950s; therefore a few Shaker buffs consider the hired men to have been the source of *all* improper artifacts. This ignores the fact that the artifacts found during the archeological digs date to the nineteenth and early twentieth centuries.

My favorite response, though, appears in the recent detective book *Shaker Run* by Karen Harper, set in an imaginary Shaker village in Ohio. Harper had clearly read "New Window on Shaker Life," which mentioned our discovery of the bottle of World's Hair Restorer in Hog Heaven, and so she added an archeologist to her story. In the book, the archeologist—named Dr. Myron Scott—upsets the Shakers at "Shaker Run" by discovering various "improper" artifacts, including the hair restorer, perfume bottles, and even wine, beer, and whiskey bottles. While I enjoyed the addition of an archeologist to her tale, I must admit that I wish she hadn't given him (me!) an earring.

Chapter Four

Blacksmithing and Pipe Smoking

Blacksmithing

Eldress Bertha Lindsay sadly described the Church Family blacksmith shop as having been her favorite building at Shaker Village (personal communication, 1978). Unfortunately, it had been removed in 1952, marking the end of nearly 160 years of Shaker blacksmithing. Eldress Bertha's sense of loss was understandable because blacksmith shops were practically ubiquitous in the nineteenth century, and the Town of Canterbury had as many as nine or ten. These included one at each of the families at Shaker Village. According to James Otis Lyford's *History of the Town of Canterbury, New Hampshire, 1727–1912*,

The Shakers have always maintained one or more blacksmith shops, and for a number of years each of the three families had one of its own. Some of the buildings are still standing. If there was no one of that trade among the members some one was employed from outside. One shop [probably the one at the Church Family] now does the work for the entire community.

Blacksmith shops were critical through the late nineteenth century for the manufacture of nails, horseshoes, and oxshoes (all from bar iron), and for the repairs performed on barrel hoops, shovels, axes, and every conceivable type of farm implement. Generally speaking, the processes involved in blacksmithing are well known, as are the tools and spatial layouts of specific smithies. Still, archeology at blacksmith shops has rarely been published, with the notable exception of work by John Light and Henry Unglik at the Fort St. Joseph Blacksmith Shop in Ontario, Canada.

The Shaker blacksmith shops are now gone, but the undisturbed foundations of two of them—at the Church and Second Families—are still clearly visible and covered with artifacts. I knew that excavations within these shops had the potential to recover smithy tools, farm machinery that had been taken in for repair, and evidence for a variety of crafts or occupations. I also relished the chance to compare two Shaker blacksmith shops, hoping to discover whether each had been "assigned" specific tasks not represented in the other. There also was the opportunity to look for evidence of some of the activities that had been "banned" by the Shakers in the mid–nineteenth century, such as the consumption of tobacco.

There were still other research opportunities, in that the large size of the Church Family blacksmith shop suggested that some craft manufacturing, and not just traditional blacksmithing, may have been going on inside this structure. For example, Eldress Bertha had stated that tinware was manufactured there, and this implied that dumps scattered either around or within the blacksmith shop foundations might shed light upon previously undocumented craft activities. Finally, there was the question of who had actually been living and working within the shops. Not only were most of the blacksmiths unknown, but it was unclear whether the blacksmiths and their assistants actually lived within these buildings. Clearly the quantities and types of refuse found—whether industrial or domestic or both—might give some insights into whether these had been residences as well as workplaces.

The Second Family Blacksmith Shop

We first explored the blacksmith shop at the Second Family, where all that survived was a rock- and brush-

4-1. The foundation of the Second Family blacksmith shop as excavated in 1996 (facing southwest).
The sole surviving Second Family building, a barn, is visible at the rear center.

covered foundation (figure 4-1). The Second Family at Canterbury Shaker Village had been gathered on November 10, 1800, at which time members consecrated their personal possessions for the collective use of the entire family. The Canterbury Second Family was home to Shakers who were neither the most powerful nor the most recent arrivals. Rather, they were full-fledged Shakers who simply had not attained the senior status of those in the Church Family. Because the only extant accounts of the Second Family are in journals kept by members of the Church Family, they nearly always refer to instances of monetary or physical assistance. For example, the first recorded instance of direct monetary assistance to the Second Family was in December of 1817, when the deacons and ministry agreed to support and maintain four elderly or handicapped Second Family members with $200.00 yearly or until some of them died. Another type of financial assistance was to give one family a monopoly over a particular industry, as in 1819, when the Church gave the Second Family sole selling rights in twenty-one towns for their garden seed business.

Such accounts give the impression that the Second Family was closely tied to, and somewhat dependent upon, the dominant Church Family, but this view may be

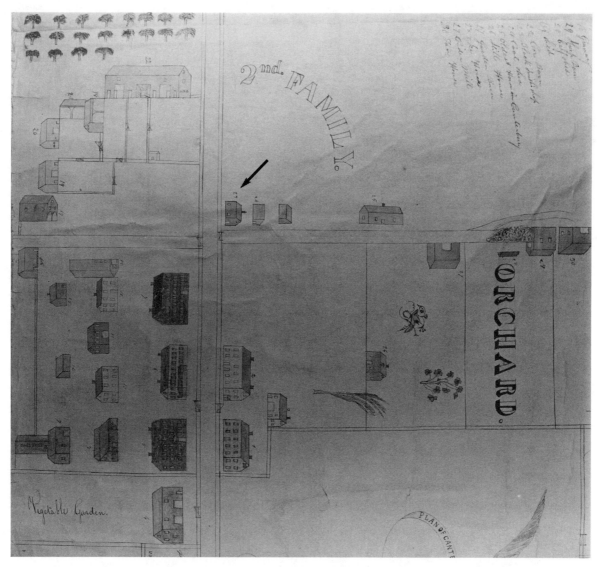

4-2. A detail from a watercolor of Canterbury Shaker Village drawn by Elder Henry C. Blinn in 1848, showing buildings of the Second Family. The arrow points to the Second Family blacksmith shop. Courtesy of Canterbury Shaker Village Archives.

the result of a biased sample and not truly reflective of the integration of the Second Family into the larger Canterbury Shaker community. However, financial and recruitment problems persisted, and in 1871, after several conferences among the trustees, ministry, elders, and eldresses, they decided to make the Second Family a branch of the Church. Most of the brethren and sisters moved to the Church Family, although a few sisters were left to care for the buildings. It was not until January of 1915 that the actual process of closing the Second Family began. The livestock were sold, and during the following spring the remaining sisters moved to the Church Family.

In 1951 David Curtis and William Meeh purchased most of the Second Family land, and Curtis erected his own house on the west side of Shaker Road, atop the foundation of the Second Family sisters' brick shop. One Shaker Second Family building has survived until today, and it originally served as a barn or shed. Many of the Second Family building foundations on the west side of Shaker Road have been bulldozed. However, the east side of the road has been less disturbed, and the surfaces of several foundations are now covered with brush and poison ivy. Of the dozens of foundations from buildings known to have existed in the Second Family before its closing in 1915, we had enough time to test and map only three during an archeological survey in 1996, one of which was the site of the Second Family blacksmith shop.

Given the importance of smithing to the residents of Canterbury, the Second Family blacksmith shop was probably constructed soon after the gathering in 1800. The shop is depicted on Elder Henry Blinn's 1848 watercolor of the village, as is a coal shed just east of it (figure 4-2). It appears again in the background of photographs dating to the early twentieth century, and it was probably taken down about the time the Second Family folded in 1915. Most likely the only Shaker blacksmith shop in use after that time was the one at the Church Family.

When we mapped the surface of Shaker Village from 1978 to 1980, I had identified this Second Family foundation as site 6:N2E0. During our more recent research, I personally removed a rich carpet of poison ivy from its surface in 1996 while dressed in a Tivec smock and rubber boots! As the surface became clearer, we found that the southern half of the foundation was covered with round fieldstones, probably deposited there after many plowings of the surrounding field. Curtis said he had never disturbed the foundation after purchasing it in 1951 except for pushing over one large stone, which he thought was the base for an anvil. As the surface was cleared, I noticed that the northern half of the foundation was covered with a dense scatter of iron artifacts, creating the impression that the building had been burned or abandoned with everything still in situ. The possible anvil base was located in the west center of the foundation, while a deep stone trough stretched across the north end of the foundation.

We gridded the surface of the foundation with pins at 1-meter intervals and then mapped all of the foundation stones, fieldstones, and artifact scatters (figure 4-3).

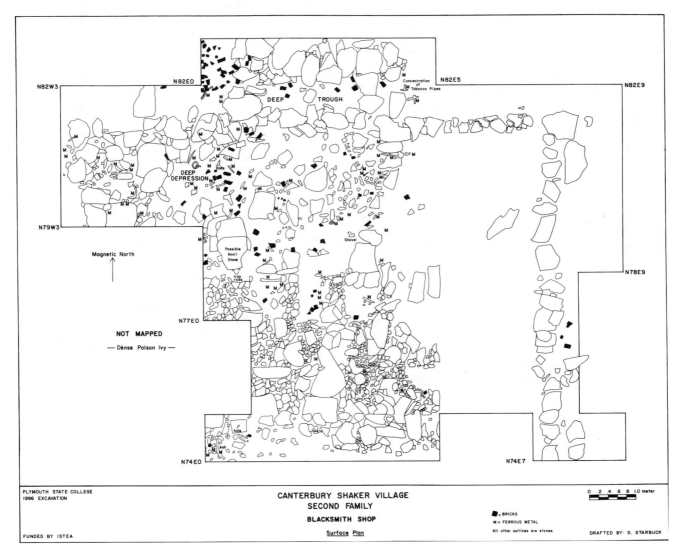

4-3. Plan view of the foundation of the Second Family blacksmith shop in fig. 4-1.

4-4. The foundation of the Second Family blacksmith shop during excavation in the fall of 1996 (facing southwest toward Shaker Road).

None of the test pits could be mapped in the southwest corner, because the poison ivy was so dense, but everywhere else we found iron artifacts lying just below the grass. Notable among these were oxshoes and a couple of drills, suggesting that a drill press may have been in use inside the shop. As our excavations proceeded (figure 4-4), we gradually discovered that this was not merely the site of a typical blacksmith shop, with a mix of broken tools and parts undergoing repair, but that a significant craft industry had been practiced here. Both inside and outside the northeast corner of the foundation there was an extensive waster dump filled with warped and asymmetrical bowls of redware tobacco pipes (figure 4-5), as well as a lesser number of waster

Table 4-1
Tobacco Pipes Found within the Second Family Blacksmith Shop

Total fragments

white (ball) clay	573
red earthenware	2,037
marbleized	421
Total	3,031 fragments

Minimum Number of Pipes

white (ball) clay	14
red earthenware	249
marbleized	142
Total	405 pipes

Bore diameters (when measurable)

White (ball) clay		Red earthenware		Marbleized	
		$4/64''$	3		
$5/64''$	1	$5/64''$	1		
		$7/64''$	28	$7/64''$	1
$8/64''$	45	$8/64''$	7	$8/64''$	2
$9/64''$	6	$9/64''$	3	$9/64''$	2
$10/64''$	6	$10/64''$	19	$10/64''$	6
$11/64''$	13	$11/64''$	186	$11/64''$	117
$12/64''$	4	$12/64''$	17	$12/64''$	7

pipes of white clay. Wasters are the rejects, the pipes that never made it to market, and pipes of both colors were large-bored and intended to have a separate reed stem inserted into the bowl. Both the red and white pipes have much the same dimensions (see table 4-1), and the white pipes were probably being made in the same molds as the redware pipes. Because white clay was the preferred color for pipes throughout the nineteenth century, it may well be that the Shakers started out importing white clay from a distance (perhaps from England), but because of cost gave up and then switched to the local, cheaper red clays that are ubiquitous throughout New England.

Shaker blacksmith shops were sometimes the location for pipe manufacture, with a pipe kiln in one corner of the shop to maximize use of the heat. The pipes would have been held by pipe kiln racks of wrought iron while they were being fired. From the pipe waster fragments that we excavated (figure 4-6), we concluded that pipes were clearly manufactured at the Second Family in the early or mid–nineteenth century. Some of the redware pipes contained bits of white clay, creating a marbleized or mottled effect (figure 4-7). The white clay may have

4-5. An intact redware pipe bowl from the waster dump located behind the Second Family blacksmith shop.

4-6. Some of the redware pipe bowl fragments found behind the Second Family blacksmith shop.

4-7. Marbleized (mottled) redware tobacco pipes found behind the Second Family blacksmith shop.

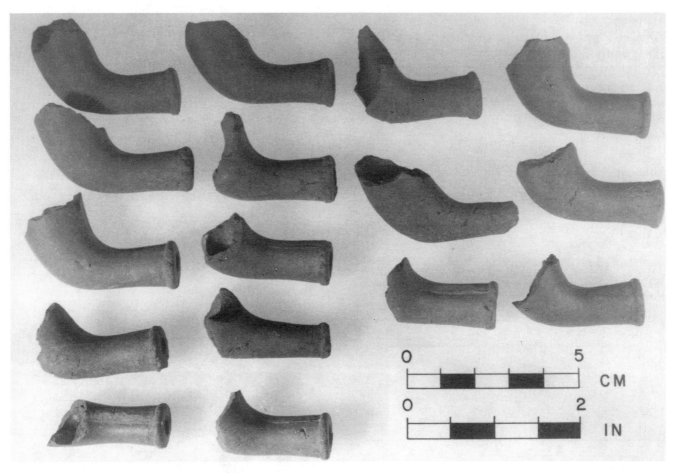

4-8. Some of the more intact redware tobacco pipes found behind the Second Family blacksmith shop.

been mixed in for aesthetic reasons, or perhaps the Shakers were merely trying to use up the white clay. This resulted in pipe wasters that ranged from perfectly red, to slightly speckled with white clay, to some that were totally awash in white. The redware pipes were much plainer in form and finish than the pipes manufactured after 1864 by John Taber and son at their factory in East Alton (and later in Wolfeboro), New Hampshire, which until now had been the only known pipemaking establishment in New Hampshire. The marbleized red-and-white pipes of Canterbury are not typical of local pipe manufacture, and it seems doubtful that the unusual-appearing, marbleized pipes would have sold very well. Because none of the Shaker pipes are decorated, unlike most contemporary pipes used by the World's People, it may well mean that they were produced strictly for the Shakers' own consumption. All of the pipes are amazingly similar, but the different bore diameters provide proof that more than one mold was used.

The Shakers are known to have manufactured great quantities of tobacco pipes at other Shaker Villages, notably at Mount Lebanon and Watervliet, New York, but no historical references have ever been found that describe pipemaking in Canterbury. During their early history, many of the Shakers were extremely fond of smoking, and according to the Canterbury *Historical Record*,

At this date [1800] it was almost the universal custom for the Brethren and Sisters to smoke tobacco, and quite a number of the pipes were taken into the social gatherings & the tobacco smoke, no doubt, filled the room. This was, however, soon discontinued, as already some were to be found who could not endure the nauseating fumes of tobacco, and on this account would leave the company.

The *Historical Record* further records that even after tobacco was banned,

We occasionally find a person who uses a pipe, but the cases are rare. The fumes of tobacco are not to be found in any of our buildings. It has proved to be a decided blessing to us that its use was not recommended by Believers.

Because the revised Shaker Millennial Laws of 1845 were starting to place limitations on the use of tobacco, it appears most likely that the wasters discovered at the Second Family represent craft production before that date. The evidence for Canterbury pipemaking was unexpected, and because it consisted of imperfect wasters in the dump, the activity it revealed was not simply a matter of Shaker brothers sneaking out to the blacksmith shop to have a smoke where the sisters would not catch them! These were pipes that had become defective during the manufacturing process, before firing was completed, and many of the pipe bowls had distorted and were no longer round in outline. The 3,031 pipe fragments recovered in 1996 (table 4-1) represent a minimum of 405 discrete pipes that had been discarded. This total is based on counting the number of "elbows" among the pipe fragments, that is, the point where the bowl meets the stem. Many of the pipes were nearly complete (figure 4-8), but there were no traces of the long willow stems that would have been inserted into the bowls for use.

We also found a host of tools inside the Second Family blacksmith shop that pertained to the more typical activities of the smithy, including tongs, files, calipers, and hundreds of iron objects that were being shaped or repaired. These included many stove parts (figure 4-9), barrel hoops, horseshoes, oxshoes, one corrective horseshoe, shovel blades, an ax head, a drawknife, teeth from a mowing machine, and much more. There were modest numbers of tin cans and bottle fragments, numerous sherds of unrefined stoneware, whiteware, and redware, and a circa 1860 dime was found on the northern edge of the foundation.

The blacksmith site was richest in the northwest corner where we excavated a large, cellar-like depression to a depth of over 1.2 meters. This depression (nearly 2 meters on a side) was literally packed with tongs, files (figure 4-10), horseshoes and oxshoes, barrel hoops, stove plates, stove legs, and sherds from either one or two gray stoneware jugs. I do not know what the function of this area was originally, before it was converted to a dump.

All together, we excavated twenty-one 1-meter-square test pits in and around the foundation. Throughout the foundation, the soil layers consisted of a thin surface lens of recent topsoil, underlain by a thicker (10–15 centimeter) band of dark, charcoal-stained earth that contained most of the iron artifacts. Underneath this was coarse yellow subsoil that was essentially sterile. We found no evidence for either a wood or stone floor within the shop foundation, although it seems likely that there would have been a wood floor. Also, we did not do any work on the site of the coal shed located about 6–7 meters to the east, but we observed that the ground there was covered with charcoal.

4-9. A cast-iron stove plate found in the northwest corner of the Second Family blacksmith shop. It reads "PALACE ARCAND."

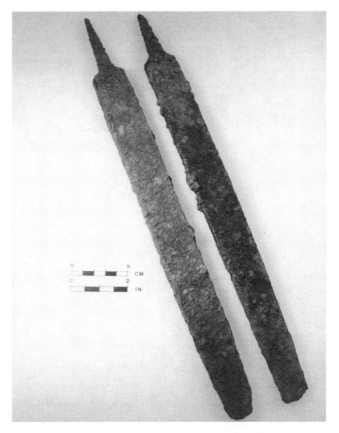

4-10. Examples of files discovered in the foundation of the Second Family blacksmith shop.

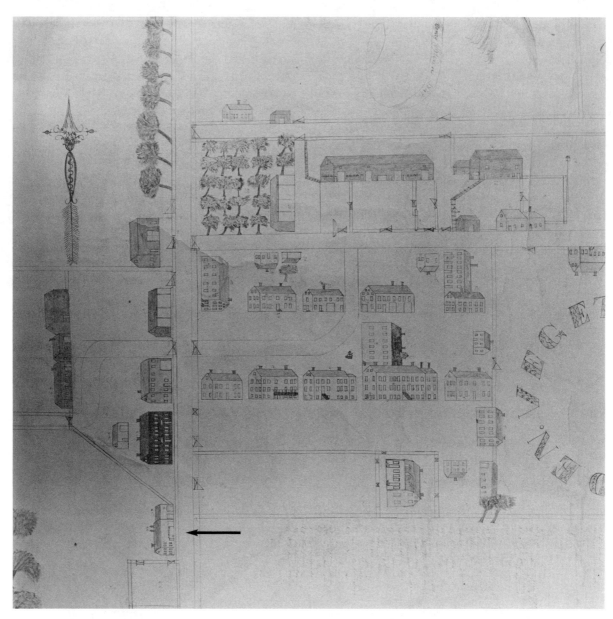

4-11. A detail from a watercolor of Canterbury Shaker Village drawn by Elder C. Blinn in 1848. This shows buildings of the Church Family, and the arrow points to the Church Family blacksmith shop and the adjacent ox shed. Courtesy of Canterbury Shaker Village Archives.

The Church Family Blacksmith Shop

The largest of the Canterbury blacksmith shops was built at the Church Family in 1811, on the west side of Shaker Road and just to the south of the trustees' office. This shop replaced one that had been erected in 1793 on the east side of Shaker Road, in between the infirmary and the brethren's shop. An excellent early graphic representation of the 1811 shop appears in Elder Henry Blinn's 1848 watercolor of Shaker Village (figure 4-11).

Other early views of the shop, drawn by Peter Foster and Joshua H. Bussell, appear in Robert Emlen's *Shaker Village Views*. Each of these drawings also shows a small ox shed that was attached at the north end of the shop, and apparently the shoeing of oxen was one of the shop's primary activities.

The 1811 blacksmith shop measured 28 × 50 feet. It contained a brick forge, and Brother Irving Greenwood wrote that it had "1 story and attic and basement." The Shakers later removed the forge in 1849 and replaced it with two cast-iron forges and an iron stack, put in at a cost of $200.00. Also, the Canterbury *Historical Record* noted:

The old brick forges at the Blacksmith shop are taken away and two cast iron forges take their places. This is the first change or improvement that has been introduced into this place for a great many years. The floor is relaid and it presents a better appearance. The building finally became so much out of repair that in 1860 the roof was raised and a jst [*sic*] added. The whole front of the building was remodeled by enlarging the doors and by adding large windows in place of the old shutters. The underpinning was also repaired and the building painted, after which it was no discredit to the family.

Later modifications to the building appear to have been minor, and subsequently the ox shed was taken down in 1900. The blacksmith shop itself was removed in 1952, and Sister Edith Clark recorded that it was "Sold to a Mr. Sloan of Mass. Taken down in April by Mr. Noyes & helper also from Mass."

After 1952, there were no further journal references to the Church Family blacksmith shop, or the site upon which it had stood, but Eldress Bertha Lindsay remembered how the blacksmith shop had still been well stocked with tools in the 1940s. Also, in the 1970s she provided a detailed description of the interior:

the upper room, a very large room, at the north end of the building here was used for the shoeing of the oxen and so forth, and then there was [*sic*] two little steps leading down to another level where they made the tinware. Then another little level led downstairs where you could go right outdoors at the south end of the building.

Fifty years of inactivity at the blacksmith site came to an end in the year 2000 as the modern museum village began to make plans to reconstruct the blacksmith shop on its original site in order to house a new restaurant for visitors. I was asked to do an archeological excavation there to define exactly the footprint of the blacksmith shop and the contiguous ox shed, and this required locating and sampling any surrounding dumps (figure 4-12).

The surface of the blacksmith shop foundation was not as rich as that at the Second Family, but it was littered with fragments of metal and glass, broken bricks, leather shoe fragments, a chisel, a knife blade, several ox shoes, and chunks of wood, some of which may have postdated the removal of the building in 1952 (figures 4-13, 4-14). We cleared the surface in June of 2000 and found that the foundation consisted of two parts: (a) the northern two-thirds, consisting of thousands of field-stones bounded by large blocks of quarried granite; this had the appearance of a filled-in cellar hole; and (b) the southern one-third, which was a deep, open cellar, capable of being driven into from the south side of the building. At the southeast corner of the cellar, there was a vertical, poured concrete support, which appears to have been a brace against the south wall of the foundation. In fact, we found a couple of additional poured concrete supports lying atop the stone pile, suggesting that during its final years of use, several braces had been employed to keep the foundation, and the building that sat atop it, from shifting and ultimately collapsing.

The large, quarried, foundation stones had been laid up only one or two courses high, and these "floated" atop the pile of smaller fieldstones. While this may have been adequate to support the weight of a building that was originally only one story high (with an attic), by the time it had been expanded to its final three-story height (still with an attic) the weight of the blacksmith shop must have far exceeded the capacity of its unstable foundation.

Initially, I assumed that the pile of fieldstones represented a cellar that had been filled in after the Shakers removed the blacksmith shop. However, after a Caterpillar "excavator" was used to completely hollow out the interior of the foundation, we found no artifacts below the surface of the stone pile. The excavator proved that the quarried stones merely sat atop the pile and were not a "shell" or "form" into which the fieldstones had been thrown. The foundation of the blacksmith shop was essentially a giant man-made platform of fieldstones, with a single layer of sill stones positioned at ground level around the perimeter. Retaining walls made from extremely large granite blocks were stacked up on the south and west to hold in all of the loose fieldstones. Everything was dry-laid, and the fieldstones became progressively deeper toward the south, which had been necessary to keep the surface of the foundation level since it had been constructed on a steep downhill slope.

Great quantities of brick covered the surface of the cellar area at the south end of the blacksmith shop foundation, including many that were slagged from facing inside the firebox. We excavated test pits there and exposed the substantial stone base of a fireplace, overlain with a tremendous scatter of bricks. Because the later 1849 forges inside the blacksmith shop were made of cast iron (and purchased from the outside world), our discovery in the cellar was no doubt the original 1811 forge base, perhaps the one that lay underneath the

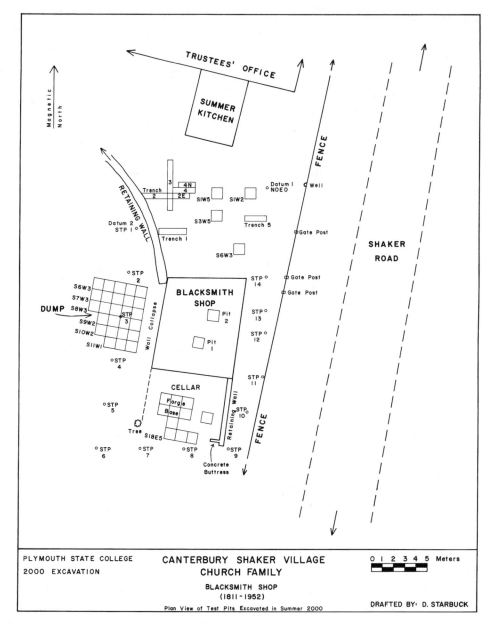

4-12. A plan view of the Church Family blacksmith shop and its associated dump as mapped and excavated in 2000.

southernmost chimney that Elder Henry Blinn portrayed in his 1848 watercolor of the village. The forge base measures 1.35 meters (east-west) by 1.07 meters (north-south) and is in excellent condition (figure 4-15). It appears to be the only surviving feature from the early period of the blacksmith shop. Scattered throughout the cellar we found nails, sherds of whiteware and redware, tin cans, bits of sheet metal, a hinge, a chisel, a file, glass bottle fragments, one tobacco pipe bowl of white ball clay, and chunks of charcoal, rotted wood, and plaster.

Most of these are artifact categories that would be found within any nineteenth- or early-twentieth-century building foundation at Shaker Village.

As the excavator scooped out the interior of the shop foundation, its treads cut several centimeters into the charcoal-stained sod on the west side of the building, kicking out pieces of worked soapstone, ceramic sherds, tobacco pipes, bottles, metal fragments, small pieces of tin, and butchered animal bones. This proved to be the main dump for the blacksmith shop, so we dropped

4-13. The surface of the Church Family blacksmith shop foundation prior to excavation in the summer of 2000 (facing southwest). Each scale board is marked in 10-cm increments.

4-14. The surface of the Church Family blacksmith shop foundation prior to excavation in the summer of 2000 (facing southeast). Each scale board is marked in 10-cm increments.

4-15. The excavated 1811 forge base in the cellar of the Church Family black-smith shop (facing south). The scale board is marked in 10-cm increments.

everything else and began salvaging as much as we could. In the weeks that followed, we excavated a total of 26 square meters of the dump, finding that the rich black fill was loaded with coal ash, burnt coal, cinders, and chunks of burnt wood. Virtually all of the dump was underlain by a single layer of fieldstones (figure 4-16). This "midden" was thickest against the west wall of the foundation, and that was also where the artifacts were richest. Pockets of brown soil lay underneath the coal and charcoal layer, and domestic artifacts were most common in this underlying soil, whereas industrial arti-facts were usually found mixed in with the charcoal and cinders.

The Blacksmith Shop dump contained an immense quantity of domestic and industrial artifacts. We were excited to find many fragments of tin, lead, and brass (in-cluding one brass ruler [figure 4-17]), occasional pockets of butchered bones, 97 leather harness or shoe frag-ments, 2 grindstone fragments, 9 whetstone fragments (figure 4-18), 6 window weight fragments, 72 cast-iron stove fragments, 24 cast-iron pot fragments, 17 pintle-type hinges, 1 ax head, 2 hoe blades, 25 fragments of iron files, 1 bull nose ring, 6 knives, 1 watch chain swivel, 20 buttons, 15 buckles, 1 porcelain drawer "pull," 1 grape-fruit spoon, many hunks of barbed wire, 1 pair of sugar tongs, a splitting wedge, and a mason's cross peen hammer (figure 4-19), 2 candlesnuffers (figure 4-20), and many large pieces of mica.

Unquestionably the largest artifact category in the shop's dump was nails, including thousands of cut (5,536) and wire (2,258) nails, moderate numbers of T-headed (139), L-headed (303), and rosehead (68) nails, some 447 roofing nails, and 2,534 horseshoe or oxshoe nails. The shoeing of animals was one of the most important activities carried on within this shop, and while no horseshoes were recovered, there nevertheless were

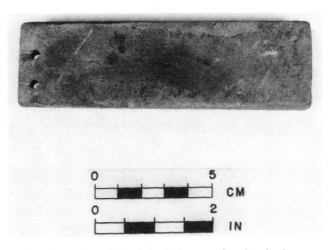

4-18. A whetstone with two holes for hanging, found in the dump west of the Church Family blacksmith shop.

4–16. The excavated dump on the west side of the Church Family blacksmith shop (facing northeast). Each scale board is marked in 10-cm increments.

4-19. A splitting wedge (*top*) and a mason's cross peen hammer excavated from the dump west of the Church Family blacksmith shop.

4-17. A fragment of brass ruler excavated from the dump west of the Church Family blacksmith shop. The gradations read from right to left.

4-20. A candlesnuffer excavated from the dump west of the Church Family blacksmith shop.

27 complete ox shoes found in the dump and in the ox shed area to the north. We also found 111 fragments of iron rod stock and 123 fragments of iron bar stock in the dump.

There were over 8,000 pottery sherds in the dump, suggesting that the blacksmith shop had been used as a dwelling. These included large quantities of plain and transfer-printed whiteware, some creamware and pearlware, vessels with annular decoration, many sherds of unrefined gray stoneware, stoneware sherds from beer or ginger beer bottles, and much redware. Many of the sherds were from plates, but nearly every other vessel form was represented here as well, including several stoneware jugs. The dating of this assemblage ranged from early through late nineteenth century, but most of the sherds fell between about 1820 and 1860.

Some of the more distinctive artifacts in this assemblage were those that pertained to smoking. Whereas few of the tobacco pipes found at the Second Family blacksmith shop showed the telltale signs of use (charcoal stains inside the bowl), here the interiors of the bowls were heavily encrusted with carbon. We found nine white ball clay bowls with the letters "TD" impressed on the side of the bowl facing the smoker. These were no doubt manufactured by the McDougall Company of Glasgow, Scotland, and some of the stem fragments were marked with either "McDougall" or "Glasgow." There were dozens of other pipe bowl and stem fragments, including some made of white ball clay, many of redware (figure 4-21), and some of burnished redware (figure 4-22). Since most of the tobacco pipes were mixed in with the cinders in the dump's fill, and also showed signs of burning on the outside, it appears that when they broke, the blacksmith(s) simply threw the pipes into the fire. A few of the pipes were highly decorative, including an effigy pipe depicting the face and cap of a band member (figure 4-23). We did not find any pipe wasters in this dump, so there is virtually no evidence for tobacco pipes having been manufactured at the Church Family. Based on our findings, the Second Family may well have had a monopoly on pipe production. There of course remains the question of whether the blacksmith(s) were smoking tobacco in the Church Family blacksmith shop before or after tobacco was banned in the 1840s. However, while the dump spans a long time period, it really cannot be determined stratigraphically because little soil built up.

Some of the other artifacts included a "Shaker No. 1 bottle," the base of a large candlestick, much window

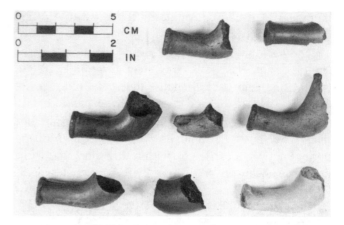

4-21. Examples of red earthenware tobacco pipes, probably manufactured by the Shakers, excavated from the dump west of the Church Family blacksmith shop.

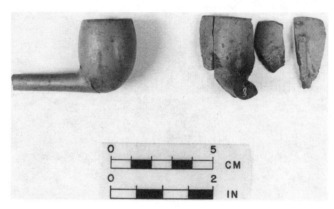

4-22. Examples of burnished, non-Shaker redware tobacco pipes excavated from the dump west of the Church Family blacksmith shop.

4-23. An effigy pipe bowl excavated from the dump west of the Church Family blacksmith shop.

4-24. Eight of the gunflints excavated from the dump west of the Church Family blacksmith shop.

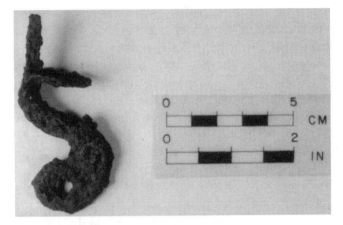

4-25. The cock from a musket excavated from the dump west of the Church Family blacksmith shop.

4-26. Examples of worked soapstone from the surface of the dump west of the Church Family blacksmith shop.

glass, quite a few fragments of wine or cider bottles, many fragments of medicine bottles, and a few glass vials. But our most surprising discovery came in the form of twelve gunflints and the cock from a musket (figures 4-24, 4-25), suggesting that firearms were being repaired here in the blacksmith shop. The historical literature for the Canterbury Shakers simply does not deal with the subject of firearms, and while guns were unquestionably used by the Shakers, it was nonetheless satisfying to finally find direct evidence for the presence of flintlocks.

Another surprise came in the form of hundreds of cut and shaped fragments of soapstone that were scattered throughout the dump (figure 4-26). Most are approximately 2.5 centimeters in thickness, and some are curved corner pieces that bear a very strong resemblance to the soapstone gravestones that were commonly used by the Shakers. (There is no evidence that the Canterbury Shakers made either soapstone stoves or sinks.) It thus appears that the Church Family blacksmith shop was the primary location where the Shakers cut their gravestones to shape, certainly a significant industry given the village's population of two hundred or more at any given time, many of whom were elderly. The dump also contained one fragment of a soapstone pipe and two fragments of soapstone molds or crucibles.

We excavated enough of the dump that it appears our assemblage must have included traces of nearly all of the activities ever performed inside the Church Family blacksmith shop. However, the dating of a majority of the artifacts suggests that this dump may not have seen much use in the twentieth century. Since dumps tend to reflect best the *final* years of their use, it may be that the later Shaker blacksmiths decided that it was not hygienic, or sightly, to dump refuse so close to the building and started carrying their trash farther away. The dump is also distinctive in that many of the artifacts suggest maintenance activities such as repairing pipes and hand tools, replacing handles, sharpening with files and whetstones, and shoeing oxen, rather than actual craft manufacture.

Final Thoughts

We were surprised and pleased when our search for new information about Shaker blacksmithing led us to unexpected evidence that the Canterbury Shakers had manufactured tobacco pipes at the Second Family blacksmith shop. At the same time, we found many excellent examples of blacksmith shop tools and learned that the Shakers had been busily maintaining their farm equipment.

Many of the redware pipes manufactured by the Shakers contained bits of white ball clay, and these were some of the strangest-looking pipes I had ever seen! Neither documentary research nor previous excavations had

Table 4-2
Selected Artifacts Recovered from the Second and Church Family Blacksmith Shops

	Second Family	Church Family
Ceramic sherds		
whiteware	73	5,567
pearlware	0	49
creamware	0	204
redware	51	1,122
stoneware (all types)	290	524
Tobacco pipe fragments	3,031	187
Metal		
knives	13	6
spoons	1	1
shovels/spades	7	0
drawknives	1	1
files	25	25
ax head	1	1
hoe blades	0	2
scythe fragments	0	1
gouges	4	0
wedge fragments	0	13
splitting wedges	0	2
punches	26	42
chisels	22	52
blacksmith tongs	5	0
cast-iron stove fragments	23	72
drills/drill bits	5	11
oxshoes	14	27
horseshoes	17	0
hinges	15	17
door latches	7	1
pail bails	8	2
barrel hoops	40	0
cutter bar teeth	9	4
wagon/carriage parts	40	3
metal chain links	43	64
manure spreader parts	3	0
buttons	2	20
buckles	19	15
tin can fragments	35	12
musket parts	0	1
Other		
gunflints	0	12
grindstone fragments	0	2
whetstone fragments	0	9
soapstone fragments	0	225

ever suggested the local manufacture of pipes in Canterbury, and we had not anticipated the presence of that industry even after we had discovered pipe fragments at the West Family in the late 1970s. The foundation outline of the Second Family shop was complete, and the interior suggested that all of the contents had been left in place when the building was removed, probably between 1910 and 1915.

The archeological evidence was rather different at the Church Family blacksmith shop, where the building had been sold and removed from the site in 1952. We were able to determine the outline of the blacksmith shop and establish that the large rock pile there was a base under the shop (rather than a filled-in cellar hole), and we were able to excavate the original forge base inside a cellar at the south end of the foundation. The dump on the west side of the shop was an unexpected and exciting discovery, with all of its evidence for shoeing oxen, for working soapstone into gravestones, for smoking tobacco, and for repairing firearms. The Church Family shop appears to have housed a broader range of activities than the shop at the Second Family, and at least half of the artifacts in the dump pertained to domestic activities. Clearly the smith(s) actually lived in this shop, while there simply was not enough evidence to make that determination at the Second Family.

The contrasts between the Second Family and Church Family blacksmith shops (table 4-2) really suggest a great deal of variability in activities from family to family and building to building. While Canterbury Shaker Village was a communal society with tightly controlled behavior, it appears that digging just one example of a particular building category—in this case, blacksmith shops—is not going to predict the activities or contents of other buildings of the same type. While this is partially due to the multifunctional nature of Shaker buildings, whereby multiple tasks might have been encompassed within a single building, it may also reflect the Shakers' desire to reduce competition and duplication of efforts among families. Every Shaker site thus has the potential to be different, and each one needs to be explored as a possible source of very new information.

Chapter Five

Some Final Thoughts

Over the past twenty-five years my research at Canterbury Shaker Village has evolved from a passive acceptance of the Shakers' own self-image, and the image created by modern Shaker scholars, to a systematic use of material culture to examine the frequent changes that occurred throughout the history of the Shaker experience. This research suggests that the Canterbury Shakers need to be viewed with a fresh set of eyes, for it appears that they were far more changeable and acquisitive than is usually suggested. Consequently, *Neither Plain nor Simple* was selected as the title for this book because these often-used terms really do not do justice to the complexity of Shaker life.

The ongoing archeological research at Canterbury Shaker Village suggests that the Shakers should not be viewed as simple aesthetes who practiced self-denial. While this may have been true of some Shakers at some moments in time, both the historical and the archeological record suggest that many of the latter-day Shakers knew how to enjoy some of life's comforts. While it may have been impossible to repeal the Millennial Laws governing their behavior, there nevertheless was a tendency for the Canterbury Shakers to bend and adapt as needs and desires changed.

To the degree that material culture mirrors behavior, the Canterbury dumps suggest that the Shakers had become almost indistinguishable from the outside world a full century ago. Mother Ann Lee and the others who began Shakerism in the mid–eighteenth century might not have recognized the middle-class consumers who followed them in the late nineteenth and twentieth centuries. We have yet to find dumps from the earliest years of the Shaker experience, but it now appears that archeology's chief contribution to Shaker research is to show how the strict, somber image of the early years was gradually replaced by a less rigid lifestyle that allowed for more individual expression and more consumer choices.

It should not be assumed in the two hundred years that Shakers lived in Canterbury that somehow they never changed. Yet the image is sometimes conveyed on guided tours and in mass-market books that the Shakers were fatally frozen in time. This impression may be unavoidable when most visitors to a museum village have only a few hours to learn about the entire Shaker experience. Yet the Shakers underwent constant change, and there were periods when they drank, smoked, ate pork, played with dogs and cats, and enjoyed little frills and luxuries. It is impossible to review the huge corpus of Shaker photographs without drawing the conclusion that in the early twentieth century the Canterbury Shakers drove very fine automobiles, owned excellent horses and boats, and had the means to buy the latest and finest technology in all of its forms. There certainly was nothing wrong with this, but I would argue that this is not the image that most Shaker scholars or enthusiasts have chosen to convey. In the same way that Shaker journals and photographs suggest a growth in consumerism, the artifacts found in the Canterbury dumps provide direct evidence for attractive dishes, "quack" medicines, personal knickknacks, beauty aids, and the occasional consumption of alcoholic beverages and tobacco. None of these taken alone is inherently scandalous, but it would appear that not all of the Shakers were leading an other-worldly lifestyle. And while a few of these artifacts may have been discarded into the dumps by hired men, that does not alter the fact that a host of "worldly" influences had entered into what had formerly been a tightly controlled community.

Fortunately, the ability of archeology to examine societies as they change over long periods of time may now

5-1. Eldress Gertrude Soule holding a cake—shaped like the Church Family meetinghouse—on Mother Ann's Day in 1979.

Students on the Boston University team had baked the cake in honor of the Canterbury eldresses.

be helping to dispel some of the myths about the Shakers. Archeological work conducted at Canterbury Shaker Village is helping to give the Shakers back some of their humanity, as opposed to the overly sanitized portrait imposed upon them. The picture that is now emerging suggests that for at least the second half of their existence, the Shakers were developing a higher degree of individuality and a greater willingness to try a host of consumer products obtained from the outside world. As the Shakers changed and welcomed new technology, they were never able to create a totally new and independent society. Rather, archeology now suggests that the Shakers inevitably became more like us, neither plain, nor simple, nor frozen at one moment in time.

Throughout the course of my research, and within the pages of this book, I have attempted to show how the Canterbury Shakers dealt with processing industries at their mills (chapter 2), with the consumption of "worldly" goods (chapter 3), with maintenance activities such as blacksmithing (chapter 4), and with the built and natural landscape (part II). This research is what any archeologist would do at any historical community, but it is especially rewarding to study the Shakers because of the degree to which their lives were carefully scripted for them. Any deviation from "the rules" is something that archeologists are only too eager to examine.

Ironically, the last three Shakers who lived in Canterbury were not always a very accurate source of information. They remembered drinking a little wine at the dinner table when they were young, but there was sometimes a tendency to repeat the stories they had learned from Shaker enthusiasts—that the Shakers didn't drink, the Shakers didn't smoke, and so forth. They no doubt remembered the customs of their youth, but it may have been increasingly hard for them to separate their own memories from the warm and wonderful stories that had been created about them.

The legacy of the Shakers will hopefully continue to evolve in unexpected ways as more archeology is conducted at their former villages. The patterns observed in Canterbury may not have occurred at all of the other Shaker Villages, yet they suggest research questions that may be asked elsewhere. I hope that other archeologists who study the Shakers will have the opportunity to sample dumps from all phases of the Shaker experience, and to compare the material culture from recent converts with that of Shakers who were more mature in their faith. In the same vein, it would be useful and perhaps controversial to discover whether elders and eldresses consumed, ate, and "enjoyed life" any differently from rank-and-file believers. Archeology should also make it possible to compare artifacts from work and living areas that were devoted specifically to men's or women's activities to determine whether there were gender-related differences in consumption patterns and in the degree to which the Millennial Laws were observed. These are the sorts of questions that we archeologists ask at all of the past settlements that we study, and I hope that the Shakers will continue to provide us with thought-provoking answers!

After twenty-five years of conducting above- and belowground archeology in Canterbury, our work is far from over. As the modern museum rebuilds structures on their original foundations, as repairs are needed on existing buildings, and as utility lines or culverts are laid, digging will always be required to "rescue" archeological sites. Sometimes the findings will be very mundane, but the occasional discovery of a "Hog Heaven" is justifica-

tion enough for having archeologists present whenever the ground is disturbed. And, as more financial resources become available for "pure" research, archeology should be used to challenge existing models about Shaker life. This may be done by digging into more dumps, more cellar holes, and into sites created during the first twenty to thirty years of the Shaker experience, when the passion of the early believers was so very strong. It is possible that archeology will then be able to make its greatest contributions, perhaps even demonstrating that the early Shakers possessed the very plainest examples of material culture, with striking contrasts to the more affluent Shakers who followed.

I have tried to present our archeological findings in a nonjudgmental way. Archeologists typically collect the material culture of the past, identify the objects, present some possible interpretations, and then—if the evidence merits it—we will enthusiastically challenge popular stereotypes. The result for me has been an ever changing perception of who the Canterbury Shakers were—and what they consumed or produced—over a long period of time. It has not been the intention in *Neither Plain nor Simple* to criticize the Shakers in any way, although perhaps some criticisms are warranted for those who have created "warm and fuzzy" stories about Shaker perfection. Rather, I have tried to let archeology tell the story of unexpected discoveries and new perspectives, and to show just how dynamic, adaptable, and technologically exciting the Canterbury Shakers really were. After so many years of working in this most stimulating setting, I am looking forward to more research opportunities and new insights in the years ahead.

PART II

Surface Archeology: The Shaker Landscape

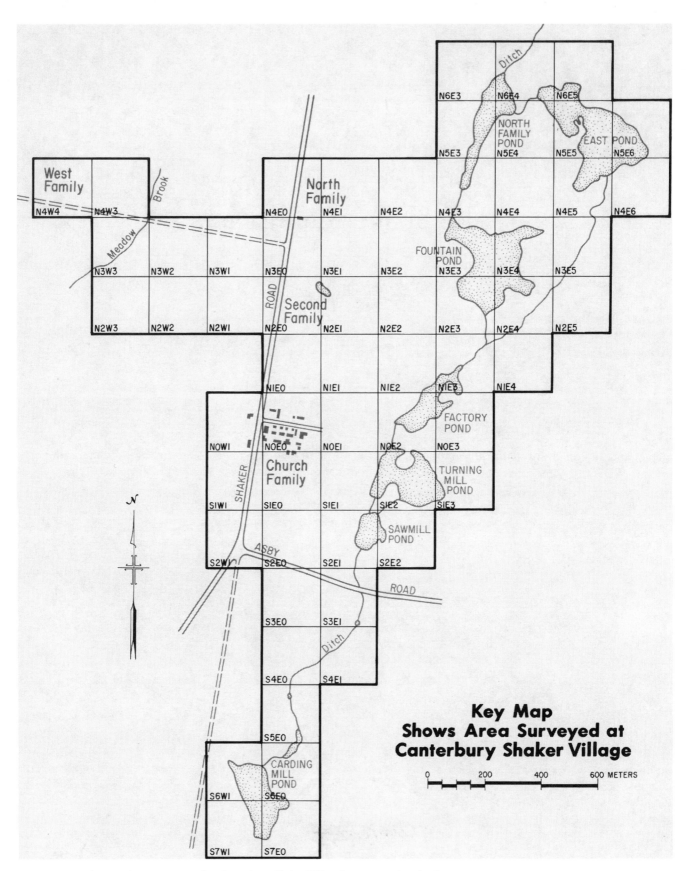

A-1. Key map showing the area surveyed at Canterbury Shaker Village between 1978 and 1982.

The Shaker Mapping Project

Mapping a Historic Landscape

In the late 1800s Canterbury Shaker Village grew to a maximum extent of about 3,000 acres. The Shaker landholdings have shrunk a great deal since then, but there have probably been fewer modifications to this landscape than to that of any other Shaker Village. Because of its size and complexity, recording the uniquely "Shaker" aspects of this landscape has required the preparation of a comprehensive series of maps that depict and identify every significant natural and culture feature. Similar types of mapping have been conducted at other archeological sites, most notably at the city of Teotihuacán in central Mexico (A.D. 1–750), where the remains of thousands of buildings were mapped across an 8-square-mile area by the Teotihuacán Mapping Project in the 1960s. I was one of the proofreaders of the Teotihuacán maps, and the scope and comprehensiveness of that project was definitely the catalyst for what I set out to do in Canterbury.

Between 1978 and 1982, we thoroughly mapped over 600 acres at Canterbury Shaker Village, showing just those areas that were most intensively modified by the Shakers. More recently, we updated five of these maps in 2001 (N0W1, N0E0, N0E1, S1W1, and S1E1) to show some of the most significant later changes. The base maps depict the fields and woods that surrounded the four Shaker families, as well as the extensive system of mills and artificial millponds that the Shakers created along the eastern side of their village. We mapped the landscape as blocks of 200 × 200 meters and prepared sixty-one contour maps that can be combined to form a single large grid of the Shakers' central landholdings (figure A-1). We prepared each original drawing at a scale of 1:500, and most drawings represent the surface of the settlement in the year 1982.

I initially employed teams of students from Boston University and the University of New Hampshire to obtain the field information that went into the maps, and in 1980 I hired a professional surveyor, Peer Kraft-Lund, to direct the surveying effort from that time forward. We used transits and foot surveys because of the "richness" of surface information and the density of ground cover. Aerial mapping of the landscape would have been quicker but probably not as accurate, because many of the wooded parts of the village and the mill system were lushly overgrown with trees, vines, and poison ivy. House foundations, ponds, and raceways that stood in open fields in the eighteenth and nineteenth centuries had reverted to forest in the twentieth century, and many features are now covered with dense secondary or tertiary growth. Transit maps and surface reconnaissance were to prove extremely time-consuming when documenting such a large area, but at the same time they guaranteed a higher level of accuracy in the recording of smaller historical features that were minimally exposed.

Our sixty-one contour maps delineate all standing structures, foundations, wells, millponds, dams, marshes, dumps, borrow pits, roads, lanes, stone walks, wire fences, stock fences, wood rail fences, granite fence posts, stone walls, ditches, orchards, herb gardens, solitary fruit trees, and fields (see legend of symbols). We prepared site reports for hundreds of these features, integrating historical information with the modern-day appearance of each site. Even open fields were treated as "sites" because the Shakers' journals and daybooks gave detailed information about the changing names and uses for each field. We used historical information both as a predictor and as an identification guide for features mapped on the surface. We then number-coded each site onto its corresponding map.

We calculated measurements and elevations relative to a permanent datum point (N0E0) established at the southwest corner of Meeting House Lane in the Church Family, and Datum N0E0 was arbitrarily said to be "0.0 meters" in elevation. We then plotted contours at 1-meter intervals on the sixty-one base maps and at 5-meter intervals on a final composite map of the entire village (figure I-3).

While these maps do not cover all of Shaker Village's original landholdings, they nevertheless do include all of the standing buildings or foundations from buildings at the Church, Second (Middle), North, and West Families, together with adjacent fields and the extensive Shaker mill system. For many of these features there is considerable historical documentation available in journals and diaries, and the information presented here is only a preliminary guide to this source material. Some 694 acres of the Shakers' original landholdings are listed on the National Register of Historic Places, and the National Register Registration Form prepared by Lisa Mausolf (August 1992) is an excellent source of architectural information for the village's still-standing buildings.

Site Inventory

Site 1:N6E3. North Family Pond ("North Family Wood Mill Pond"). See map on p. 123. In 1802 the Shakers purchased Tibbets Brook, and in 1814 they created a pond there. In the same year they constructed two mills south of the pond, one for sawing firewood and the other for turning furniture. Each mill had its own dam. The pond has been well maintained until the present and is still filled with water. It measures 4.62 acres in surface area.

Site 1:N6E4. North Family Pond (see 1:N6E3). See map on p. 124.

Site 2:N6E4. East Pond ("Runaway Pond"). The Shakers created East Pond in 1836 by the erection of two dams that flooded what had been called the "Muffett Swamp." On January 18, 1843, the east dam broke, apparently due to muskrats or frost, and the Shakers repaired it the next

year. In 1923 they repaired two leaks. There were no mills on this pond, and it served solely as a reservoir for mills farther south in the system. This was the largest of the Shaker ponds, and it measures 16.45 acres in surface area.

Site 3:N6E4. Dam on the north side of North Family Pond. This dam consists of earth fill with a stone facing, and it was probably constructed in 1814. In 1935, 230 feet of this dam were rebuilt. Portions of this dam are slumping, and there are numerous leaks. The dam ranges between 1.4 and 2.7 meters (4.6 and 8.9 feet) in height.

Site 4:N6E4. The "Long Ditch." In 1800 the Shakers dug a canal to deliver water from Lyford Pond to East Pond, although Brother Irving Greenwood noted that north of the Ham pasture no ditch was needed, because the land was swampy. (Ham was a neighbor who lived just north of the Shakers.) According to Brother Francis Winkley, in 1816 the Shakers extended the ditch from Upper (North Family) Pond to the "road east of Huckins—a Costly Jobb." Between 1839 and 1840 they widened, straightened, and deepened the ditch for a stretch of two miles. Also at this time they built nine stone bridges across the ditch so that Ham could reach his pastures to the east of the ditch. In 1885 they constructed another pond, called "New Pond," at a cost of about $5,000; the Shakers dug a ditch containing a 12-inch iron pipe to connect the two ponds, thus assuring a much larger water supply for the Long Ditch than before. According to the "Historical Record of the Church Family," the Shakers cleaned the ditch and fixed the banks in 1908 and again in 1911. The ditch is currently dry, and no water has run through it for some years.

Site 5:N6E4. Overflow ditch running from North Family Pond to East Pond. Water carried by the "Long Ditch" into North Family Pond flowed downhill through this ditch into East Pond.

Site 1:N6E5. East Pond (see 2:N6E4). See map on p. 125.

Site 1:N5E3. North Family Pond (see 1:N6E3). See map on p. 126.

Site 1:N5E4. North Family Pond (see 1:N6E3). See map on p. 127.

Site 2:N5E4. East Pond (see 2:N6E4).

Site 3:N5E4. Dam on the north side of North Family Pond (see 3:N6E4).

Site 4:N5E4. Overflow ditch (see 5:N6E4).

Site 1:N5E5. East Pond (see 2:N6E4). See map on p. 128.

Site 1:N5E6. East Pond (see 2:N6E4). See map on p. 129.

Site 2:N5E6. Modern tent platform on a sandy beach.

Site 3:N5E6. Beach (post-Shaker).

Site 4:N5E6. Borrow pit (post-Shaker).

Site 5:N5E6. Dam on the east side of East Pond. The Shakers built this earth and stone dam in 1838 and referred to it as the "Muffett dam." The dam broke in 1843, probably due to muskrats or frost, and they rebuilt it in 1844. According to Brother Francis Winkley, the dam broke "with tremendous noise sweeping everything in its course and such terrified our religious neighbors who live east of us who thought the day of judgment had commenced many fell on their knees imploring for mercy. . . ." This dam is 6–7 meters (20–23 feet) wide and 2.7–3.7 meters (9–12 feet) high.

Site 1:N4W4. West Family house foundation. See map on p. 130. Prior to 1979, all four walls of this foundation were visible on the surface of the ground, although the cellar hole was completely filled with fieldstones. Because the surface of this field was to be bulldozed in 1979, we decided to excavate both in and around the foundation before it was completely covered over. We placed a total of eight trenches inside the foundation and excavated eleven 1-meter-square pits outside it on the north, west, and east sides. We found large quantities of redware pottery and much smaller amounts of whiteware, creamware, and pearlware, along with cut nails, window glass, and animal bones. The foundation measured 11.7 meters (38 feet) east-west by 8.65 meters (28 feet) north-south, and there were entrances in the centers of both the north and east walls. The bulldozing in 1979 completely buried this foundation, apparently without damaging it. While we believe that this was the site of a Shaker house, historical records for the West Family are too vague to permit a correlation between the excavated material and any specific structure.

Just northeast of this foundation is a small well with an inside diameter of 0.65 meters (25 inches) and an open shaft going down 6.6 meters (22 feet). The well was not touched in 1979, and it is still exposed.

In 1979 we observed a second house foundation about 30 meters east of the first, and this, too, was due to be bulldozed. Unfortunately, the second foundation had already been severely disturbed, and our single trench and two 1-meter-square pits failed to define the walls or to collect an adequate artifact sample. The 1979 bulldozing completely covered this foundation.

Site 2:N4W4. West Family house foundation. Before commencement of excavations in 1980, we found this foundation to be covered with fallen trees, brush, and sod. During surface clearing, we exposed a well (0.65 meters, or 25 inches, inside diameter) just north of the foundation, and then we discovered stone rubble from a chimney base inside the foundation. We excavated a total of fourteen 1 × 1–meter pits in and around the foundation, and we recovered redware, creamware, bricks, animal bones (pig), nails, buttons, clay pipe stems, and glass. There had been no cellar here—only a crawl space beneath the floor—and the small quantities of artifacts suggested a relatively brief occupation at the beginning of the nineteenth century. This appears to have been a Shaker structure, measuring 11.3 meters (37 feet) by 12.5 meters (41 feet), but its specific function is still unknown. The foundation is quite intact.

Site 3:N4W4. Mound of earth fill. This mound represents earth bulldozed from the surface of the adjacent (east) field in 1979 as part of recent farming activities.

Site 1:N4W3. Water backed up to the north of the road running to the West Family. See map on p. 131. This body of water has been created by a beaver dam and is of recent origin.

Site 2:N4W3. West Family well. This large well or cistern stands alone in the middle of the field, and a few stones lying nearby on the surface of the field suggest that a house once stood close by. It has an inside diameter of 1.115 meters (44 inches).

Site 3:N4W3. Mound of earth fill. This mound represents earth bulldozed from the surface of the adjacent (west) field in 1979 as part of recent farming activities.

Site 1:N4E0. North Family horse barn foundation. See map on p. 132. This barn is identified on Elder Henry Blinn's 1848 watercolor of Shaker Village. The dates of its construction and removal are unknown. The surviving foundation is only partially exposed and is covered with trees and bushes. It measures about 14 meters (46 feet) east-west.

Site 2:N4E0. North Family blacksmith shop foundation. This blacksmith shop is identified on Elder Henry Blinn's 1848 watercolor of Shaker Village. The dates of its construction and removal are unknown, but it was definitely gone by circa 1918. The foundation is today covered with grass, and only a few of the foundation stones are visible.

Site 3:N4E0. North Family brethren's shop foundation. This shop is identified on Elder Henry Blinn's 1848 watercolor of Shaker Village. The date of its construction is unknown; it was taken down circa 1918. The foundation is today covered with grass, and only a few of the foundation stones are visible.

Site 4:N4E0. North Family infirmary foundation. The exact date of this building's construction is unknown, but according to Brother Irving Greenwood, it was in use at the West Family by 1805: "The Infirmary originally was the Dwelling House at [the] West Family & was moved to the North family in 1826. [It was] Fitted up in [the] basement for the hat business & [the] rest of [the] house as an Infirmary." In 1884 the building was remodeled and used solely as an infirmary. The Shakers took it down circa 1918. Today the foundation is covered with grass, and only a few of the foundation stones are visible. It measures about 16.8 meters (55 feet) north-south by about 14 meters (46 feet) east-west.

Site 5:N4E0. Small garage owned by the Meeh family (recent). This garage measures 2.15 meters (7 feet) north-south by 4.4 meters (14.5 feet) east-west. It was built circa 1963.

Site 1:N4E1. North Family barn ramp. See map on p. 133. It is unknown exactly when the Shakers constructed this cow barn, but it was removed circa 1918. The cow barn was 105 feet long and 60 feet wide, and the main body of the barn was to the east of the ramp. The surviving barn ramp measures 15.8 meters (52 feet) north-south by 29.6 meters (97 feet) east-west. The four apple trees north of the barn are Baldwins, planted by the North Family Shakers.

Site 2:N4E1. Recent barn (1954) atop the foundation of the North Family laundry (wash house). The Shakers constructed the North Family laundry and sisters' shop in 1831, and they were combined into a single three-story building that measured 60 x 40 feet. This cost $2,200 and was paid for by the Church Family. The Shakers took down the laundry in the early twentieth century, and much later, in 1954, the Meeh family constructed a barn on top of the old foundation. They later built a second story for the barn in 1980. The new barn now measures 12.2 meters (40 feet) east-west by 41.1 meters (135 feet) north-south.

Site 3:N4E1. North Family "Pickle Establishment" foundation. This building is identified on Elder Henry Blinn's 1848 watercolor of Shaker Village. The dates of its construction and removal are unknown. The foundation today is heavily overgrown with brush and briars and measures about 6.1 meters (20 feet) north-south.

Site 4:N4E1. North Family foundation. This possible foundation contains only a few trees and bushes and is easily visible; however, the foundation walls for this structure do not appear to be complete.

Site 5:N4E1. North Family well. This well is still filled with water, but the large stones covering it make it impossible to measure the diameter.

Site 6:N4E1. North Family well. This well is still filled with water and has an inside diameter of 0.91 meters (3 feet).

Site 7:N4E1. North Family well. This well is still filled with water and has an inside diameter of 1.37 meters (4.5 feet).

Site 8:N4E1. North Family well. This well is still filled with water and has an inside diameter of 1.1 meters (4.2 feet).

Site 9:N4E1. North Family orchard. In 1840 this orchard was described by Isaac Hill as follows: "seven hundred grafted trees of the best varieties . . . ," and these included Greenings, Baldwins, and Russets. It is unknown when the Shakers planted this orchard or when it was removed.

Site 1:N4E2. Sugar house (recent). See map on p. 134. This structure measures 7.6 meters (25 feet) north-south by 4.3 meters (14 feet) east-west. The current property-owners, Tim Meeh and Jill McCullough, built it in 1976.

Site 2:N4E2. Wood shed (recent). This shed measures 4.19 meters (13.75 feet) north-south by 8.43 meters (27.66 feet) east-west. It was built at the same time as the sugar house.

Site 1:N4E3. North Family Pond (see 1:N6E3). See map on p. 135.

Site 2:N4E3. North Family sawmill (wood mill) foundation. The Shakers built this sawmill in 1814 to saw firewood, and in 1824 they added a dining room to the mill. In 1894 they removed the sawmill's flat roof, and they put on a pitched roof. Between 1902 and 1905 the Shakers made various improvements at both the dam and the mill, such as the installation of a new penstock (1902), the purchase of six lumber rolls (1902), the installation of a wood pulley (1903) and two drag saws (1903), and the addition of a new slide gate (1903). They installed a well pump under the mill in 1911. These alterations notwithstanding, the Shakers tore down the remains of the old mill in 1912 and burned them. The sawmill foundation measures about 7.2 meters (23.6 feet) wide by 10.3 meters (33.8 feet) long, while the wheel pit measures 1.25 meters (4.1 feet) wide by 6.25 meters (20.5 feet) long. There are no artifacts or equipment visible in the wheel pit.

Site 3:N4E3. North Family turning mill foundation. Built in 1814, the Shakers described this mill in the "Historical Record of the Church Family" as "a mechanics' shop with water power for various machinery." In 1840 Isaac Hill noted that the Shakers added "an additional building over the stream with the apparatus and machinery requisite for the ready construction of common family water tubs. . . ." Years later, Brother Irving Greenwood described the turning mill as used for "making tables, chairs, beds & tubs & pails." The Shakers removed the mill by 1891 because it was in poor repair. The 15-inch penstock that brought water into the mill is still intact, and water continues to flow through it into the foundation. This foundation measures about 7.2 meters (23.6 feet) east-west by 10.3 meters (33.8 feet) north-south. Also, the dam that formed the north wall of the mill is still in excellent condition and measures about 2.5 meters (8.2 feet) in height above the wheel pit and 65 centimeters (2.1 feet) in thickness. There is no equipment visible in the wheel pit.

Site 4:N4E3. Dam on the south side of North Family Pond. The Shakers constructed this dam in 1814 to supply water

A-2. The dam at the southern end of North Family Pond, with the North Family sawmill (wood mill) foundation in the foreground (facing north).

to the North Family sawmill, and it has been well maintained to the present day. In 1912 the Shakers dug out the center of the dam, removing the remains of old wooden pipe (penstock), and putting in iron pipe with a 4-inch valve on the end. This gate valve is still present, recessed into the base of the dam wall, and it is leaking badly (figure A-2). The dam as it borders on the North Family sawmill (2:N4E3) is about 3.2 meters (10.5 feet) high, 6.2 meters (20.3 feet) wide, and 20.3 meters (66.6 feet) long.

Site 5:N4E3. Overflow channel. This 1-meter-wide channel carried water south from North Family Pond around the two mill sites and into Fountain Pond. Along most of its length the channel is open and lined with stone walls, but a short stretch in the center is subterranean.

Site 6:N4E3. Shed (recent). Construction of this cabin began in 1964, and it has gradually been added onto. (Note: This structure collapsed sometime between 1980 and 1984.)

Site 7:N4E3. Peach orchard. According to Eldress Bertha Lindsay, this orchard received its name "because in those early days they planted peach or pear trees between the apple trees. Being short-lived, the peach trees were cut down, and the apple trees were trees that lasted many, many years longer. Now in the Peach Orchard were the Rhode Island Greenings and Baldwins." It is unknown when the Shakers commenced this orchard or when they removed it. The only evidence for it now consists of small circles of stones that the Shakers placed around the base of each tree.

Site 1:N4E4. Pleasant Grove ("Fountain Ground," "Feast Ground," "Holy Ground"). See map on p. 136. In the early 1840s every Shaker Village experienced a religious revival and selected—under spirit influence—a place for worship. In Canterbury this occurred in 1842 when a company of ministry, elders, and others selected a place east of the North Family and about one-half mile northeast of the Church Family. They cleared the spot, removed timber, and leveled it by plowing and carting dirt, and then they built a house at the northwest corner of the enclosure. They built a fence around the Feast Ground that they painted white, and they planted fir trees around this (figure A-3). A road was constructed from the Church Family to this spot between 1842 and 1844, although Shakers from the North and Second Families would sometimes go there directly from their homes and enter Pleasant Grove on the north side. According to Brother Irving Greenwood, "The first meeting was held Oct. 15, 1843. Meetings were held here until 1860. In 1861 the house, stone & fence were removed & the place has not been used since."

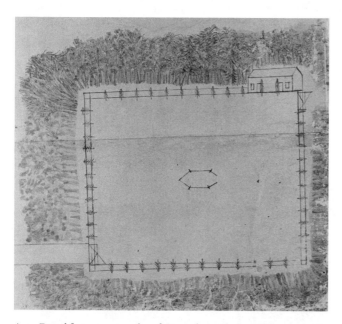

A-3. Detail from a watercolor of Canterbury Shaker Village drawn by Elder Henry C. Blinn in 1848. This section shows the Shaker Holy Ground, "Pleasant Grove," surrounded by fir trees and with a house for shelter at the northwest corner (*upper right*). Courtesy of Canterbury Shaker Village Archives.

A-4. The raised platform that was erected in 1842 to support Pleasant Grove.

Pleasant Grove currently appears as a raised, artificial platform, lightly covered with trees (figure A-4), and an overgrown road still connects it to the foot of the lane that runs west up to the Church Family.

Site 2:N4E4. Base of the altar in the center of Pleasant Grove. According to Brother Irving Greenwood, "There was a marble slab 6' long 3' wide 3" thick set in a stone base in center of the lot with an inscription engraved on it. This slab had a railing around it. Set in place June 1848." Engraved on this "Fountain Stone" were the words: "The Lord's Stone. Written and placed here in 'Pleasant Grove' by command of our Lord and Saviour, Jesus Christ. Erected June 24, 1848. Engraved at Canterbury, N.H." According to Elder Henry Blinn, the stone "remained on the grounds for nineteen years, & was removed on the 7th of Oct. 1861." Until at least 1980, a small cluster of stones in the approximate center of Pleasant Grove marked the location of the altar. Unfortunately, these have been removed.

Site 3:N4E4. Foundation for a small house at the northwest corner of Pleasant Grove. This house was raised in October of 1844, and according to Brother Irving Greenwood, it was "a 1 story bld'g 20' × 60 ft in case of rain." According to Elder Henry Blinn, this was clapboarded and painted white, was unfinished on the inside, and had a good floor. There were two doors on the front, separate entrances for the brothers and sisters. Blinn also noted that the house was "in good repair till Mar. 4th 1861 when the roof of the building fell in, & it was soon

A-5. The foundation for the house that was erected at the northwest corner of Pleasant Grove.

ascertained that the center or tie beam had been eaten off by large black ants. The building was removed soon after. . . ." The foundation is clearly visible today, but no artifacts appear on or around it (figure A-5).

Site 4:N4E4. Peach orchard (see 7:N4E3).

Site 1:N4E5. East Pond (see 2:N6E4). See map on p. 137.

Site 2:N4E5. Dam on the east side of East Pond (see 5:N5E6).

Site 3:N4E5. Overflow and ditch running south from East Pond. This overflow controlled the level of water in East Pond, and the ditches sent water south to Factory Pond. The dam is about 3.0 meters (9.8 feet) in height at the outlet, but the gate valve has been removed. Water slowly escapes from the pond at this point.

Site 1:N4E6. East Pond (see 2:N6E4). See map on p. 138.

Site 2:N4E6. Dam on the east side of East Pond (see 5:N5E6).

Site 1:N3W3. Meadow Pond. See map on p. 139. The manufacture of bricks began in 1824 on the east side of Meadow Pond, and according to Elder Henry Blinn, "several hands were employed at work in the business. The clay was of excellent quality. . . ." Brother Irving Greenwood noted, "there was built a dam, brick shed & a house for workmen at the North end of the Church Lake meadow. Bricks had been made here before but not as a regular business. For several years a large number of bricks were made. Some years 150 to 250 thousand. Clay is of fair quality. The bricks for all our brick bldg's were made here." According to Eldress Bertha Lindsay, "it was on the shores of this pond that much of the clay that was made into bricks, and into little pipes for sale, was gathered. These ponds, in my day, was [sic] stocked with fish, so that we could fish." We have not been able to determine the exact location of the brickyard.

Site 2:N3W3. West Family sawmill foundation. In 1805 the West Family built a sawmill that contained two turning lathes atop a dam at the foot of West Hill on Meadow Brook. In 1850 the Shakers repaired the dam and rebuilt the sawmill, and it was taken over by the Second Family. It is not known when they ceased to use the sawmill or took it down, but foundation stones from the mill and dam now litter the bottom of Meadow Brook.

Site 3:N3W3. West Family dam. This dam was built by the West Family in 1805 and rebuilt by the Second Family in 1850. It has been breached for an unknown length of time, and Meadow Brook is unimpeded as it passes through the dam (figure A-6). There is little evidence left for the pond that was once held back by this dam. At its highest, the dam measures 3.8 meters (12.5 feet) in height, and about 7.3 meters (23.8 feet) in thickness.

A-6. The breached 1805 dam across Meadow Brook (facing northwest).

A-7. The North Family trustees' office, west elevation.

Site 4:N3W3. Overflow. This massive, stone-lined spillway is located at the westernmost end of the West Family dam. The channel measures about 5.1 meters (16.75 feet) in width and 6.8 meters (just over 22 feet) in length, and as water rose in the pond and flowed over the edge of the spillway, it dropped about 1.5 meters (59 inches) to the ground below before flowing on to Meadow Pond.

Site 5:N3W3. Site of excavation trenches in 1980. We excavated three 1 × 1–meter pits here in 1980 so as to locate the northern edge of the overflow, but no edge was found. Artifacts were few but suggested an early-nineteenth-century date.

Site 6:N3W3. Overflow channel. This lengthy channel carried runoff from the West Family dam to Meadow Pond. Substantial stone walls on either side guided the water until it merged with Meadow Brook.

Site 7:N3W3. Shallow overflow channel. A poorly marked channel, possibly predating the overflow to the northwest (6:N3W3).

Site 1:N3W2. West Family foundations. See map on p. 140. There are several scatters of foundation stones on the surface here, but these remains are fragmentary. It is impossible to reconstruct the outlines of individual structures without subsurface excavations.

Site 1:N3E0. North Family trustees' office. See map on p. 142. The Shakers built the North Family office in 1826, and this is the only North Family building still standing. William Meeh purchased this house from the Shakers in 1950, and it was subsequently owned and occupied by

his son Tim Meeh and Jill McCullough. Currently it is owned and occupied by Greg Meeh and Hillary Nelson. The building measures 41 × 34 feet, has two stories and a basement, and was made of 71,000 bricks furnished by the Church Family. Prior to 1950 the Shakers were no longer able to maintain the house; it had become run down, and locally it received the nickname of the "Bee House" because so many people had lived there successively. The interior burned in 1961, and much of the original interior woodwork is gone. However, the house still has original window casements, doors, stairs, and banisters, and a few of the second-story rooms retain their built-in furniture (figure A-7).

Site 2:N3E0. North Family infirmary foundation (see 4:N4E0).

Site 3:N3E0. North Family dwelling house foundation. This house was built in 1815, and after being further enlarged in 1817 it measured 46 × 36 feet and was three stories high on the south side and two stories on the north. In 1843 the Shakers made an addition to the east end, nearly as large as the other part of the dwelling. They made an addition of another 30 feet to the east end in 1846. Also in 1846, the Shakers dug a well under the dwelling house that was 25 feet deep and lined with brick; this well is still visible inside the foundation today. The structure was vacated in 1894, and the Shakers finally removed it circa 1918. The foundation is today covered with grass, and only short sections of the foundation stones are visible. Eldress Bertha Lindsay described the North Family dwelling house as having been almost as large as the dwelling house still standing at the Church Family (3:N0E0).

Site 1:N3E1. North Family foundation. See map on p. 143. Unidentified. This foundation is today covered with grass, and only a few of the foundation stones are visible.

Site 2:N3E1. Recent barn atop the foundation of the North Family laundry (see 2:N4E1).

Site 3:N3E1. North Family sisters' shop foundation. This is identified on Elder Henry Blinn's 1848 watercolor of Shaker Village. The date of its construction is unknown, but the Shakers took it down circa 1918. The cellar hole today stands open and is filled with briars. It measures about 10.35 meters (34 feet) east-west by 7 meters (23 feet) north-south. In 1996 we excavated three test pits

A-8. The foundation of the North Family sisters' shop as it underwent excavation in 1996 (facing northeast).

inside the cellar and two outside, but we found very few artifacts (figure A-8).

Site 4:N3E1. North Family foundation. Unidentified. Elder Henry Blinn identified this location in his 1848 watercolor as the site of a hog pen. There is a great deal of scattered stonework here, but it does not form a clear outline, and the surface is covered with trees and brush. The stone foundation walls suggest a building that was 13 meters (44 feet) east-west by 24 meters (80 feet) north-south. In 1996 we excavated a total of eleven test pits here, and the artifacts included redware pipe fragments, indicating that the Shakers had smoked here. The artifacts did not suggest a date of construction nor the date of removal of this building, and there was nothing to indicate whether this had been a "Hog Pen."

Site 5:N3E1. North Family apple orchard. We do not know when the Shakers planted this orchard. The surviving trees include ten Rhode Island Greenings, two Baldwins, and three Winesap.

Site 1:N3E3. Fountain Pond (Chestnut Pond). See map on p. 145. This is one of the largest (12.57 acres in 1982) and best preserved of the Shaker ponds, but no record has survived for its date of construction. The only journal citation for this pond notes that the Shakers repaired two bad breaks in the pond's dam in 1923. The dams on this pond have little height, but they are in good condition, and leakage is fairly minor. Beavers are presently

quite active here. No mills were located on the pond, and it stored water for mills farther south in the water-power system.

Site 2:N3E3. Submerged wall or dam in Fountain Pond. This appears to have been a retaining wall or dam that predated the present configuration of the pond. It is below water and cannot be examined closely.

Site 3:N3E3. Peach orchard (see 7:N4E3).

Site 1:N3E4. Fountain Pond (see 1:N3E3). See map on p. 146.

Site 2:N3E4. Peach orchard (see 7:N4E3).

Site 1:N3E5. Ditch running south from East Pond (see 3:N4E5). See map on p. 147.

Site 1:N2W3. Meadow Pond (see 1:N3W3). See map on p. 148.

Site 1:N2W1. House owned by Dudley and Jacqueline Laufman (recent). See map on p. 150.

Site 2:N2W1. Garage owned by Dudley and Jacqueline Laufman (recent).

Site 3:N2W1. Second Family laundry (wash house) foundation. This building is identified on Elder Henry Blinn's 1848 watercolor of Shaker Village. The dates of its construction and removal are unknown (figure A-9). The foundation stones are not clearly visible, but the laundry appears to measure 23.5 meters (77 feet) east-west.

A-9. The Second Family laundry before removal. Courtesy of Canterbury Shaker Village Archives.

Site 4:N2W1. Cabin (recent). This building is a study built by David and Midge Wyman in 1958 and measures 10.25 feet north-south by 12.5 feet east-west.

Site 1:N2E0. House owned by David Curtis (recent). See map on p. 151. This house was built in 1959 by David Curtis (36.25 × 26.33 feet) on the approximate site of the Second Family sisters' brick shop, built in 1838. Isaac Hill described the brick shop in 1840 as follows: "Here the females were busily engaged, some in plying the hand wheel and others drawing out the numerous threads of the jenny: others were at the needle making up garments either for domestic use or sale, and others were preparing the curd, pressing the fresh cheese in the hoop, or turning those which had been taken out." The Second Family sisters' brick shop burned down in World War II, at which time it was being used as an air raid–watching tower.

Site 2:N2E0. Barn owned by David Curtis. This barn was formerly a shed owned and built by the Shakers. The date of its construction is unknown. It is currently the only Second Family structure still standing, measuring 20 × 57.5 feet.

Site 3:N2E0. Second Family laundry (wash house) foundation (see 3:N2W1).

Site 4:N2E0. Garage owned by Dudley and Jacqueline Laufman (recent).

Site 5:N2E0. Second Family orchard. It is unknown when these trees were planted.

Site 6:N2E0. Second Family blacksmith shop foundation. This shop is identified on Elder Henry Blinn's 1848 watercolor of Shaker Village. It was probably constructed soon after 1800 and may have survived until about 1915, when the Second Family closed. In 1996 we removed brush and poison ivy from the surface, mapped the foundation stones, and excavated a total of twenty-one test pits in and around the foundation. These revealed many iron tools and thousands of fragments of redware tobacco pipes that had been manufactured here.

Site 7:N2E0. Curtis Pond (recent). This small pond was dug by David Curtis in 1952.

Site 8:N2E0. Shed owned by David Curtis (recent). This shed was raised in the mid-1950s and measures about 8 feet north-south by 12 feet east-west.

A-10. The foundation of the Second Family dwelling house during excavation in 1996 (facing northwest). The house owned by David Curtis (1:N2E0) appears in the background.

Site 9:N2E0. Second Family dwelling house foundation. According to Brother Francis Winkley, this house was first occupied in 1796: "the Second Order Moved into Second Dwelling House—the Boys & Girls added to it—22 male 23 female." This wood-framed dwelling had two chimneys and two doors facing west toward Shaker Road. The Shakers probably removed it circa 1915 when the Second Family closed. The western foundation wall is still quite intact, and the interior of the cellar is covered with scattered stones and bricks. In 1996 we excavated nine test pits inside the cellar as well as trenches at the corners of the foundation (figure A-10).

Site 10:N2E0. House owned by David and Midge Wyman (recent). The Wymans built this house in 1956, with additions in 1958 and 1960. It measures 28 feet north-south by 40 feet east-west.

Site 11:N2E0. Shed owned by David and Midge Wyman (recent). This shed was built in 1958 and measures 20.5 feet east-west by 12 feet north-south.

Site 12:N2E0. Second Family trustees' office foundation. The date of this building's construction is unknown, but the structure is identified on Elder Henry Blinn's 1848 watercolor of Shaker Village. In 1918 the Shakers lifted the Second Family office off its foundation and transported it to the Church Family, where it stands today as

A-11. One of the 1996 excavation pits inside the foundation of the Second Family trustees' office, revealing an intact stone floor in the cellar (facing west). The scale boards are marked in 10-cm increments.

the Enfield House (4:N0E0). We excavated eleven test pits inside the open cellar hole in 1996 and discovered an intact stone floor that survives in the cellar close to the western foundation wall (figure A-11).

Site 13:N2E0. Second Family brethren's brick shop foundation. The date of construction for the brethren's brick shop is unknown, but the building is identified on Elder Henry Blinn's 1848 watercolor of Shaker Village. A fire destroyed the brethren's brick shop in 1900 (figure A-12). This site is now covered with a large pile of brick and stone rubble.

Site 1:N2E1. Curtis Pond (see 7:N2E0). See map on p. 152.

Site 2:N2E1. Second Family cider mill or tan house foundation. Elder Henry Blinn's 1848 watercolor shows both of these buildings in this approximate location. It is impossible to tell which of these buildings is now represented by foundation stones on the surface, but the foundation measures about 7.9 meters (26 feet) north-south by 12.8 meters (42 feet) east-west.

Note: There is no map N2E2.

Site 1:N2E3. Fountain Pond (see 1:N3E3). See map on p. 153.

Site 2:N2E3. Dams on the south side of Fountain Pond. Two earth and stone dams are located on the south and southeast sides of Fountain Pond. One of these contains a gate valve (3:N2E4) for controlling the level of water in the pond, and the dam is about 3.5 meters (11.5 feet) in height at the gate valve. It is not known when the dams were built.

Site 3:N2E3. Ditch running south from Fountain Pond. This shallow ditch guides water south to Factory Pond.

Site 1:N2E4. Fountain Pond (see 1:N3E3). See map on p. 154.

Site 2:N2E4. Dams on the south side of Fountain Pond (see 2:N2E3).

Site 3:N2E4. Gate valve. This valve, recessed into the base of the dam, controls the flow of water into ditches south of Fountain Pond. Ditching then carried water some 428 meters (1,404 feet) south to Factory Pond. The name of the manufacturer—Chapman Valve Mfg. Co. —is on the valve (figure A-13).

Site 4:N2E4. Small pond. This pond may originally have been part of Factory Pond (1:N1E2), but it presently appears as an isolated body of water about 167 meters (548 feet) northeast of Factory Pond.

Site 5:N2E4. Small earth and stone dam.

A-12. The Second Family brethren's brick shop after it burned in 1900. Courtesy of Canterbury Shaker Village Archives.

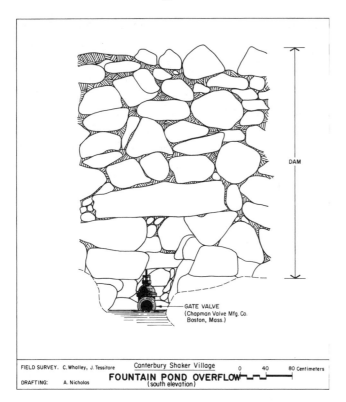

FIELD SURVEY. C. Wholley, J. Tessitore   Canterbury Shaker Village

DRAFTING: A. Nicholas   **FOUNTAIN POND OVERFLOW**
                                    (south elevation)

0   40   80 Centimeters

A-13. The gate valve built into the dam on the south side of Fountain Pond.

Site 6:N2E4. Ditch running south from East Pond (see 3:N4E5).

Site 1:N2E5. Ditch running south from East Pond (see 3:N4E5). See map on p. 155.

Site 1:N1E0. Shaker cemetery. See map on p. 156. The Shakers erected the stone wall around this cemetery in 1798. In 1840 Isaac Hill described the appearance of the cemetery as follows: "Recently tomb stones designating the name and age of all who have died since the United Brethren sat down upon this ground . . . excepting two burials in a distant field, have been erected. . . . the graves are disposed in rows in a direct line, those in each successive row behind those of the front row."

In 1900 the Shakers removed the individual tombstones from the cemetery, although they kept a sketch showing the relative placement of the graves. In 1903 they enlarged the cemetery and walled it in with a 32-inch-high iron fence (made by the Enterprise Fence and Foundry Co. of Indianapolis, Indiana). In 1904 Mrs. J. O. Shaw, Jr., presented to the Shaker Society a monument of Rockport granite that now stands in the center of the cemetery (figure A-14). It has the word "Shakers"

carved in raised letters on the side facing Shaker Road. In 1992 Sister Ethel Hudson became the last Shaker to be buried in the cemetery.

Site 2:N1E0. West Barn Field. This field is where the horses were pastured.

Site 3:N1E0. North Barn Field. This field received its name from being adjacent to the Church Family's successive cow barns (21:N0E0). It is easily the most level field for miles around.

Site 4:N1E0. Second Family horse barn foundation. The date of its construction is unknown, but the horse barn is identified on Elder Henry Blinn's 1848 watercolor of Shaker Village. In 1900 a fire destroyed the horse barn. The surviving foundation now measures 19.2 meters (63 feet) north-south by 12.2 meters (40 feet) east-west.

Site 5:N1E0. Shaker Road. The Shakers laid out the stone wall on the east side of the road from the trustees' office to the Second Family in 1797 and 1798 and rebuilt it in 1834 and 1903; the west wall was rebuilt in 1851 and again in 1903. In May of 1855 the Shakers set out maple trees that lined either side of the road as it runs from the Church Family's trustees' office north to the Second Family.

Site 6:N1E0. Well. This Second Family well measures 0.91 meters (3 feet) in inside diameter and is 18 feet deep. The well is located inside a poorly defined founda-

A-14. The monument in the center of the Shaker cemetery (facing west).

tion that may have been a shed attached to the horse barn. The foundation measures about 6.7 meters (22 feet) north-south by 7.9 meters (26 feet) east-west.

Site 1:N1E1. North Barn Field (see 3:N1E0). See map on p. 157.

Site 2:N1E1. Cisterns. The Shakers built these cisterns in 1866 and pumped water to them from a pump in the clothiers' mill (weaving mill) (6:N0E2) just south of Factory Pond. According to Brother Irving Greenwood, "There were 6 of them 8 ft. in diam [*sic*] & 6 ft. deep. They have arched tops above the 6 foot height. They are brick & covered with cement inside & out & connected by small arched tunnels large enough for a man to crawl through. They have a total capacity of 13000 gallons. They were filled the first time Oct. 5, 1866. Their full water level is 75 ft. above pond level." The total cost of building this system was $3,000, and the Shakers pumped water from the mill to the cisterns and then south to the Church Family through a 2-inch iron pipe. In 1876 they noted having to clean out the cisterns, which "had four or five feet depth of mire in bottom"; they no doubt required frequent cleaning.

In 1929 the Shakers laid 600 feet of 6-inch cast-iron pipe from the pump mill to the cisterns at a cost of $921.60, at which time they also installed six new fire hydrants throughout the Church Family. Today the cisterns are no longer in use.

Site 3:N1E1. North Orchard. Brother Francis Winkley wrote that in 1795 the Shakers "Set out Orcharding North of tan house this Spring & Last." He also noted that the Shakers expanded this orchard in 1798 when "the East part of the Orchard North of the Tanhouse [was] set out this Spring." According to Brother Irving Greenwood, the North Orchard originally covered 6 acres and "was partly cut down in 1828 but the greater part of it stood until 1864 when all but a few trees were cut down." The cutting of many of the trees in 1828 was a direct result of the abolition of cider drinking in that year.

Eldress Bertha Lindsay observed, "On the west side of the North Orchard were peach trees for a great many years. After the peach trees failed to give fruit, they were cut down, the land here was terraced, and on these terraces were built grape arbors, so for many years we had beautiful grapes here." In recent years this has been used as a hay field and for pasturage.

Site 4:N1E1. Night Pasture. According to Eldress Bertha Lindsay, "This was where the cows spent the night in the summertime."

Site 1:N1E2. Factory Pond (Tan House Pond, Wood Mill Pond, Bark Mill Pond, and Ice Mill Pond). See map on p. 158. The Shakers constructed this pond in 1802 and erected a 25 × 25–foot fulling mill nearby in 1804. In the early twentieth century, a wood mill and a combination ice mill and threshing mill stood at the south end of the pond. The pond presently covers 4.52 acres, but based upon surrounding topography it appears that it was considerably larger when originally in use.

Site 2:N1E2. Night pasture (see 4:N1E1).

Site 1:N1E3. Factory Pond (see 1:N1E2). See map on p. 159.

Site 2:N1E3. Ditch running south from East Pond (see 3:N4E5).

Site 1:N1E4. Ditch running south from East Pond (see 3:N4E5). See map on p. 160.

Site 1:N0W1. Church Family trustees' office. See map on p. 161. The present trustees' office, built between 1830 and 1832, was the third office to have been built for the trustees. It measures 72 × 42 feet, is two stories in height, and has a full cellar and an attic. It is the only brick building in the Church Family (see 1:N3W3) and was the first building at the village to have a slated roof (rather than shingles). The cost of the building's construction was $7,440.57. The trustees' office became a U.S. Post Office in October of 1848 with David Parker as the postmaster, and it always served as the office for the Lead Ministry. The Shakers added Colonial Revival–style porches and Doric columns in 1914.

They added the south kitchen in 1880, and in 1906 they built the "Express Office" or "Annex," 30 × 30 feet, on the north end of the trustees' office to be used for packing and storage. In 1909 the Shakers built the second-story porches on the west side and a bridge connecting the trustees' office with an adjacent wood shed. They later removed them circa 1940. Until the opening of the Marcia and John Cooper Hubbard Visitor Education Center in 2001, the museum used the "Express Office" as the admissions office for visitors to Shaker Village, while the trustees' office was the final residence for

A-15. The Church Family trustees' office with the "Express Office" or "Annex" at its north end (facing southwest).

Eldresses Bertha Lindsay and Gertrude Soule. The trustees' office is presently used chiefly as a residence for museum staff (figure A-15).

Site 2:N0W1. Church Family ministry horse barn. In 1819 the Shakers constructed the horse barn, covered with large shingles, on the west side of Shaker Road, at which time it measured 60 × 40 feet. It was on the site of an earlier 1798 horse barn. They built an addition measuring 49 × 27 feet onto its northeast corner in 1824. It underwent other remodelings in 1880, 1901, and 1927. The Church Family originally kept horses in the southern part of the barn and the trustees' horses in the north, but the 1927 renovation greatly altered the interior. In 1991 the museum remodeled the horse barn to its 1901 appearance (figure A-16).

Site 3:N0W1. Church Family carriage shed (horse stand)/ Hubbard Visitor Education Center. In 1834 the Shakers built the original carriage shed to accommodate the horses and carriages of visitors to the village. They added a second story in 1850 for storage and made an addition onto to the west side of the building in 1853. They sold

A-16. The Church Family horse barn (facing west).

the carriage shed to the Shelburne Museum in Shelburne, Vermont, in 1951, and it was removed at that time. Archeology was conducted there in 2000 as a prelude to building a major visitor center on this site in 2001. The new Marcia and John Cooper Hubbard Visitor Education Center is now the starting point for all guided tours of Shaker Village.

Site 4:N0W1. Church Family hired men's shop (workmen's lodge) foundation. The Shakers constructed this building in 1822 as a wood house and subsequently converted it to a "Boys' Shop," a dwelling for children. They moved it to its present location in 1902 to provide quarters for the hired men whose lodge had been destroyed by fire in 1901. An earlier horse mill stood in this same spot (see 9:N0W1).

The original building measured 31 × 45 feet and had one story. The Shakers added a second story and a 10-foot addition in 1843. It previously had been positioned where the creamery is today (8:N0E0), before it was moved to its final location northwest of the trustees' office. The Shakers sold the hired men's shop and removed it in 1959 to save on property taxes. Some of the foundation stones are still visible, and today the surface of the foundation is kept clear of brush. A large, flat stone lies just east of the former entry into this building.

Site 5:N0W1. Church Family swine or hog house foundation. The Shakers built their hog house in 1817, at which time it measured 32 × 51 feet. According to a later source, Isaac Hill, this was enlarged to "a one-story building eighty feet long by forty feet in width. At one end is a well and pump, a chimney with kettle and apparatus for boiling potatoes and other roots, a machine for mashing them when boiled, a meal room with lock and key, and a cellar underneath in which potatoes and other articles that will not bear frost shall be preserved. The pens for the hogs are apartments of some twelve by twenty feet on either side of an alley running the length of that end of the building. . . ." The building probably ceased to be used in the 1840s, when the Shakers' Millennial Laws banned the consumption of pork. However, it appears that they did not remove the hog house until as late as circa 1905. The 1996 excavation of a trench for a culvert rediscovered this foundation, and our subsequent archeological excavation recovered tens of thousands of artifacts from the filled-in cellar (see chapter 4).

Site 6:NoW1. Earth road (recent). This modern road takes visitors to parking areas behind the trustees' office and the Hubbard Visitor Education Center.

Site 7:NoW1. Church Family blacksmith shop foundation. The Shakers built this blacksmith shop in 1811, and it measured 25 × 50 feet. It replaced an earlier shop, erected in 1793, that had stood between the infirmary and the brethren's shop. In 1849 the Shakers removed the old brick forges and installed two cast-iron forges; the building later underwent an extensive remodeling in 1860. According to Eldress Bertha Lindsay, "the upper room, a very large room, at the north end of the building here was used for the shoeing of the oxen and so forth, and then there was [*sic*] two little steps leading down to another level where they made the tinware. Then another little level led downstairs where you could go right outdoors at the south end of the building."

The Shakers finally sold the blacksmith shop and had it removed in 1952, but all four stone foundation walls are still visible. In 2000 I conducted an extensive salvage excavation inside the foundation and in the shallow industrial dump that lies to the west. Plans are now under way to build a modern restaurant on this site (see chapter 4).

Site 8:NoW1. Blacksmith Shop Field ("office garden"). This field contained an orchard of 200 apple trees that were set out in 1881. Until recently this field was used as pasturage, but now it is a parking lot for visitors to the village.

Site 9:NoW1. Millstone. We found no structural remains close to this millstone (6.5 feet in diameter), but according to "A Historical Record of the Society of Believers in Canterbury, N.H.," the earliest known mill at Shaker Village was a gristmill constructed just east of this location in 1797: "a building 36 × 36 was raised on the west side of the highway and designed for a mill in which to saw wood, grind corn and grain and for wood turning. Four horses were used on this circular sweep." This mill appears to have been taken out of service in 1800 when the first grist- and sawmill was built south of Sawmill Pond (see 4:S2E1), and the Shakers removed the last remains of the mill in 1902 when they constructed the hired men's shop (4:NoW1).

Site 10:NoW1. Church Family orchard. The Shakers planted this apple orchard in 1917, and some of the orig-

inal trees still stand. Eldress Bertha Lindsay stated that this orchard was called "Paradise." "Paradise is where they grew the Russets, the Astrachans, the Pearmains, and a lovely yellow Golden Ball." Many of the original trees have now been replaced using historically appropriate varieties.

Site 11:NoW1. Lane. This narrow, overgrown lane connected the Church Family with a sugar bush and, eventually, with Meadow Pond. Much early- to mid-twentieth-century trash is scattered along the sides of the lane.

Site 12:NoW1. West Barn Field (see 2:N1Eo).

Site 13:NoW1. "Wiggin Lot." Chase Wiggin owned the farm that became the Second Family's land.

Site 1:NoEo. Church Family children's house (East House, "Old Trustees' Office"). See map on p. 162. The Shakers built this house in 1810, measuring 28 × 38 feet, and it is two stories high with an attic. It was originally used as a trustees' office in the same location as the present trustees' office (1:NoW1). They moved it in 1833 to its present location, where it was first called the "East House" and, more recently, the "Children's House." Elder Henry Blinn, writing much later, noted that "a spinning jenny [of 80 spindles] was placed in the basement & all the wool that passed through the machines at the Carding Mill, for the Church family, was spun at this place [in the basement]. The first loft was appropriated to the Garden seed business, for assorting, papering, packing, etc. The second loft was used by the Caretakers & little girls, as a workshop and for sleeping apartments. The whole building has for many years been used for the little girls." After that, the house continued to be used as a dwelling for girls, and it was designed to accommodate eight girls at a time, as well as two sisters. In 1916 some of the sisters created a small darkroom for photography in the basement. Today the children's house is used as a residence by the museum's director.

Site 2:NoEo. Church Family sisters' shop ("New Spin Shop," "House A"). The Shakers raised this building between 1816 and 1817 as a spin shop measuring 50 × 32 feet, and it has two stories and an attic. They built it on the site of an older spin shop, raised in 1795, which was moved north and became part of the laundry (11:NoEo). After the Shakers brought an end to spinning here in the 1830s, the sisters used the building for workshops and

A-17. The Church Family sisters' shop, north elevation.

A-18. The Church Family dwelling house, west elevation.

for musical instruction. Tailoring was perhaps the most important activity conducted here. In 1891 Elder Henry Blinn noted that the cellar was the best storage place at the village for winter apples and sauces. The elders occupied the western half of the first story, while the large east room was used for instruction in musical instruments. The sisters used the northwest room on the second story for making dresses, and the other rooms were general workrooms. The eldresses' confession room was located here, where sisters made their weekly confession to the eldresses. Today the sisters' shop is open to the public (figure A-17).

Site 3:N0E0. Church Family dwelling house ("House D"). In 1793 the Shakers raised their massive dwelling, measuring 32 × 42 feet, but many additions and roof changes have been made since then. They added a domed cupola containing a Paul Revere bell in 1832 to call the family to meals and meetings, but because of its large size—which offended the ministry at New Lebanon—they lowered the cupola by 5 feet 5 inches in 1842. In 1837 they built a large meeting room or chapel on the north side of the dwelling that measures 52 × 43 feet. Water closets were first installed in 1887. The Shakers moved the village's library, begun in 1853, to here in 1917, and the Shaker school operated here from 1921 until 1934. The dwelling eventually expanded to fifty-six rooms and is the largest building at Shaker Village. The first floor held Shaker Village's butcher shop, bakery, kitchen, and dining room; the second and third floors contained bedrooms; and the attic served as a huge, handcrafted storage area. Sister Ethel Hudson spent her final years living here alone before passing away in 1992. Today the dwelling is nearing the end of years of restoration work

and is about to be opened to the public for the first time (figure A-18).

Site 4:N0E0. Enfield House. Enfield House was originally constructed as the office in the Second Family in 1826 (12:N2E0), but the Shakers moved it about 400 meters south to the Church Family in 1918, at which time they added two elevated entrance porches on the south side. After masonry work, cementing, and plastering on the new foundation, the project of relocating this building cost a total of $7,405.38. The Shakers then moved into the house in November of 1921, and it later became the most popular residence for Canterbury Shakers in the twentieth century because it was more modern than the old dwelling house. They named it "Enfield House" because it subsequently housed elderly

A-19. Enfield House (formerly the Second Family trustees' office) (facing southeast).

A-20. The Church Family infirmary, south elevation.

A-21. The Church Family carriage house (facing northwest).

sisters who moved here from the Shaker Village in Enfield, New Hampshire, in 1923. The house measures 62 × 29 feet, is 2½ stories high, and has an attic and a full cellar. The cellar was the location of the village's poplar wood industry. Today Enfield House is used for collections and archival storage (figure A-19).

Site 5:NoEo. Church Family infirmary ("House I," nurse house). The Shakers originally constructed the infirmary in 1811 as a dwelling for visitors and as living quarters for the trustees on nights and Sundays. They subsequently converted it to an infirmary in 1849, and they tinned the roof in 1850. They built it with two stories plus an attic, 40 × 32 feet, and the first water closet in the village was installed here in 1852. They later added a 2½-story ell to the northwest corner of the building in 1892. After 1892, the first floor of the infirmary housed nurses' quarters, a pharmacy, a nurses' sitting room and office, and the dentist's office. Patients' rooms were upstairs, and the attic contained medical supplies and a mortuary. The building's use as an infirmary ended in 1937 with the death of the last nurse. The infirmary is now open to the pubic and used to interpret Shaker medical history (figure A-20).

Site 6:NoEo. Church Family carriage house ("Yellow Building," "House Y"). The carriage house was erected for storage purposes in 1825. It has two stories and an attic and measures 40 × 70 feet. The east side has three sets of double carriage doors, and the north side just one set of double doors. The gable roof is covered with slate shingles. Various rooms held carriages, a paint shop, a wood house for the infirmary, a granary, and rooms for storing medicines and lumber. The attic floor was used

for drying herbs. The garden seed business was briefly located in this building in the 1840s. Today the carriage house contains the village's gift shop, along with craft and exhibition areas (figure A-21).

Site 7:NoEo. Church Family brethren's shop (brethren's north shop, farmers' shop, "House U"). The Shakers erected the brethren's shop in 1824; it measures 48 × 36 feet, and it has two stories with an attic. They placed it on the site of an earlier (1795) wheel shop, and it was originally occupied by the farmers, spinning wheel makers, shoemakers, and physicians. The physicians occupied the eastern half of the first floor, and the Shakers used the cellar for storing apples, cider, and wine. They also used the northeast room on the first floor as a printing office from 1869 to 1877. In 1921 they purchased a large, 3-ton, walk-in safe in Concord, New Hampshire, and installed it on the first floor. The brethren's shop now contains Shaker Village's administrative offices (figure A-22).

A-22. The Church Family brethren's shop, north elevation.

A-23. The Church Family creamery, south elevation.

A-24. The Church Family north shop (facing northeast).

Site 8:N0E0. Church Family creamery. The Creamery measures 30 × 45 feet, and it was built between 1903 and 1905 under the direction of a non-Shaker carpenter, S. H. Mead. He constructed the building with two stories, an attic, a full cellar, and a gable roof of slate. In 1905 the Shakers purchased a steam heating plant for the building, an 8-horsepower Kinney safety boiler and engine. In 1919 they installed a new heating plant in the cellar at a cost of $1,890.25, and in 1938 they added a new Smith 9 sec. #27 steam boiler at a cost of $833.50. The sisters who were engaged in dairying lived upstairs in the creamery. Today the creamery building houses the village's "Creamery Restaurant" (figure A-23).

Site 9:N0E0. Wood deck of water tower. The combined tank and tower, completed in January of 1901, was 92 feet in height; the tank alone was 16 feet in height. The tower was of steel, and the tank, made of unlined cypress wood, had a capacity of 22,000 gallons. It was built atop a 50-foot-deep well that had been dug at the corner of the dwelling house in 1822 to supply water in case of fire. Atop the tank was a 12-foot Halladay Standard Wind Mill. All together, the cost was $1,979.00. In 1911 the Shakers took down the windmill because repairs had become too expensive, and they purchased a 3-horsepower electric motor with which to run the pump.

Site 10:N0E0. Church Family north shop ("House G"). The Shakers constructed the north shop from 1841 to 1842 on the site of an earlier wood shed (1798–1841), and the building measures 40 × 80 feet. It has two stories plus an attic, and it was built under the direction of a

non-Shaker, Lynus Stevens of Claremont, New Hampshire. The Shakers used most of the first story as a wood house and the west end as a store room for the deacons and deaconesses. The second story contained workrooms for the sisters and was equipped with hand looms for the weaving of cloth. They used two lofts in the attic for the drying of herbs, especially those needed for making sarsaparilla, which was distilled in the syrup shop (12:N0E0). Today the north shop sees only light use for storage and special events, and it is one of the least-altered buildings at Shaker Village (figure A-24).

Site 11:N0E0. Church Family laundry ("House L"). The oldest section of the laundry building began in 1795 as a 1½-story "Spin Shop," measuring 24 × 32 feet, and located on the site of the present-day sisters' shop (2:N0E0). The Shakers moved it to its present location in 1816, where it now is located at the south end of what has grown into a far larger, L-shaped laundry building.

A-25. The Church Family laundry (facing northwest).

The present laundry took the place of an earlier wash house that had been on the same site and which the Shakers took down in 1816. They operated the original laundry with horse-powered machinery, including a 1-horsepower treadmill. In 1844 they replaced this with a steam boiler and engine, and in 1852 they added a steam-drying room with movable racks. A flue boiler was added in 1860, and this required the addition of a tall brick smokestack. They constructed a dry house, for drying food, at the east end of the laundry in 1879 and then rebuilt it in 1880. They constructed a knitting shop at the north end of the laundry in 1886, after which they used the dry house for finishing sweaters and storing yarn. They later used the combined first floor of the laundry and dry house for repairing automobiles, and an adjacent space became a woodworking shop. The vast laundry complex, after many years of modifications, has now been renovated, and much of its original equipment is still intact (figure A-25).

Site 12:NoEo. Church Family syrup shop (grain store, granary, still house, "The Distillery"). The 22 × 24–foot center of this building appears to be the oldest standing pre-Shaker building at Shaker Village and probably was either the residence of (1775–1782) or a granary for Benjamin Whitcher, who donated his property to the Shakers after they began arriving in 1783. This structure originally stood northwest of the north shop (10:NoEo), and the Shakers moved it to its current location in 1841. It became known as "The Distillery," and they used it for distilling syrup of sarsaparilla. The Shakers added 13 feet to the north end of the building in 1847 and 18 feet to the south end in 1848, where they bottled and packed the syrup. The sarsaparilla kettles were taken out in 1919 and 1920, and they added a brick, wood-burning stove for use

A-26. The Church Family syrup shop (facing southwest).

A-27. The Church Family steel garage (facing southeast).

in the canning business, which continued here until 1958. During this period the Shaker artist Sister Cora Helena Sarle (1867–1956) used the southernmost room on the second floor as a painting studio. More recently, the modern herbalists at Shaker Village have used the syrup shop (figure A-26).

Site 13:NoEo. Church Family steel garage. The Shakers purchased this prefabricated steel garage in 1923 from the Penn. Metal Co. of Boston for $618.00, and it cost another $250.00 to erect. The Shakers picked it up at the factory in Cambridge, Massachusetts. It measures 30 × 24 feet, and was the last building to be raised in the Church Family. The building has a single room and three pairs of double doors (figure A-27).

Site 14:NoEo. Church Family powerhouse. The Shakers built their powerhouse in 1910 with a wooden frame and pressed metal shingles, and it measures 24 × 36 feet. The electric generating system in the powerhouse consisted of storage batteries and a Nash 30-horsepower gasoline engine that ran a 125-volt, 144-ampere Crookes Wheeler direct-current generator. Two 500-gallon gas tanks and one 1,500-gallon gas tank were located outside the building. This system initially powered electric lights in sixteen buildings, and the cost of the complete plant was about $8,000. The Shakers brought the 7-ton engine and generator here from the railroad in Belmont, New Hampshire. Later, in 1925, the Shakers paid Concord Wiring and Supply Co. about $6,000 to run an alternating-current electric line from Loudon, New Hampshire, to the powerhouse (a distance of 5 miles). They then

A-28. The Church Family powerhouse contained the village's direct-current generator and storage batteries (facing northwest).

purchased electricity directly from the New Hampshire Power Co. but kept the powerhouse ready for emergencies. The Shakers began using alternating current on December 11, 1925. Finally, in 1937 they decided it would cost too much to replace the plates and separators in the powerhouse, so they sold the batteries that year and sold the gasoline engine in 1940. They then renovated the building, and it was used as an office by the farm manager, Richmond McKerley. Today the powerhouse is open to the public as a summer kitchen (figure A-28).

Site 15:NoEo. Church Family firehouse (garage). The Shakers built their firehouse as a combined firehouse and

A-29. The Church Family firehouse was built with a wood frame and pressed metal siding. It contained the village's fire engine (facing northeast).

garage in 1908 at a cost of $1,000. It measures 28 × 28 feet and originally contained the village's first automobile, a 1908 Reo. In 1916 they enlarged the garage by cutting it apart in the center, moving the eastern half over 12 feet, and filling in between. This is a wood-framed building with pressed metal shingles, tin and asbestos interior walls and ceiling, and a cement floor (figure A-29). The shingles were manufactured by the Cortright Metal Roofing Company of Philadelphia.

Site 16:NoEo. Church Family carpenter shop (broom shop, herb house, old visiting shop, visitors' house, entertaining house, new shop). The Shakers built their carpenter shop in 1806 as a dwelling house for visiting Shakers, and it was first located where the children's house (1:NoEo) now stands. It measures 32 × 24 feet and has one story with an attic. Between 1815 and 1832 they used it as a spin shop, and then they moved it to its present location. They added a cellar in 1850. According to Elder Henry Blinn, this shop was used for many years as "a storage for herbs and also as a place to press and pack them for market. A few years since [1877] the whole building was rebuilt on the inside and fitted for a broom shop and is used for that business." The broom-making business lasted until 1890. Hired men lived here between 1901 and 1903, and after 1903 the Shakers used the east room as a carpenters' shop and the rest of the building for storage. They renovated the building in 1951 and briefly used it as a residence. Today the carpenter shop houses several industries, including dovetailing and the manufacture of baskets, oval boxes, and brooms (figure A-30).

A-30. The Church Family carpenter shop (facing northeast).

Site 17:NoEo. Church Family schoolhouse. The Shakers built their schoolhouse in 1823 and first occupied it in 1824. It originally measured 24 × 34 feet and was one story high. According to Elder Henry Blinn's "Church Record," "The North half of the room [was] used for the pupils, with three rows of desks, and six desks in a row. These accommodated two pupils each. The first row was on a platform, raised one step from the floor; the second row raised another step, and the third row another making a rise of three steps to the rear row of desks. In a central position on the south side of the room was the teacher's desk."

In 1863 the Shakers moved the schoolhouse 3 rods south, jacked it up 12 feet to become the second story, built a new schoolroom underneath, and added a wood shed at the east end. The enlargement of the schoolhouse may have been more a result of increasing numbers of non-Shaker pupils arriving from the outside world, rather than implying an increase of children within the Shaker community.

The new schoolroom had the pupils facing north, toward the teacher's desk, which was placed on a low platform. The Shakers subsequently used the second story as a gymnasium, a meeting room for singers, and a recitation room. Later, in 1880, they purchased an organ for the schoolroom. The fence around the schoolhouse yard was manufactured by the Anchor Fence Post Co., and the Shakers erected it in July of 1909 at a cost of $180.00. In 1921 they moved classes from here to the dwelling house (3:NoEo) in order to save wood and because of the difficulty in keeping paths open during the winter. The Shaker school closed in 1934, and today the schoolhouse is the end point for guided tours through

A-32. Archeology students exploring the crawl space underneath the schoolhouse in 1980.

Shaker Village, where guides conclude their presentation of the Shaker experience in Canterbury (figure A-31).

There is a crawl space underneath the schoolhouse, and our archeology team explored this in 1980 (figure A-32). Underneath the building we discovered numerous ink bottles, quill pens, a watercolor set, slate roof tiles, and a complete cat skeleton.

Site 18:NoEo. Church Family cart shed. The Shakers built their cart shed in 1840 with granite posts to hold up the gable roof and vertical planks on its sides. It measures 110 × 25 feet. For many years they used the north end of the shed as an icehouse, and the center of the shed held farm wagons. They installed 5-ton Fairbanks scales in the south end of the cart shed in 1862, in order to weigh farm wagons and, later, trucks; they rebuilt the scales in October of 1928. In the winter of 1982–1983 the roof of the cart shed collapsed, and the structure had to be extensively rebuilt. Today it is used for small exhibits and storage (figure A-33).

A-31. The Church Family schoolhouse with the wood shed at its east end, south elevation.

A-33. The Church Family cart shed, facing northwest. The Fairbanks scales were located inside the enclosed portion on the left.

A-34. The Church Family bee house in its present location, facing northeast.

Site 19:NoEo. Church Family bee house. The Shakers originally constructed the bee house 400 feet to the east in 1837 as a drying house, first for drying apples and later for drying lumber. Elder Henry Blinn changed it to a house for the beekeepers in 1865. It measures 12 × 25 feet and was built with a ventilator atop its gable roof. The Shakers moved it to its present location in 1940, and in 1977 the museum added a concrete ramp on the south side and cut a second door into the east side (figure A-34).

Site 20:NoEo. Church Family wood shed. The Shakers built this, the "East Woodshed," in 1861 just south of the cow barn. It is of post and beam construction and is sheathed in vertical boards. Three open bays originally alternated with four closed bays. The barn fire in 1973 (see 21:NoEo) destroyed a companion wood shed, the "West Woodshed." Today the shed is kept well stocked with wood (figure A-35).

A-35. The east wood shed of the Church Family, facing northeast.

A-36. The north side of the Church Family cow barn. Courtesy of Canterbury Shaker Village Archives.

Site 21:NoEo. Church Family cow barn foundation. The Shakers built their final and largest cow barn in 1858, measuring 200 feet long and 45 feet wide. They constructed 25-foot ramps at either end of the barn, bringing the total length to 250 feet (figure A-36). It was located in the vicinity of an earlier barn, constructed between 1801 and 1803. They built two silos inside the barn in 1894 and 1895, measuring 11 × 13 feet and 33 feet high. An 85-ton-capacity "Green Mountain" silo, measuring 14 × 26 feet, was built at the northeast corner of the barn in 1900, and then moved to the north center of the barn in 1907 and placed next to a new silo. When the barn was consumed by fire in 1973, the fire also burned an attached south walk and toolshed, plus a nearby sheep barn (built in 1860) and a wood shed. Today the open cellar hole of the cow barn and its two ramps are still among the most imposing features at Shaker Village. We conducted small excavations into the ramp at the east end of the cow barn in 1998 and 2000, discovering many tens of thousands of artifacts dating to circa 1900. This was one of the Shakers' richest dumps (see chapter 3).

Site 22:NoEo. Church Family arboretum. Elder Henry Blinn planted the arboretum in 1886, and it is said to have contained examples of every tree found in New Hampshire. A sign positioned within the arboretum identifies it as follows: "On this site in 1885–1886 Elder Henry Blinn of the Canterbury Shakers planted New Hampshire's first arboretum."

Site 23:NoEo. North Barn Field (see 3:N1Eo).

Site 24:NoEo. Church Family vegetable garden ("Kitchen Garden," seed garden field). Up until the 1840s this was the field where the Church Family raised seeds for its commercial seed business. According to Brother Irving Greenwood," In 1813 we find the 1st record of a brother having charge of the veg. garden, although we understand that the same piece of land, about 3 acres, was laid out soon after the Church was organized and was called the Kitchen Garden." Later, Eldress Bertha Lindsay noted that this field was "three acres large; it was three hundred and eighty feet long. At the south end of this field was a stone wall and a gate, and it was here that there were two beautiful mulberry trees." This field has now been restored to its original use as a vegetable garden.

Site 25:N0E0. Stone walk. The Shakers laid out this walk from the vegetable garden to the trustees' office between 1832 and 1835.

Site 1:N0E1. Church Family garden barn and garden barn shed. See map on p. 163. The Shakers raised the 30 × 40–foot garden barn in 1828 for use by the gardeners in the vegetable garden, originally the Shaker seed garden (24:N0E0). This barn had two stories with an attic and a full cellar. They took it down in the 1950s, and the cellar hole was subsequently filled with twentieth-century trash. I directed an archeological field school here in 1994, at which time we placed several pits inside the cellar and exposed the tops of most of the foundation stones. The museum fully reconstructed the attached garden barn shed in 1999 for use as storage, and the garden barn itself is now (2002) in the process of being reconstructed for use by the gardeners.

Site 2:N0E1. Church Family bee house foundation. This was the original site of the bee house (19:N0E0), which was moved from this site in 1940 and set in its present location south of the cow barn. Its stone foundation is still visible in this spot, and we used archeology in 1994 to expose the corners of the foundation.

Site 3:N0E1. Earth road (recent). This road was added in 1988 as part of the museum's fire protection system.

Site 4:N0E1. North Barn Field (see 3:N1E0).

Site 5:N0E1. Church Family botanical garden field. The Shakers cultivated plants here to be made into medicine. The Shaker physician Thomas Corbett commenced this garden circa 1804, and new medicinal plants were added until the garden covered an acre and a half and contained about two hundred varieties. Today the herbalists at Shaker Village are again cultivating an extensive herb garden in this field.

Site 6:N0E1. Church Family vegetable garden (see 25:N0E0).

Site 7:N0E1. Tan House Field. This field received its name from a tannery that was erected here in 1792 and measured 26 × 36 feet. The Shakers processed hides they had purchased as well as hides from their own animals. In 1815, after their business had expanded, they moved the tannery to the side of Factory Pond so they could take advantage of the waterpower.

Site 8:N0E1. Apple trees. It is unknown when these trees were planted. Approximately five survive, with tiny, wormy apples.

Site 9:N0E1. North Orchard (see 3:N1E1).

Site 10:N0E1. Night pasture (see 4:N1E1).

Site 1:N0E2. Factory Pond (see 1:N1E2). See map on p. 164.

Site 2:N0E2. Turning Mill Pond. This pond was constructed in 1817. The "Long Ditch" supplied much of the pond's water, but it has always been fed by local streams as well. Brother Irving Greenwood described how the Shakers augmented the flow: "We buy water rights of Nathaniel and James Ingalls Feb 5 1817 for $140.50. This gave us the right to divert water into this pond that formerly ran through their land." The pond was long an excellent site for fishing, and in 1990 it measured 8.39 acres in area. Today, with the Shaker dam at its southern end replaced by a modern dam in 1988 as part of the fire protection system, the pond is brimming with water, and a white swan has made the pond its home.

Site 3:N0E2. Tan House Field (see 7:N0E1).

Site 4:N0E2. Raceway carrying water from Factory Pond to the 1905 pump mill. Most of this 51-meter-long (167 feet) headrace is subterranean, and it presently is clogged with leaves and debris washed in from the pond. The mouth of the raceway is filled with fallen, rotting timbers.

Site 5:N0E2. Trash rack that filtered the water that ran to the pump mill. This consisted of a vertical iron grate that allowed water to pass on to the pump mill but trapped leaves and branches before they could reach and clog the waterwheel. Large tree roots and cows destroyed this trash rack in 1983 or 1984.

Site 6:NoE2. Pump mill. The Shakers erected their pump mill here in 1905 at a total cost of $1,162.69. It was on the site of an earlier clothiers' or weaving mill that measured 26 × 36 feet. They had built the clothiers' mill here in 1828, and according to Isaac Hill this was "where the beautiful woollen cloths and flannels manufactured by the sisters are fulled and dressed. Here were samples of all wool, mixed worsted and cotton cloths. . . ." Elder Henry Blinn described the clothiers' mill as measuring 26 × 36 feet, and in 1848 the Shakers added a third story to this mill to accommodate power looms. The clothiers' mill was powered by an overshot wheel, with a gasoline engine in reserve in case of low water, and in 1884 the Shakers installed a 6 × 12–inch Douglass pump, along with a 24-inch iron penstock to bring water to the mill. After 1866 the clothiers' mill contained a water-powered pump to pump pond water up to the cisterns (2:N1E1) in the North Orchard, and after the Shakers removed the clothiers' mill in 1905 (figure A-37), pumping water became the sole function of the new pump mill.

The pump mill was one story, measured 26 × 24 feet, and contained a Douglass Triplex single-acting pump with 5 by 8–inch cylinders, 3-inch suction and 2½-inch

A-37. Dismantling the 1828 Church Family clothiers' mill. This was where the Canterbury sisters fulled and dressed woolens and flannels, but in 1905 the mill was torn down and a pump mill was constructed in the same location. Courtesy of Canterbury Shaker Village Archives.

discharge valves. The Shakers installed a new Douglass Triplex pump in 1921 and installed new overshot wheels in 1912 and 1931. They built the original waterwheel of cast iron but replaced it with one of chestnut in 1912 because of problems with rusting. They removed the last waterwheel circa 1951 and sold it to the Shelburne Museum in Vermont. The roof of the pump mill was allowed to collapse into the foundation, and the building sat in ruins until 1996, when the museum restored the pump mill and replaced the roof.

Site 7:NoE2. Wooden trash rack that filtered the water that ran to the wood mill. This trash rack, consisting of vertical wooden members set in the water and ringing the entrance to the penstock, prevented any floating debris in the pond from entering the mill's power system. The sticks formed a rectangular framework of 1.04 × 1.18 meters (3.4 × 3.9 feet), secured at their bottoms for stability. In 1982 the trash rack was missing a few of its sticks but was still in remarkably good condition in spite of its repeated exposure to the sun and temperature changes. Unfortunately, Factory Pond regained some of its water soon after that, and the trash rack was completely washed away in 1984.

Site 8:NoE2. Sluice gate that controlled the flow of water into the wood mill. This wooden gate was positioned against the open mouth of the iron penstock, prohibiting the flow of water when the gate was lowered and permitting water to flow into the turbine when it was raised. In 1982 the sluice gate was still in position, though in dilapidated condition, but in 1984 the gate finally collapsed, leaving the mouth of the penstock exposed.

Site 9:NoE2. Wheel pit of the Church Family wood mill. The Shakers built this mill in 1915 on the site of a series of earlier wood mills that dated back to 1812. The best account of one of these earlier mills appears in "A Historical Record of the Society of Believers," dating to 1840: "[the] building covered a tannery and bark-mill in the basement story, and a mill for the manufacture of shingles and a thrashing machine room. The last machine was an invention of the Shakers and had been used by them for thrashing their grain for more than twenty years. . . . The head and fall at this mill is fifteen feet in 1840."

The Shakers had built an earlier mill on this site in 1886 with a 24-inch Tyler wheel, whereas the 1915 wood mill had a penstock built of 4-inch chestnut and a 15-inch Hercules wheel that had originally been installed inside the turning mill (6:S1E1). The 1915 wood mill measured 29 × 30 feet, was one story in height, and was built at a cost of $800.00. The Shakers began sawing here in May of 1916, using a circular saw purchased from the Lane Mfg. Co. of Montpelier, Vermont. A road ran past the wood mill to the east so the Shakers could bring logs here more easily. The turbine box for the wood mill presently contains many burnt timbers and fallen dam stones, and no machinery survives. However, metal artifacts litter the site. The wheel pit measures 1.9 meters (6.2 feet) wide by 5.4 meters (17.7 feet) long by 1.4 meters (4.6 feet) deep.

Next to one of the earlier wood mills, the Shakers erected a combination threshing mill and icehouse in 1876, measuring 40 × 50 feet. In 1914 they removed the threshing mill from the building and enlarged the ice rooms so as to occupy the entire structure. Not long afterward, in 1929, they removed the ice rooms due to the arrival of electric refrigeration and modified the building for other types of storage. They later sold both the wood mill and the ice house in 1952 to Maurice Kimball of Concord, New Hampshire. It is not clear whether any foundation stones presently visible on this site pertain to the icehouse.

Site 10:N0E2. Dam on the south side of Factory Pond. The Shakers constructed this earth and stone dam in June of 1802, and soon afterward it was used to supply water to a fulling mill. Its thickness is about 6.0 meters (20 feet) along most of its length, expanding to about 13.0 meters (43 feet) thick at the wood mill (9:N0E2). In 1924 a leak in this dam caused the Shakers to place a cement wall 10 feet long and 12 inches thick inside the dam at the point where the penstock went through to the wheel in the wood mill. Leaks in the dam for this pond were a chronic problem until 1988, when the museum partially rebuilt the dam during construction of the fire protection system. Factory Pond is now full of water year-round.

Site 11:N0E2. Night Pasture (see 4:N1E1).

Site 1:N0E3. Factory Pond (see 1:N1E2). See map on p. 165.

Site 2:N0E3. Overflow and ditch. This spillway and its associated ditch carried water south from Factory Pond to Turning Mill Pond. The overflow is crudely built, consisting of stone cobbles and bricks, loosely mortared together. Because of poor construction, the width and length of the overflow are difficult to ascertain, but the stone-lined floor appears to be 2.9–4.0 meters (9.5–13 feet) in width and 2.4–4.7 meters (7.9–15.4 feet) in length.

Site 3:N0E3. Dam on the south side of Factory Pond (see 10:N0E2).

Site 1:S1W1. Church Family Blacksmith Shop foundation (see 7:N0W1). See map on p. 166.

Site 2:S1W1. Blacksmith Shop Field (see 8:N0W1).

Site 3:S1W1. Meeting House Field. This was originally part of the Benjamin Whitcher farm at the time of the "Gathering" in Canterbury. The Shakers finished building the stone wall around this field in 1799, except for the side next to Shaker Road, which was added in 1793. This field is presently used just for hay.

Site 4:S1W1. Apple trees of unknown origin. These trees may date to 1881, when an orchard was set out in Blacksmith Shop Field (see 8:N0W1).

Site 5:S1W1. Ox pasture. Eldress Bertha Lindsay stated that in this pasture "was found a spring of water, and a trough was built here to give the oxen water. This was also piped down the road to the watering trough." The ox pasture has no use today.

Site 6:S1W1. Shaker Road. The Shakers laid out the stone walls flanking the road from the trustees' office to the foot of the hill in 1793 and rebuilt them in 1851. They later set out the maple trees that lined the road from the Church Family's trustees' office south to the foot of the hill in May of 1871.

Site 7:S1W1. Earth Road (recent) (see 6:N0W1).

Site 1:S1E0. Church Family Meeting House ("Old Church"). See map on p. 167. The Shakers raised their meetinghouse in 1792, and it measured 34 × 44 feet. Moses Johnson of Enfield, New Hampshire, who had supervised the building of the New Lebanon meetinghouse in 1786, was appointed the master builder of the meetinghouse in Canterbury, and he constructed it with 2½ stories, a gambrel roof, and dormer windows. The interior woodwork was painted dark blue, and there were originally north and south exterior stairs to the

A-38. The Church Family meetinghouse, west elevation.

second-story sleeping lofts for the brothers and sisters. The Shakers removed these stairs in 1815 and replaced them with a new stairwell on the east side of the building. The ministry dwelt here and took their meals here until they completely moved into the ministry shop in 1878. The interior woodwork of the meeting room was painted light blue in 1878, the first time the room had been painted since 1815. Today the meetinghouse contains a variety of exhibits and is the first stop for visitors who take the guided tour through the museum village (figure A-38).

Site 2:S1E0. Church Family ministry shop. The Shakers erected this 2½-story building in 1848, originally measuring 36 × 24 feet, to replace an earlier ministry shop that had become too small. This building was used both as a workshop and, after 1878, for sleeping apartments for the ministry. It has a gable roof and was the first building at the village to have its roof covered in tin. The Shakers added a single-story ell to the south side of the building in 1858; this ell was first used by the physician and after 1860 by the dentist. Today the building is used as exhibit space, and it is undergoing renovation.

Site 3:S1E0. Church Family ministry barn (horse stable) foundation. According to Brother Francis Winkley, in 1794 the Shakers raised a horse stable here, measuring 15 × 56 feet, to house the horses of visiting ministries. (Elder Henry Blinn wrote that this barn measured 26 × 59 feet.) In 1829 the Shakers converted it to use as a wagon shed and wood house. The barn was still standing in 1914, but today only the foundation is left.

An intact, clapboarded privy house still stands within the foundation of the 1794 ministry barn and measures 2 × 4 meters (6.5 × 13 feet). It has two equal-size compartments, each with its own entrance on the south side of the building.

Site 4:S1E0. Meeting House Lane. The Shakers lined the lane that leads to the western entrance of the meeting-house with maple trees on the south side in 1859 and on the north side in 1860. There have been several losses, but most of these trees still stand today.

Site 5:S1E0. Church Family vegetable garden (see 25: N0E0).

Site 6:S1E0. Meeting House Field (see 3:S1W1).

Site 7:S1E0. Church Family apple orchard ("New Orchard"). The Shakers planted this orchard in 1917 in Meeting House Field at a cost of $251.60, and it originally consisted of twelve rows of 20 trees each. A harsh winter in 1934 killed approximately 123 trees, but some replanting has been done. In 1978 the orchard consisted of 140 trees (twenty varieties). Eldress Bertha Lindsay stated that "we had Delicious, McIntosh, Baldwins, the Arkansas and Canada Reds, the Yellow Transparent, the Pippin—the Newton Pippins—and the Fall Pippins; we had Winesap, Jonathan, Wealthies, Maiden's Blushes."

Site 1:S1E1. Church Family vegetable garden (see 25: N0E0). See map on p. 168.

Site 2:S1E1. Church Family apple orchard (see 7:S1E0).

Site 3:S1E1. Tan House Field (see 7:N0E1).

Site 4:S1E1. Turning Mill Pond (see 2:N0E2).

Site 5:S1E1. Dam on the south side of Turning Mill Pond. This dam was constructed in 1817 at the time the pond was created. Repairs to the turning mill dam in 1915 raised it by 9 inches and so increased the pond's capacity. Due to lack of maintenance, the dam's matrix washed out over a number of years, and the museum constructed a new dam in 1988 just north of the original dam. The original Shaker dam is about 4.5 meters (14.8 feet) in height (above the wheel pit), about 9 meters (29.5 feet) thick (at the turning mill), and runs for a distance of about 79 meters (259 feet) along the southern edge of the pond. The new dam was built as part of a fire protection system, but it looks nothing like the original Shaker dam.

Site 6:S1E1. Turning mill foundation. The Shakers built their turning mill in 1818, and it was always accompanied by several subsidiary mill buildings south and southwest of Turning Mill Pond. Isaac Hill's 1840 account described the turning mill as 40 × 30 feet and used for various purposes: "Here the Shakers have made the improved pails. . . . The water power of this building is also used for various other economical purposes; among them was a cannon ball in a mortar turned for the purpose of pulverizing barks and medical roots—a machine for polishing metals, and machines for turning and boring."

The turning mill was three stories tall and had an attic, and the Shakers made an addition of unspecified dimensions in 1823. They added machinery for making brooms in 1861, and they made hoops here for a few years beginning in 1885. While the turning mill originally contained an overshot waterwheel, they later replaced it with a Hercules turbine in 1885. In 1913 the Shakers ran an electrical line to the turning mill, but in 1914 they abandoned the mill. They sold the turning mill in 1916 to a Mr. Brake of Belmont, New Hampshire, for $25.00, and he took it down.

The dimensions of the surviving foundation are 14.9 × 9.7 meters (49 × 32 feet), and recent farm trash has been strewn over the surface. None of the original machinery survives, and the wheel pit appears to have been partially filled in in 1915 so as to support the 24-inch penstock, which ran from the turning mill dam south to the 1915 sawmill (4:S2E1). There are still two concrete supports in the wheel pit that the 24-inch penstock rested upon.

Site 7:S1E1. Mill Orchard. The Shakers set out Mill Orchard in 1848 at a location southwest of Turning Mill Pond, using trees taken from P. Foster's nursery on Ingall's Hill. Eldress Bertha Lindsay stated that this orchard contained Chenango apples and "Nonesuch apples, Sheepnoses, Banana, and an apple called the President—a small apple, a yellow apple, which was very delicious in pies or sauce, applesauce." No trees from this orchard survive today.

Site 8:S1E1. Fire pump house (recent). The pump house was built in 1988 as part of the museum's fire protection system.

Site 9:S1E1. Earth road (recent) (see 3:N0E1).

Site 1:S1E2. Turning Mill Pond (see 2:N0E2). See map on p. 169.

Site 2:S1E2. Boys' Island. The Shakers built stone retaining walls around this "island" in 1867, but it is actually a peninsula, with a road connecting it to the mills on the southern edge of Factory Pond. The "island" received this name because this was where Shaker boys grew their own small gardens. According to Eldress Bertha Lindsay, "it was here that they grew Sheepnoses and Turkey Eggs, and further on, leading down, is what they called the Boys' Garden, and this was right along the edge of the pond, and later they planted a few apple trees in there also." A few of these trees still grow on the island, along with blackberries, raspberries, and stray asparagus plants.

Site 3:S1E2. Overflow and ditch. This narrow, stone-lined spillway probably dates to 1817, and it channels excess water south from Turning Mill Pond to Sawmill Pond. The floor of the overflow consists of tightly packed stone cobbles, forming a channel 2.9 meters (9.5 feet) wide and 8.6 meters (28.2 feet) long before passing the water into the ditch that runs for 73 meters (239.5 feet) to Sawmill Pond.

Site 4:S1E2. Overflow and ditch. This massive, stone-lined spillway was built in 1915 at the west end of Ingall's Dam (5:S1E2) to take care of spring floods. If water in the pond rose suddenly, this overflow was large enough to dump a great deal of water out of the mill system very quickly. The floor of the overflow consists of stones that have been mortared together, and the stone-lined

A-39. The spillway at the west end of Ingall's Dam on Turning Mill Pond (facing north). The scale board is marked in 10-cm increments.

channel measures 5.75 meters (18.9 feet) wide by 14.1 meters (46.3 feet) long (figure A-39). Water that flowed out of Turning Mill Pond through this overflow and the associated ditching was carried out of the mill system altogether. The ditch runs about 442 meters (1,450 feet) southeast and deposits its water in a marsh just north of Asby Road.

Site 5:S1E2. Dam south of Turning Mill Pond. The Shakers constructed this earth and stone dam in 1915 in order to raise the level of water in the pond, and it was called "Ingall's Dam." There had been an older dam here, but the Shakers built a new wall in back of the earlier dam, filled it with small rocks, and covered both dams with earth. Ingall's Dam is in good condition, although it has minor leaks. The dam is 5.4–7.5 meters (17.7–24.6 feet) in width, 65.8 meters (216 feet) long, and about 2.0 meters (6.5 feet) high.

Site 6:S1E2. Tree house (recent). A sizable, though dilapidated, tree house was suspended between several trees in 1982 but has since collapsed. It was not built by the Shakers.

Site 7:S1E2. Ditch carrying water south from Factory Pond to Turning Mill Pond.

Site 1:S1E3. Turning Mill Pond (see 2:N0E2). See map on p. 170.

Site 2:S1E3. Dam south of Turning Mill Pond (see 5:S1E2).

Site 3:S1E3. Ditch carrying water south from Factory Pond to Turning Mill Pond (see 7:S1E2).

Site 1:S2W1. Meeting House Field (see 3:S1W1). See map on p. 171.

Site 2:S2W1. Stone watering trough. Micajah Tucker built this trough in 1831 so that horses and cows could drink before ascending the hill to the Church Family. Eldress Bertha Lindsay stated that "there was always fresh bubbling water here, piped down from the ox pasture. The four points [corners] to this watering trough point to the four points of the compass." The trough, which measures about 4 × 4.5 feet, has not been used as a watering trough for some years (figure A-40).

Site 3:S2W1. Ox pasture (see 5:S1W1).

A-40. The stone watering trough at the foot of Shaker Road, before the ascent up to the Church Family.

Site 1:S2E0. Meeting House Field (see 3:S1W1). See map on p. 172.

Site 2:S2E0. Church Family apple orchard (see 7:S1E0).

Site 3:S2E0. Bean Field. This field was given its name because beans were raised here for many years.

Site 1:S2E1. Sawmill Pond. See map on p. 173. The Shakers constructed this pond in 1800, and it was the very first of the Shaker-made ponds. It supplied water to a long succession of grist- and sawmills, but the pond ceased to be used in 1915. The pond currently measures only 2.28 acres in area, and it appears to have been the smallest of the ponds in the mill system.

Site 2:S2E1. Dam south of Sawmill Pond. This low earth and stone dam was probably constructed in 1800. Because this dam saw no maintenance for thirty or more years, the pond lost most of its water. The museum finally replaced it with a modern, non-Shaker dam in 1988 when constructing the fire protection system. The original dam measured about 10 meters (33 feet) in maximum thickness and about 2–3 meters (6.5–10 feet) in height. The current dam has enabled the pond to retain its water, but the very small, uniform-appearing stones look nothing like the large, quarried blocks of the original dam.

Site 3:S2E1. Headrace. Running about 41 meters (135 feet) south from Sawmill Pond to the site of the 1915 sawmill, this headrace contained a 24-inch cast-iron pipe that carried water from Turning Mill Pond to the sawmill. In the 1950s, the farm manager at that time removed this penstock and sold it as scrap. The head-race ditch is now about 1.5–2.0 meters (5.0–6.5 feet) deep.

Site 4:S2E1. Sawmill foundation. The Shakers erected several successive sawmills and gristmills in this location, typically with both functions combined in the same structure. According to Brother Francis Winkley, the original 1800 mill consisted of a gristmill that measured 24 × 30 feet and a sawmill that measured 16 × 42 feet. The Shakers tore down this mill in 1832.

The next combined grist- and sawmill was erected between 1832 and 1834, just north of the old one. In 1840 Isaac Hill described it as "an extensive building eighty feet by forty and three stories high—a building framed of stouter timber than is often found in the largest structures. This building covers a grist mill with four runs of stones, of which is one set of burrs for the manufacture of flour. This mill is visited by customers ten, fifteen and twenty miles distant, who are unable to find another so good. . . . Under the same roof and moved by the same wheel is a mill for sawing common boards from logs—a circular saw for slitting—a machine for sawing pail staves—a mill for grinding malt—also, a shop for manufacturing measures, as half bushels, pecks, etc. The great wheel which moves the machinery of this building

A-41. The foundation of the 1915–1954 sawmill while it was still filled with Town of Canterbury trash (facing southeast)

is thirty-four feet in diameter. . . . The expense laid out in constructing the buildings and machinery exceeded ten thousand dollars. . . ." Elder Henry Blinn described this same mill: "A large circular saw for the cutting of timber logs took the place of the old upright saw [in 1855], and was used for several years, but finally this was taken away and the old upright saw again brought into use as being less expensive. An overshot wheel, 33 ft in diameter was used when the mill was first built. This gave place after a few years to three Russell wheels [in 1865] and these, in turn gave place to four Tyler wheels." The Shakers had earlier replaced the overshot wheel, in 1851, "and two iron [Parker] wheels are bought for the place. The whole cost of repairs at the mill this season is some $5000.00."

Over the years the sawmill's power system thus underwent an evolution from an overshot wheel to two Parker wheels (1851) to three Russell wheels (1865) to four Tyler wheels. The Shakers periodically changed the type of saw that was used, going from an up-and-down saw, to a circular saw, to another up-and-down saw, to a "Muley" saw (an up-and-down type), and finally to a Lane 54-inch circular saw in 1893. The Lane saw cost $392.00. They also put a Tyler 24-inch turbine into the sawmill, purchased from the Fitchburg Machine Company of Fitchburg, Massachusetts, for $190.00. They removed this sawmill in 1915 to make way for the final sawmill.

The Shakers built their last sawmill in this location—in fact, the last operative mill at Shaker Village—in 1915 at a cost of about $3,000. The 1915 sawmill was one story high, measured 54 × 40 feet, and had a roof and siding of galvanized iron. The Shakers purchased an electric generator for it, run by waterpower; it had a 6-inch Register Gate wheel that developed 25 horsepower with a 54-foot head. To get sufficient head the Shakers did away with Sawmill Pond and ran a 24-inch cast-iron pipe to the sawmill from Turning Mill Pond. They sold the mill building and removed it in 1954, and the foundation was then filled with non-Shaker trash from the Town of Canterbury (figure A-41). The museum removed this recent fill with power equipment in the fall of 1995, and today there is no evidence of the Shakers' machinery or their power system inside the open stone foundation.

Site 5:S2E1. Foundation (unidentified). The function and age of this small (about 6 × 7.5 meters) foundation are unknown, but it appeared on an 1879 map of Shaker Village prepared by John McClintock. No artifacts are visible on the surface of the site.

Site 6:S2E1. Tan House Field (see 7:N0E1).

Site 7:S2E1. Sawmill Field. This field derived its name from the progression of sawmills located just to the southeast (see 4:S2E1). Its principal use has always been for pasturage.

Site 8:S2E1. Tailrace from turning mill. This channel carried water used by the turbine in the turning mill's wheel pit south into Sawmill Pond; it is partially above- and partially belowground. The subterranean part of the tailrace is about 15.0 meters (49 feet) long, and the exposed part is about 6.8 meters (22.3 feet) long. The width varies from 1.0 to 2.0 meters (3.3 to 6.6 feet).

Site 1:S2E2. Sawmill Pond (see 1:S2E1). See map on p. 174.

Site 2:S2E2. Dam south of Sawmill Pond. The dam (see 2:S2E1) is unusually wide at this point but has very little relief.

Site 3:S2E2. Overflow and ditch carrying water south from Sawmill Pond. A small amount of water currently flows through the overflow and ditch, and it joins with the water flowing through the sawmill tailrace at a point just south of Asby Road. The stone-lined portion of this overflow channel is about 4.1 meters (13.5 feet) wide by 6.0 meters (19.7 feet) long.

Site 4:S2E2. Possible overflow. This channel has been filled in with earth and is no longer operative. Still, it appears to have been a spillway, and it measures 6.25 meters (20.5 feet) in length by about 1.3 meters (4.3 feet) in width.

Site 5:S2E2. Ditch carrying water south from Turning Mill Pond into Sawmill Pond (see 3:S1E2).

Site 6:S2E2. Ditch running south from Turning Mill Pond (see 4:S1E2).

Site 1:S3E1. Sawmill foundation (see 4:S2E1). See map on p. 176.

Site 2:S3E1. Headrace (see 3:S2E1).

Site 3:S3E1. Tailrace running south from the 1915 sawmill. Most of the tailrace is subterranean, but it becomes a

steep-sided open ditch just north of Asby Road. The tailrace measures 0.6–1.0 meters (2–3 feet) in width and is 2–4 meters (6.5–13.0 feet) deep.

Site 4:S3E1. Ditch carrying water south from Sawmill Pond (see 3:S2E2).

Site 1:S4E0. Ditch carrying water south from Sawmill Pond (see 3:S2E2). See map on p. 177.

Site 1:S4E1. Ditch carrying water south from Sawmill Pond (see 3:S2E2). See map on p. 178.

Site 1:S5E0. Marsh. See map on p. 179. This marsh was originally an unnamed pond within the Shaker mill system, but it is now very nearly dry. There are only a few scattered journal references to this pond, and none to indicate when the pond was constructed or when it shrank to a marsh. It was built to supply water to a sawmill that lay just to the south (2:S6E0). The bed of the pond is now covered with grass and tree stumps.

Site 2:S5E0. Ditch carrying water south from Sawmill Pond (see 3:S2E2).

Site 1:S6W1. Carding Mill Pond. See map on p. 180. Carding Mill Pond was constructed in 1811 and was abandoned on or before 1890. The pond presently measures 5.55 acres in surface area and is well filled with water, but it will soon become just a marsh if the dam (3:S7E0) is not repaired.

Site 1:S6E0. Carding Mill Pond (see 1:S6W1). See map on p. 181.

Site 2:S6E0. Sawmill foundation. The date of construction of this mill is unknown, but Brother Francis Winkley wrote in 1824 that the Shakers "built a wood shelter at the head of the carding millpond." In 1840 Isaac Hill wrote that this was "A building with a machine for sawing wood. At this place, being near an extensive and beautiful woodlot, the fuel used by the family is prepared. . . ." The wheel pit for the sawmill now lies open, free of trash, but large rocks have fallen in from the sides. Water still flows rapidly through an iron penstock into the wheel pit and on into the tailrace. The wheel pit itself measures 2.2 meters (7.2 feet) deep, 2.5 meters (8.2 feet) wide, and 5.7 meters (18.7 feet) long.

Site 3:S6E0. Dam south of the unnamed millpond. We do not know when the Shakers constructed this earth and stone dam, but it still is in excellent condition. The dam is about 35.0 meters (115 feet) long and 5.4 meters (18 feet) thick.

Site 1:S7W1. Carding Mill Pond (see 1:S6W1). See map on p. 182.

Site 2:S7W1. Carding mill foundation. Isaac Hill described the carding mill as "A building 35 by 50 feet and two stories, containing apparatus and machinery for carding wool." The Shakers constructed their carding mill in 1812, and it also contained a trip-hammer and a furnace for casting stoves. Elder Henry Blinn described this building as "43 × 38 and two stories high. An overshot waterwheel was placed at the east end and outside of the building, and the water was conveyed from the pond in an open trough. The carding machinery were manufactured at the Society of New Lebanon. . . ." The mill housed two carding machines, a wool picker, and a shearing machine. In 1840 an "arm wheel" replaced the overshot wheel.

In 1860 the Shakers built a house at the carding mill for hired help. Prior to this, hired helpers had lived in the lower part of the mill. Also in 1860, the Shakers put a new waterwheel into the carding mill. In 1861 they sold the carding machines and purchased new ones. Finally, they sold this newer carding machinery, and it was taken away in 1881. Later, brooms were manufactured there.

In 1896 the Shakers sold the carding mill building to Frank Fellows of Belmont, New Hampshire, but the mill burned on April 20 before he could remove it. The bottom of the wheel pit in the carding mill is presently littered with foundation stones, and no machinery is visible. The wheel pit measures about 2.0 meters (6.5 feet) deep, 2.58 meters (8.5 feet) wide, and 8.55 meters (28 feet) long. The main foundation for the carding mill is surrounded by the foundations from several smaller buildings.

Site 3:S7W1. Foundation. Unidentified mill building. This open cellar hole contains a small number of ferns, and the foundation stones are well exposed all around the perimeter to a depth of about 4.5 feet (1.4 meters). The cellar hole measures 8.1 meters (26.5 feet) north-south by 6.2 meters (20.3 feet) east-west.

Site 4:S7W1. Foundation stones. The structure supported by these stones may have been either an addition onto 3:S7W1 or else a very small separate structure.

Site 5:S7W1. Foundation. Unidentified mill building. Just west of this foundation is an extremely deep open well that has an inside diameter of 75 centimeters (2.3 feet).

Site 6:S7W1. Henry Beck's land. Beck was one of the founders of Canterbury Shaker Village, and his land bordered the village on the south.

Site 1:S7E0. Carding Mill Pond (see 1:S6W1). See map on p. 183.

Site 2:S7E0. Carding Mill foundation (see 2:S7W1).

Site 3:S7E0. Dam south of Carding Mill Pond. The Shakers constructed this earth and stone dam in late 1811. The dam ranges between 1.3 and 4.3 meters (4.25 and 12 feet) in height but has slumped badly at its eastern end and will soon be totally breached. Water is pouring through the dam at this point. A dirt road once ran along the top of the dam, and it is about 46.5 meters (153 feet) long and 4.9–7.7 meters (16–25 feet) wide.

Site 4:S7E0. The southern end of the Shaker mill system. After leaving Carding Mill Pond, the water was allowed to flow south without further ditching.

Site 5:S7E0. Man-made dike and channel. Connecting Carding Mill Pond with a small marsh, this channel appears to have been a spillway at some time in the past. It measures 3.5–5.0 meters (11.6–16.4 feet) in width and about 30 meters (98 feet) in length.

Site 6:S7E0. Man-made dike. This feature and the accompanying channel (7:S7E0) may have formed a second spillway for Carding Mill Pond.

Site 7:S7E0. Shallow, unused channel.

LEGEND
Symbols and Conventions Used On 1:500 Base Maps

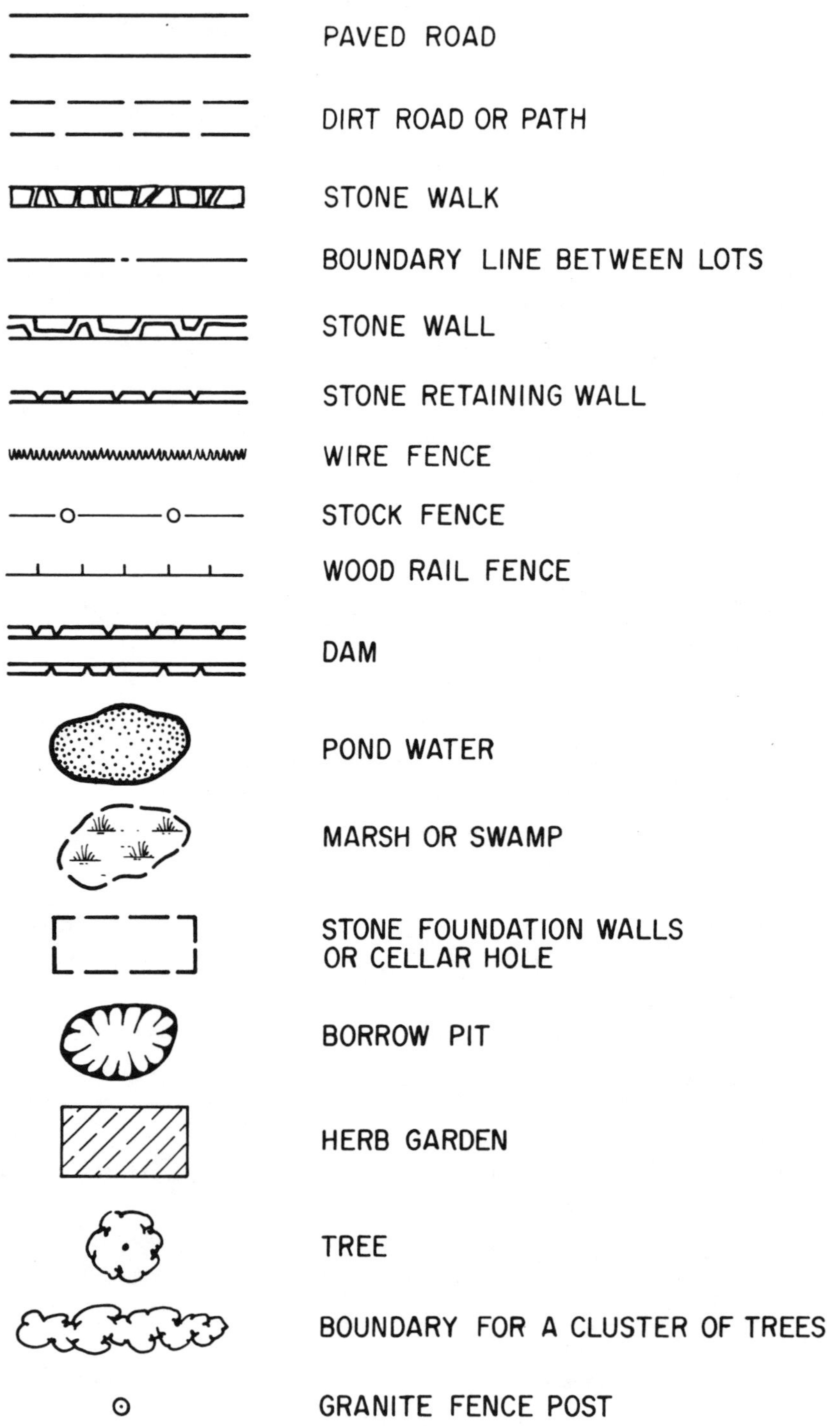

PAVED ROAD

DIRT ROAD OR PATH

STONE WALK

BOUNDARY LINE BETWEEN LOTS

STONE WALL

STONE RETAINING WALL

WIRE FENCE

STOCK FENCE

WOOD RAIL FENCE

DAM

POND WATER

MARSH OR SWAMP

STONE FOUNDATION WALLS
OR CELLAR HOLE

BORROW PIT

HERB GARDEN

TREE

BOUNDARY FOR A CLUSTER OF TREES

GRANITE FENCE POST

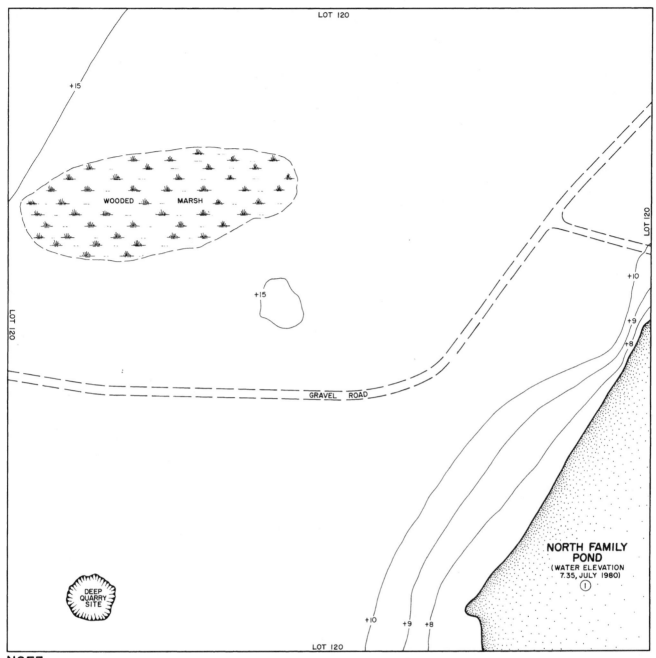

LOT 120

+15

WOODED   MARSH

+15

LOT 120

LOT 120

+10

+9

+8

GRAVEL   ROAD

NORTH FAMILY
POND
(WATER ELEVATION
7.35, JULY 1980)
①

+10   +9   +8

DEEP
QUARRY
SITE

LOT 120

N6E3

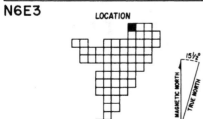

LOCATION

15½°

MAGNETIC NORTH

TRUE NORTH

CANTERBURY SHAKER VILLAGE

0   5   10   15   20   25   50 METERS

CONTOUR INTERVAL 1 METER

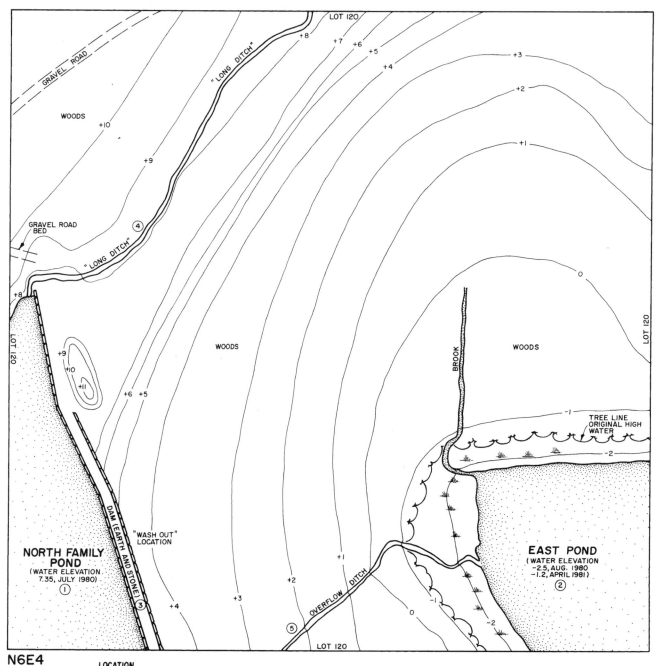

124

LOT 120

GRAVEL ROAD

"LONG DITCH"

WOODS
+10

+9

+8
+7
+6
+5
+4
+3

+2

+1

GRAVEL ROAD
BED

+8

"LONG DITCH"

LOT 120

0

+8

+9
+10
+11

WOODS

BROOK

WOODS

+6 +5

-1

TREE LINE
ORIGINAL HIGH
WATER

-2

LOT 120

DAM (EARTH AND STONE)

"WASH OUT"
LOCATION

NORTH FAMILY
POND
(WATER ELEVATION
7.35, JULY 1980)
①

③

+4

+3

+2

+1

+2

+3

+4

OVERFLOW DITCH

⑤

0

-1

-2

EAST POND
(WATER ELEVATION
-2.5, AUG. 1980
-1.2, APRIL 1981)
②

LOT 120

N6E4

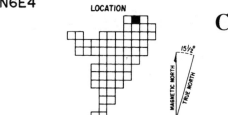

LOCATION

15½°

MAGNETIC NORTH
TRUE NORTH

CANTERBURY SHAKER VILLAGE

0 5 10 15 20 25   50 METERS

CONTOUR INTERVAL 1 METER

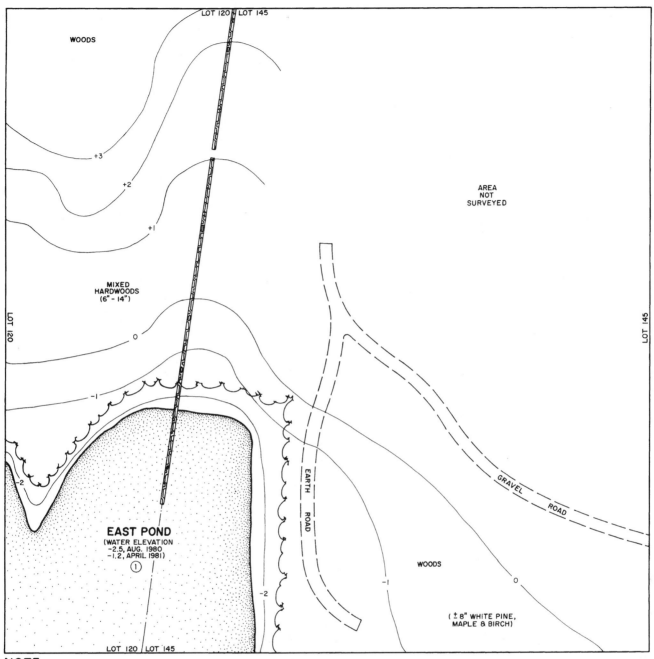

CANTERBURY SHAKER VILLAGE

N6E5

LOCATION

MAGNETIC NORTH 15½° TRUE NORTH

0 5 10 15 20 25   50 METERS

CONTOUR INTERVAL 1 METER

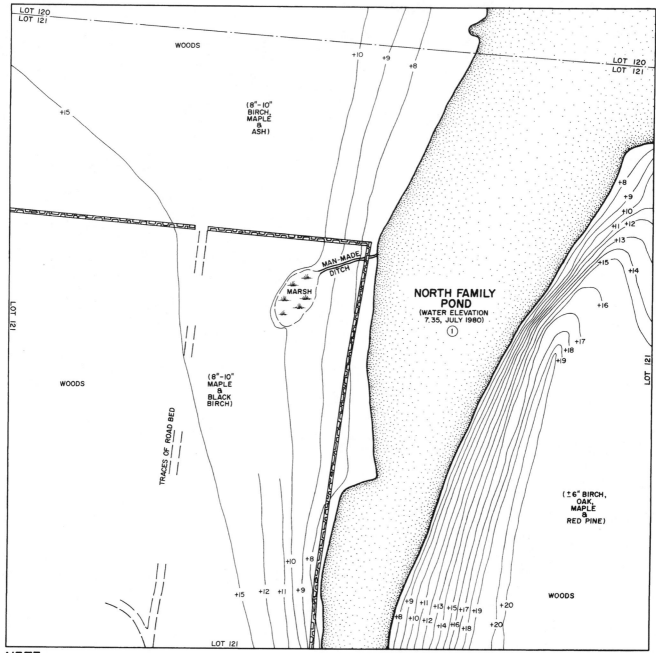

LOT 120
LOT 121

WOODS

+10 +9 +8

LOT 120
LOT 121

(8"-10"
BIRCH,
MAPLE
&
ASH)

+15

+8

+9

+10

+11 +12

+13

+15 +14

MAN-MADE
DITCH

MARSH

NORTH FAMILY
POND
(WATER ELEVATION
7.35, JULY 1980)
①

+16

+17

LOT 121

+18

+19

LOT 121

WOODS

(8"-10"
MAPLE
&
BLACK
BIRCH)

(±6" BIRCH,
OAK,
MAPLE
&
RED PINE)

TRACES OF ROAD BED

WOODS

+10 +8

+15 +12 +11 +9

+9 +11 +13 +15 +17 +19 +20
+8 +10 +12 +14 +16 +18 +20

LOT 121

N5E3

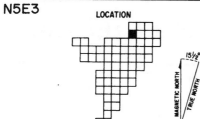

CANTERBURY SHAKER VILLAGE

15½°
MAGNETIC NORTH
TRUE NORTH

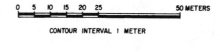

0 5 10 15 20 25   50 METERS

CONTOUR INTERVAL 1 METER

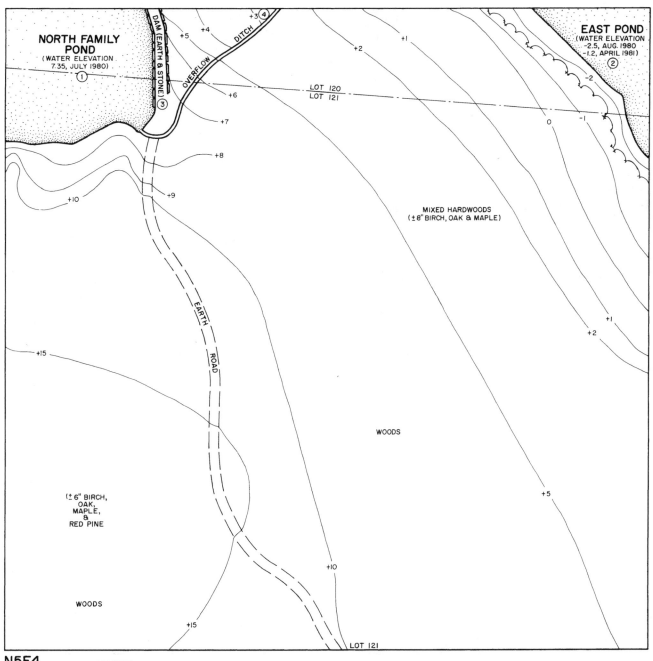

NORTH FAMILY
POND
(WATER ELEVATION
7.35, JULY 1980)
①

DAM (EARTH & STONE) ③

OVERFLOW

DITCH

④ +3
+5
+4
+6
+7
+8
+9
+10
+15

EAST POND
(WATER ELEVATION
-2.5, AUG. 1980
-1.2, APRIL 1981)
②
-2
-1
0

+2
+1

LOT 120
LOT 121

MIXED HARDWOODS
(±8" BIRCH, OAK & MAPLE)

EARTH   ROAD

WOODS

+1
+2

+5

(±6" BIRCH,
OAK,
MAPLE,
&
RED PINE

WOODS

+10

+15

LOT 121

N5E4

LOCATION

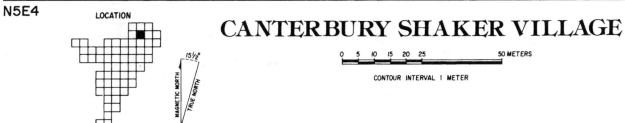

15½°
MAGNETIC NORTH
TRUE NORTH

CANTERBURY SHAKER VILLAGE

0 5 10 15 20 25   50 METERS

CONTOUR INTERVAL 1 METER

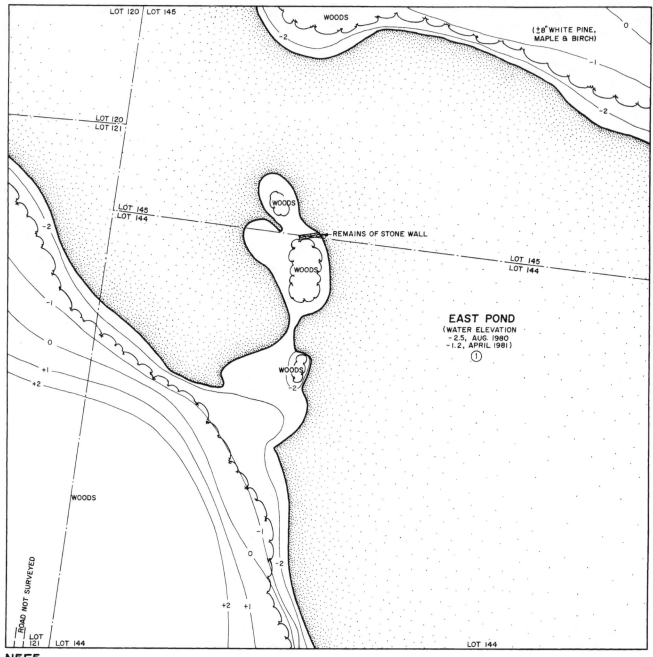

LOT 120 | LOT 145

WOODS

(±8" WHITE PINE, MAPLE & BIRCH)

−2

0

−1

−2

LOT 120
LOT 121

LOT 145
LOT 144

−2

WOODS

REMAINS OF STONE WALL

WOODS

LOT 145
LOT 144

−1

0

+1

+2

EAST POND
(WATER ELEVATION
−2.5, AUG. 1980
−1.2, APRIL 1981)
①

WOODS

−2

WOODS

−2

−1

0

+2 +1

ROAD NOT SURVEYED

LOT 121 | LOT 144

LOT 144

N5E5

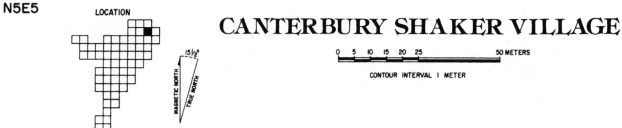

LOCATION

15½°

MAGNETIC NORTH

TRUE NORTH

CANTERBURY SHAKER VILLAGE

0 5 10 15 20 25   50 METERS

CONTOUR INTERVAL 1 METER

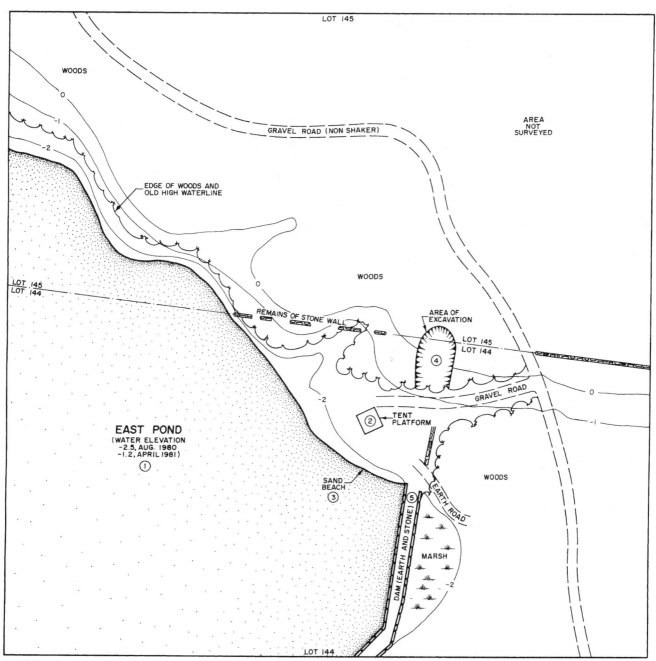

LOT 145

WOODS

GRAVEL ROAD (NON SHAKER)

AREA
NOT
SURVEYED

0

-1

-2

EDGE OF WOODS AND
OLD HIGH WATERLINE

LOT 145
LOT 144

0

WOODS

REMAINS OF STONE WALL

AREA OF
EXCAVATION

LOT 145
LOT 144

④

GRAVEL ROAD

0

-2

-1

EAST POND
(WATER ELEVATION
-2.5, AUG. 1980
-1.2, APRIL 1981)
①

TENT
② PLATFORM

SAND
BEACH
③

WOODS

⑤

MARSH

-2

DAM (EARTH AND STONE)

EARTH ROAD

LOT 144

N5E6

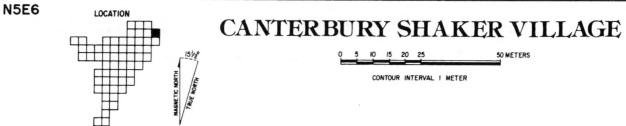

LOCATION

MAGNETIC NORTH · TRUE NORTH · 15½°

CANTERBURY SHAKER VILLAGE

0   5   10   15   20   25   50 METERS

CONTOUR INTERVAL 1 METER

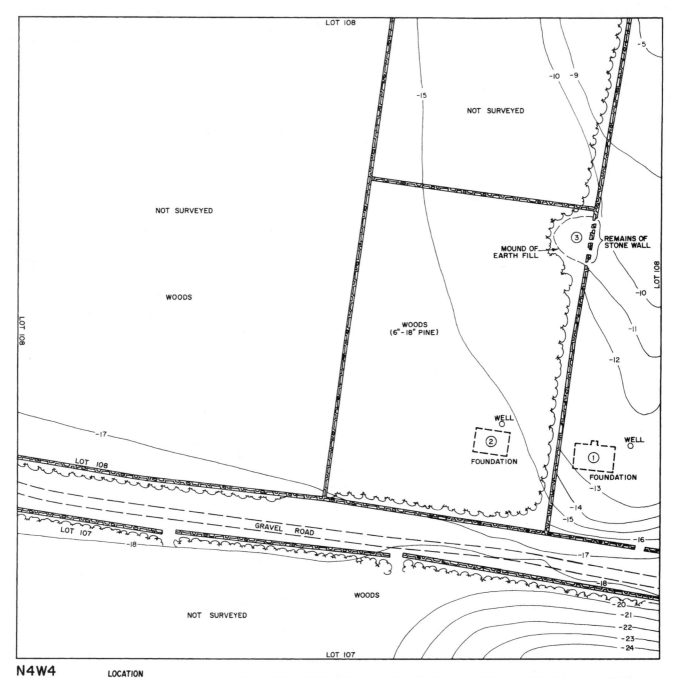

LOT 108

NOT SURVEYED

NOT SURVEYED

WOODS

WOODS
(6"-18" PINE)

MOUND OF
EARTH FILL

③

REMAINS OF
STONE WALL

LOT 108

LOT 108

WELL
○

②

FOUNDATION

WELL
○

①

FOUNDATION

GRAVEL ROAD

LOT 108

LOT 107

WOODS

NOT SURVEYED

LOT 107

N4W4

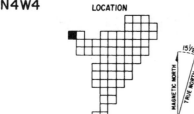

LOCATION

MAGNETIC NORTH
TRUE NORTH
15½°

CANTERBURY SHAKER VILLAGE

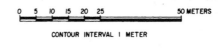

0 5 10 15 20 25   50 METERS

CONTOUR INTERVAL 1 METER

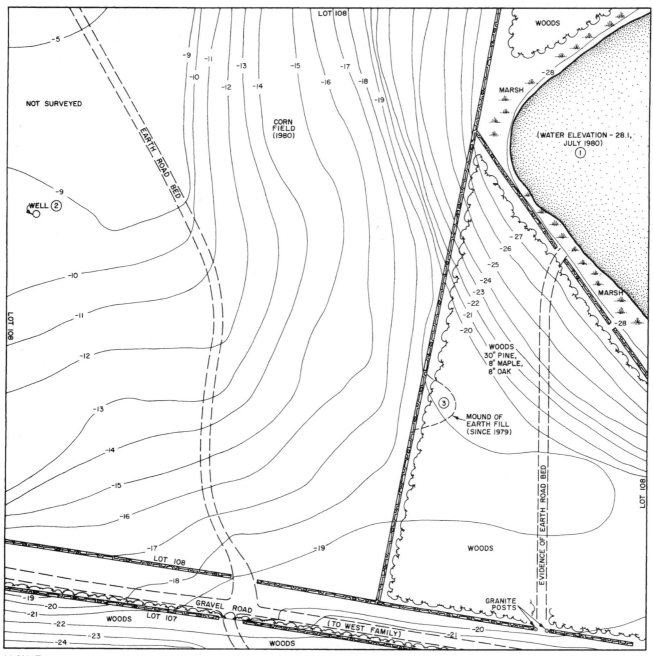

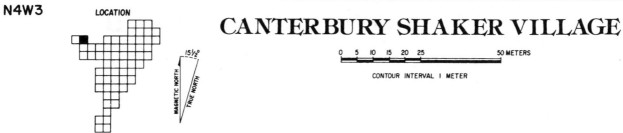

CANTERBURY SHAKER VILLAGE

N4W3

LOCATION

CONTOUR INTERVAL 1 METER

132

N4 E0

LOCATION

MAGNETIC NORTH

TRUE NORTH

15½°

CANTERBURY SHAKER VILLAGE

0 5 10 15 20 25   50 METERS

CONTOUR INTERVAL 1 METER

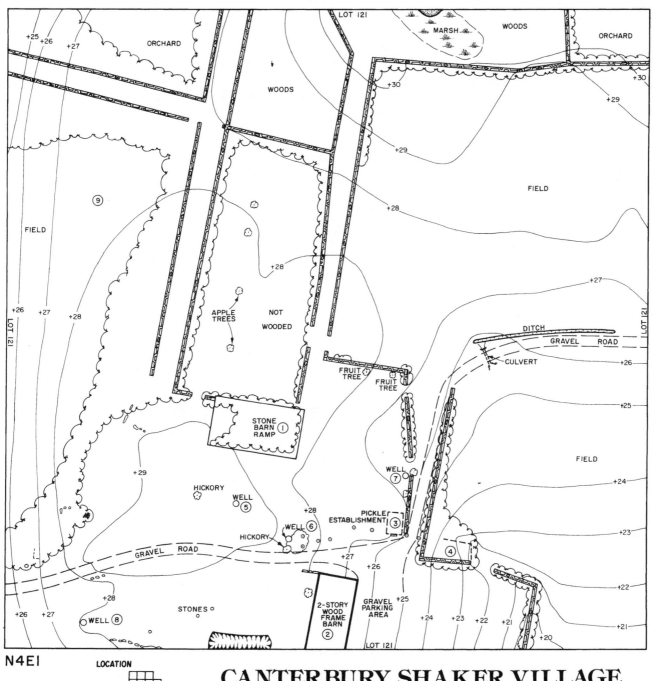

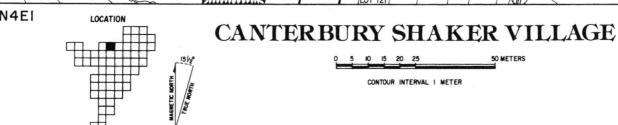

CANTERBURY SHAKER VILLAGE

N4E1

LOCATION

0 5 10 15 20 25   50 METERS

CONTOUR INTERVAL 1 METER

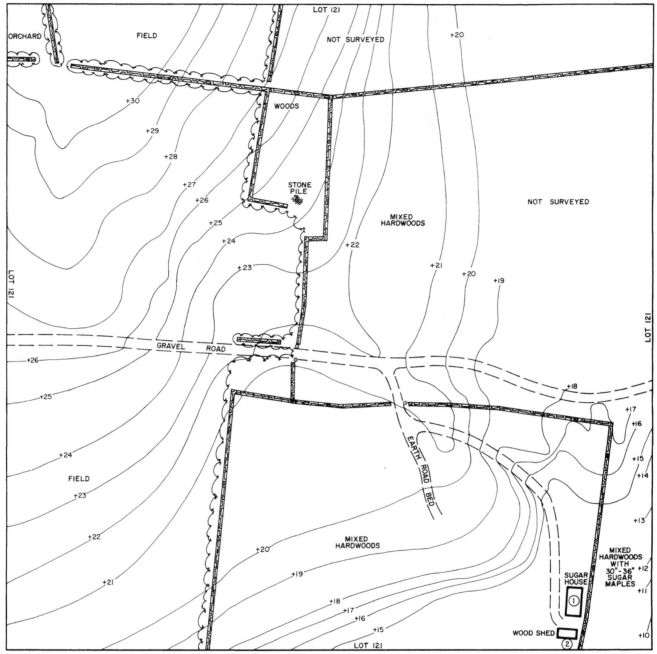

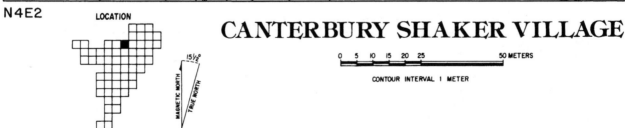

N4E2

LOCATION

MAGNETIC NORTH   TRUE NORTH   15½°

CANTERBURY SHAKER VILLAGE

0 5 10 15 20 25   50 METERS

CONTOUR INTERVAL 1 METER

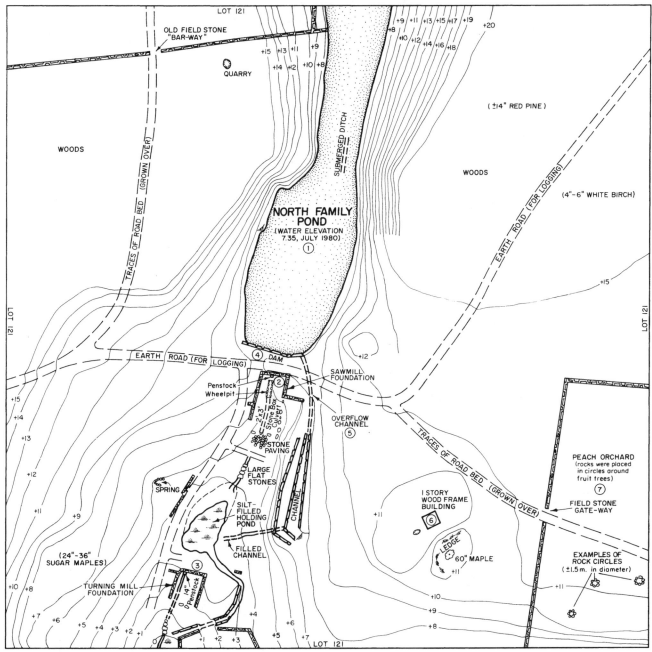

LOT 121

OLD FIELD STONE "BAR-WAY"

QUARRY

+9 +11 +13 +15 +17 +19
+8 +20
+10 +12 +14 +16 +18
+15 +13 +11 +9
+14 +12 +10 +8

(±14" RED PINE)

WOODS

WOODS

SUBMERGED DITCH

(4"-6" WHITE BIRCH)

TRACES OF ROAD BED (GROWN OVER)

EARTH ROAD (FOR LOGGING)

NORTH FAMILY POND
(WATER ELEVATION 7.35, JULY 1980)
①

+15

LOT 121

EARTH ROAD (FOR LOGGING) ④ DAM
Penstock Wheelpit ②
SAWMILL FOUNDATION
+12
+15
+14
+13
OVERFLOW CHANNEL ⑤
TRACES OF ROAD BED (GROWN OVER)
STONE PAVING
+12
SPRING
LARGE FLAT STONES
PEACH ORCHARD
(rocks were placed in circles around fruit trees) ⑦
FIELD STONE GATE-WAY
+11
SILT-FILLED HOLDING POND
CHANNEL
I STORY WOOD FRAME BUILDING ⑥
+11
LEDGE 60" MAPLE
FILLED CHANNEL
+9
(24"-36" SUGAR MAPLES)
EXAMPLES OF ROCK CIRCLES (±1.5 m. in diameter)
+10 +8
TURNING MILL FOUNDATION ③
+11
Penstock
+10
+7 +6 +5 +4 +3 +2 +1
+4
+9
+2 +3
+5 +6 +7 +8
LOT 121

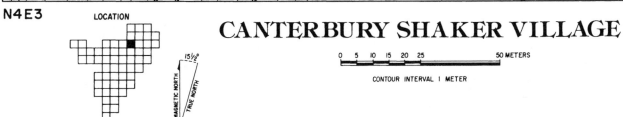

N4E3

LOCATION

MAGNETIC NORTH TRUE NORTH 15½°

CANTERBURY SHAKER VILLAGE

0 5 10 15 20 25 50 METERS

CONTOUR INTERVAL 1 METER

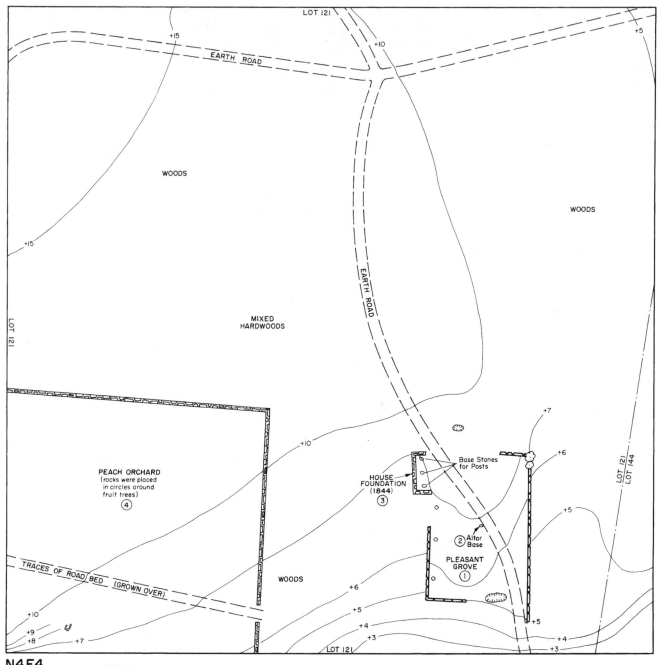

LOT 121

EARTH ROAD

WOODS

WOODS

+15

+15

MIXED
HARDWOODS

EARTH ROAD

+10

+7

PEACH ORCHARD
(rocks were placed
in circles around
fruit trees)
④

+10

Base Stones
for Posts

+6

HOUSE
FOUNDATION
(1844)
③

+5

LOT 121
LOT 144

② Altar
Base

PLEASANT
GROVE
①

TRACES OF ROAD BED (GROWN OVER)

WOODS

+6

+5

+5

+10

+9

+8

+7

+5

+4

+3

LOT 121

+4

+3

N4E4

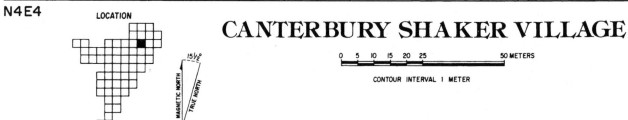

LOCATION

15½°

MAGNETIC NORTH

TRUE NORTH

CANTERBURY SHAKER VILLAGE

0 5 10 15 20 25   50 METERS

CONTOUR INTERVAL 1 METER

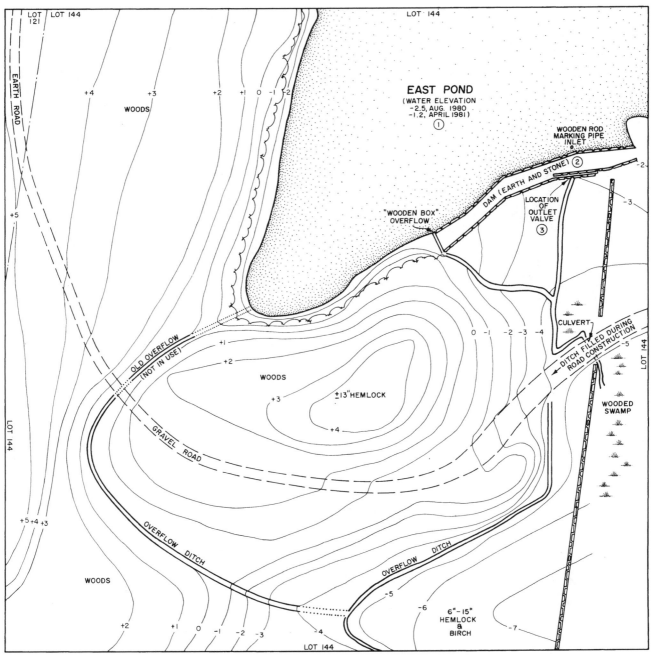

East Pond area map.

N4E5

LOCATION

MAGNETIC NORTH / TRUE NORTH 15½°

CANTERBURY SHAKER VILLAGE

0 5 10 15 20 25   50 METERS

CONTOUR INTERVAL 1 METER

Map labels: LOT 121, LOT 144, EARTH ROAD, WOODS, EAST POND (WATER ELEVATION −2.5, AUG. 1980 −1.2, APRIL 1981) ①, WOODEN ROD MARKING PIPE INLET ②, DAM (EARTH AND STONE), LOCATION OF OUTLET VALVE ③, "WOODEN BOX" OVERFLOW, OLD OVERFLOW (NOT IN USE), GRAVEL ROAD, ±13"HEMLOCK, WOODS, OVERFLOW DITCH, CULVERT, DITCH FILLED DURING ROAD CONSTRUCTION, LOT 144, WOODED SWAMP, 6"-15" HEMLOCK & BIRCH, LOT 144

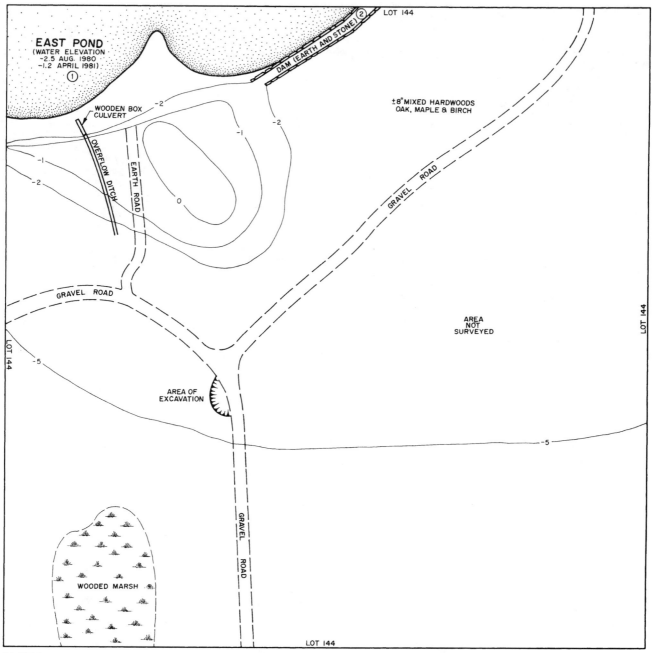

EAST POND
(WATER ELEVATION
-2.5 AUG. 1980
-1.2 APRIL 1981)

LOT 144

DAM (EARTH AND STONE)

±8" MIXED HARDWOODS
OAK, MAPLE & BIRCH

WOODEN BOX
CULVERT

OVERFLOW DITCH

EARTH ROAD

GRAVEL ROAD

GRAVEL ROAD

LOT 144

AREA
NOT
SURVEYED

LOT 144

AREA OF
EXCAVATION

-5

-5

GRAVEL ROAD

WOODED MARSH

LOT 144

N4E6

LOCATION

MAGNETIC NORTH

TRUE NORTH

15½°

CANTERBURY SHAKER VILLAGE

0 5 10 15 20 25   50 METERS

CONTOUR INTERVAL 1 METER

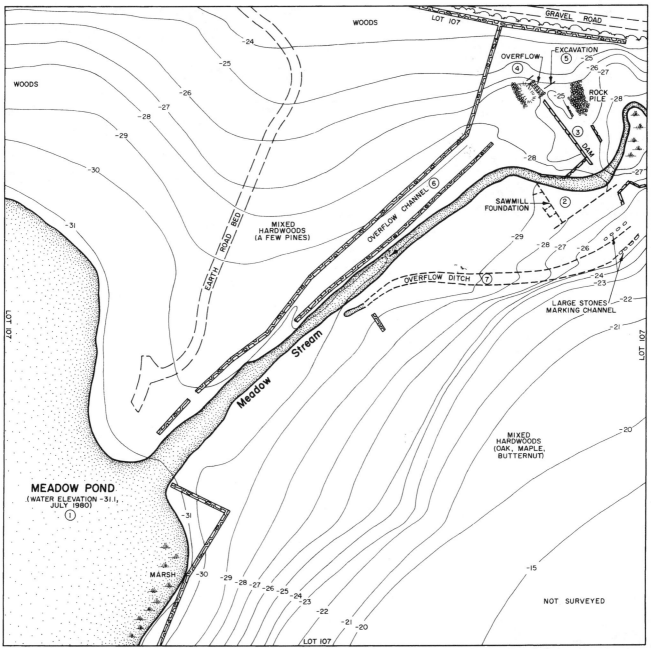

WOODS

LOT 107

GRAVEL ROAD

WOODS

MIXED HARDWOODS (A FEW PINES)

EARTH ROAD BED

OVERFLOW

EXCAVATION
⑤

OVERFLOW CHANNEL ⑥

④

⑤

ROCK PILE

③ DAM

SAWMILL FOUNDATION

②

OVERFLOW DITCH ⑦

LARGE STONES MARKING CHANNEL

LOT 107

Meadow Stream

MEADOW POND
(WATER ELEVATION -31.1, JULY 1980)
①

MARSH

MIXED HARDWOODS (OAK, MAPLE, BUTTERNUT)

NOT SURVEYED

LOT 107

N3W3

LOCATION

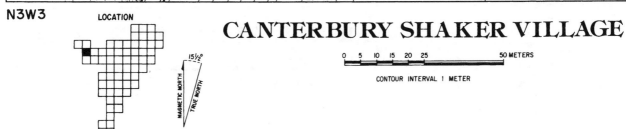

15½°

MAGNETIC NORTH

TRUE NORTH

CANTERBURY SHAKER VILLAGE

0   5   10   15   20   25   50 METERS

CONTOUR INTERVAL 1 METER

140

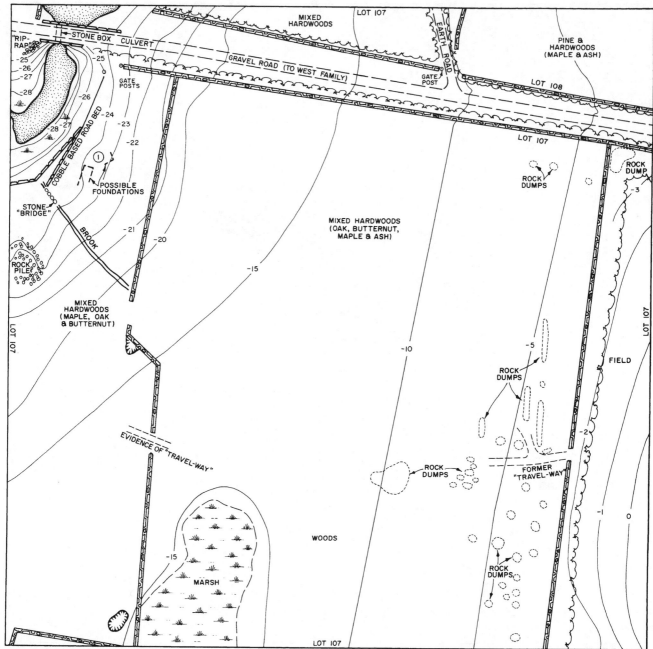

N3W2

LOCATION

CANTERBURY SHAKER VILLAGE

0 5 10 15 20 25   50 METERS

CONTOUR INTERVAL 1 METER

LOT 108

WOODS

FIELD

+8 +9 +10 +11

LOT 108

GRAVEL ROAD (TO WEST FAMILY)

LOT 107

-3

-2

-1

ROCK
DUMP

0

+1

FIELD

+2

+3

+4

+5

+6

+7

+8

+9

LOT 107

+11

ROCK
DUMPS

FIELD

+12

ROCK
DUMPS

LOT 107

N3WI

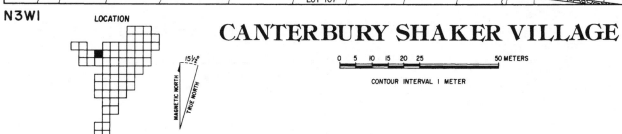

LOCATION

MAGNETIC NORTH
TRUE NORTH
15½°

CANTERBURY SHAKER VILLAGE

0 5 10 15 20 25   50 METERS

CONTOUR INTERVAL 1 METER

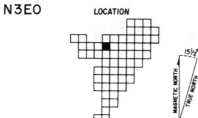

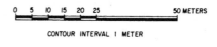

CANTERBURY SHAKER VILLAGE

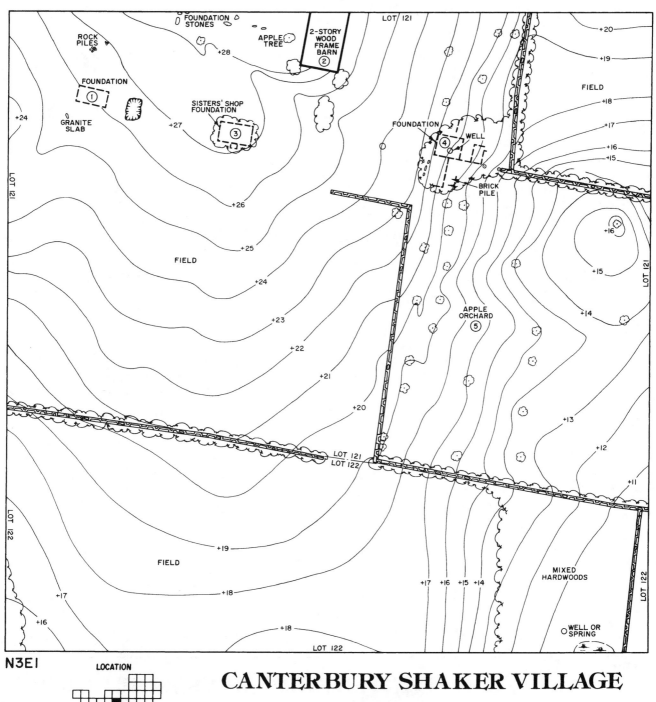

FOUNDATION STONES

ROCK PILES

APPLE TREE

2-STORY WOOD FRAME BARN ②

LOT 121

+28

+20

+19

FIELD

FOUNDATION ①

GRANITE SLAB

+24

SISTERS' SHOP FOUNDATION ③

+27

FOUNDATION ④ WELL

+18

+17

+16

+15

LOT 121

BRICK PILE

+26

+16

+25

+15

FIELD

+24

+23

APPLE ORCHARD ⑤

+14

LOT 121

+22

+21

+20

+13

+12

LOT 121
LOT 122

+11

LOT 122

+19

FIELD

MIXED HARDWOODS

LOT 122

+17

+18

+17 +16 +15 +14

+16

WELL OR SPRING

+18

LOT 122

N3E1

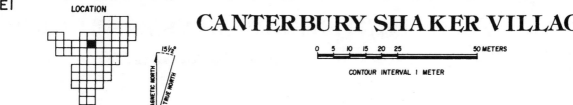

LOCATION

MAGNETIC NORTH   TRUE NORTH   15½°

CANTERBURY SHAKER VILLAGE

0 5 10 15 20 25   50 METERS

CONTOUR INTERVAL 1 METER

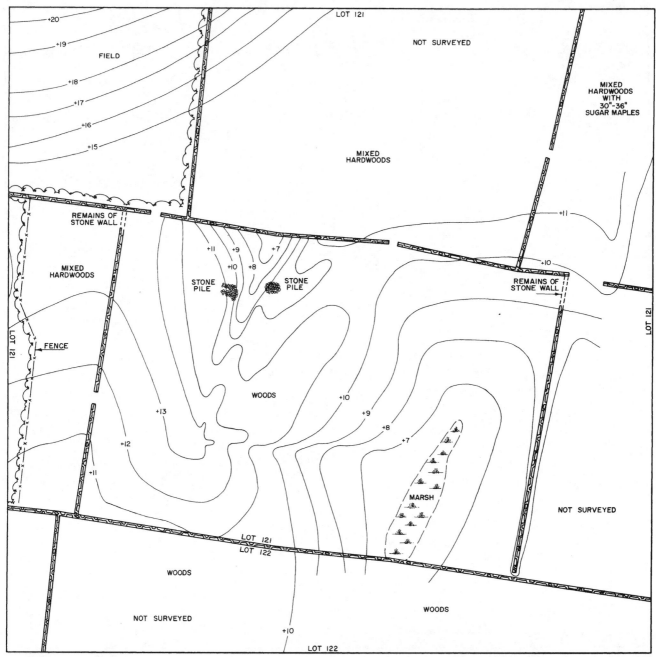

N3E2

LOCATION

CANTERBURY SHAKER VILLAGE

0 5 10 15 20 25   50 METERS

CONTOUR INTERVAL 1 METER

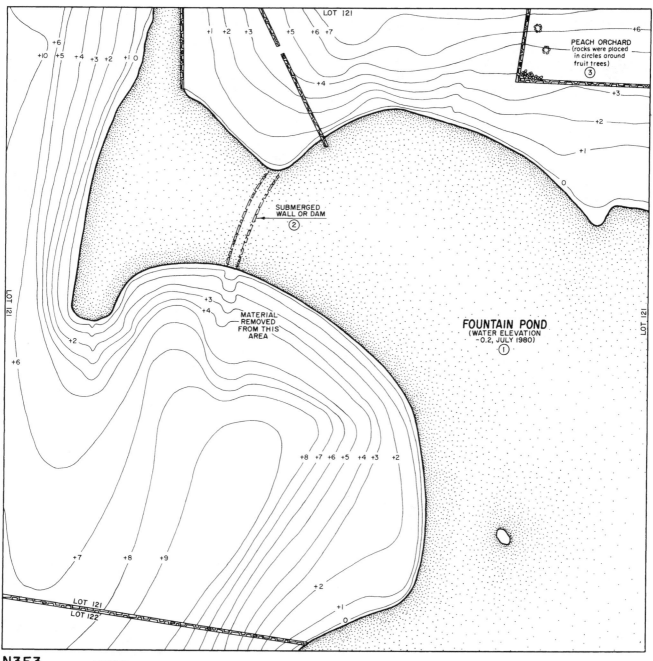

LOT 121

+6 +1 +2 +3 +5 +6 +7

+10 +5 +4 +3 +2 +1 0

+4

PEACH ORCHARD
(rocks were placed
in circles around
fruit trees)
③

+6

+3

+2

+1

0

LOT 121

SUBMERGED
WALL OR DAM
②

FOUNTAIN POND
(WATER ELEVATION
-0.2, JULY 1980)
①

LOT 121

+3
+4
MATERIAL
REMOVED
FROM THIS
AREA
+2
+6

+8 +7 +6 +5 +4 +3 +2

+7 +8 +9

+2

+1

0

LOT 121
LOT 122

N3E3

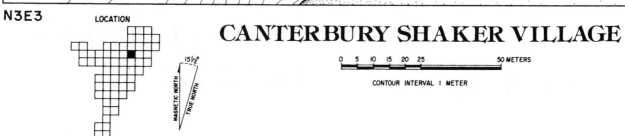

LOCATION

MAGNETIC NORTH / TRUE NORTH 15½°

CANTERBURY SHAKER VILLAGE

0 5 10 15 20 25 50 METERS

CONTOUR INTERVAL 1 METER

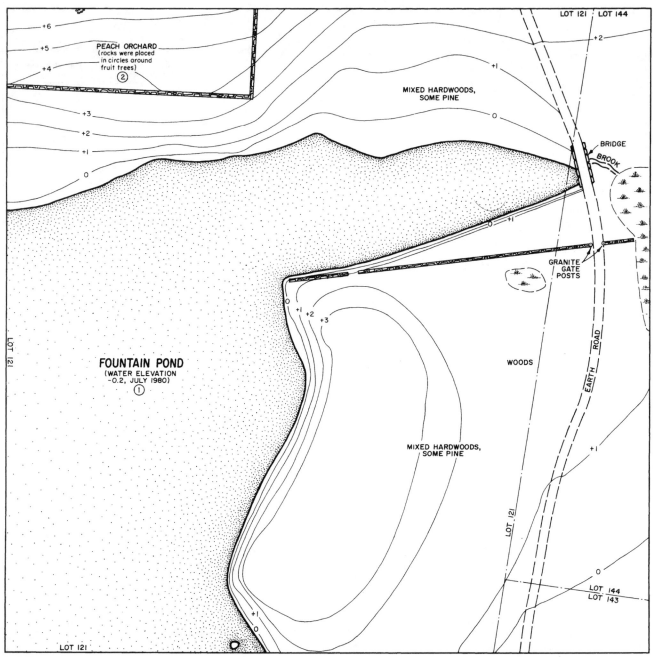

PEACH ORCHARD
(rocks were placed
in circles around
fruit trees)
②

FOUNTAIN POND
(WATER ELEVATION
-0.2, JULY 1980)
①

LOT 121

LOT 121

LOT 121 | LOT 144

MIXED HARDWOODS,
SOME PINE

BRIDGE

BROOK

GRANITE GATE
POSTS

WOODS

MIXED HARDWOODS,
SOME PINE

EARTH ROAD

LOT 121

LOT 144
LOT 143

N3E4

LOCATION

MAGNETIC NORTH
TRUE NORTH
15½°

CANTERBURY SHAKER VILLAGE

0 5 10 15 20 25   50 METERS

CONTOUR INTERVAL 1 METER

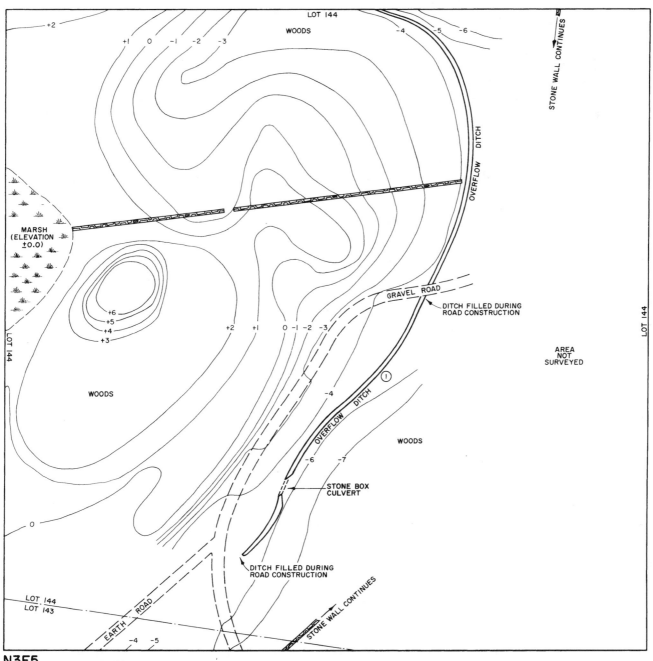

N3E5

LOCATION

CANTERBURY SHAKER VILLAGE

0 5 10 15 20 25   50 METERS

CONTOUR INTERVAL 1 METER

148

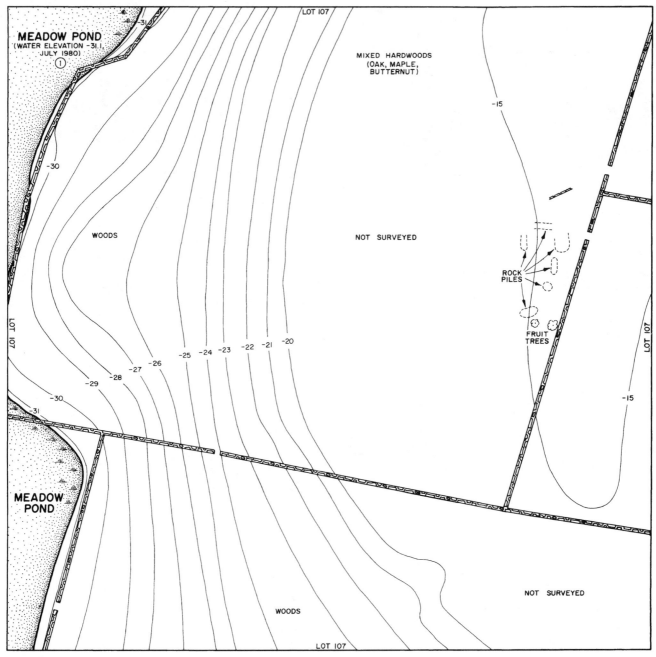

MEADOW POND
(WATER ELEVATION -31.1,
JULY 1980)

LOT 107

MIXED HARDWOODS
(OAK, MAPLE,
BUTTERNUT)

-15

WOODS

NOT SURVEYED

ROCK
PILES

FRUIT
TREES

LOT 107

-30

-25 -24 -23 -22 -21 -20

-27 -26

-28

-29

-30

-31

-15

LOT 107

MEADOW
POND

WOODS

NOT SURVEYED

LOT 107

N2W3

LOCATION

MAGNETIC NORTH 15½° TRUE NORTH

CANTERBURY SHAKER VILLAGE

0 5 10 15 20 25 50 METERS

CONTOUR INTERVAL 1 METER

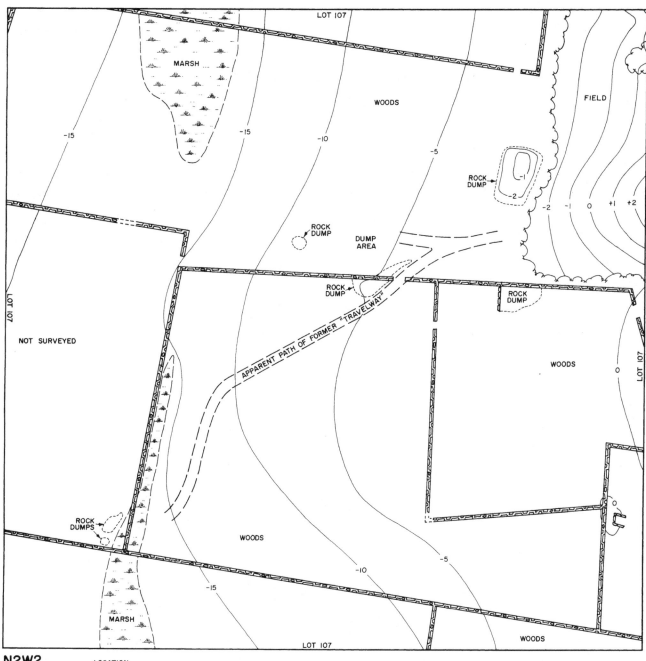

LOT 107

MARSH

WOODS

FIELD

-15

-15

-10

-5

ROCK
DUMP

-1

-2

-2

-1

0

+1

+2

ROCK
DUMP

DUMP
AREA

LOT 107

ROCK
DUMP

NOT SURVEYED

ROCK
DUMP

APPARENT PATH OF FORMER "TRAVELWAY"

WOODS

LOT 107

0

ROCK
DUMPS

WOODS

WOODS

-5

-10

-15

MARSH

LOT 107

WOODS

N2W2

LOCATION

MAGNETIC NORTH

TRUE NORTH

15½°

CANTERBURY SHAKER VILLAGE

0 5 10 15 20 25   50 METERS

CONTOUR INTERVAL 1 METER

LOT 107

LAUFMAN
HOUSE

①

②
+11

FLAT
PLATFORM

+12

③

LAUNDRY
FOUNDATION

LOT 107

FIELD

+1 +2 +3 +4 +5 +6 +7 +8 +9 +10

+4

+1 +2 +3

LOT 107

WOODS

ROCK
DUMP

+3

ROCK DUMPS

+5

④

+12

WELL

WOODS

+11

OLD TRUCK
BODY

0

ROCK
DUMPS

+4

+6 +5

+6 +7 +8 +9 +10

POND
(WATER
ELEVATION
+4.3, OCTOBER
1980)

WOODS

+1 +2 +3

LOT
107

N2W1

LOCATION

15½°

MAGNETIC NORTH

TRUE NORTH

CANTERBURY SHAKER VILLAGE

0 5 10 15 20 25   50 METERS

CONTOUR INTERVAL 1 METER

N2E0

LOCATION

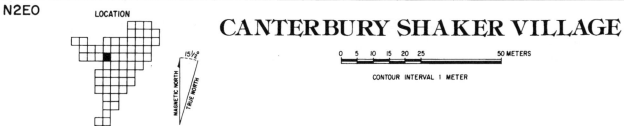

CANTERBURY SHAKER VILLAGE

0 5 10 15 20 25   50 METERS

CONTOUR INTERVAL 1 METER

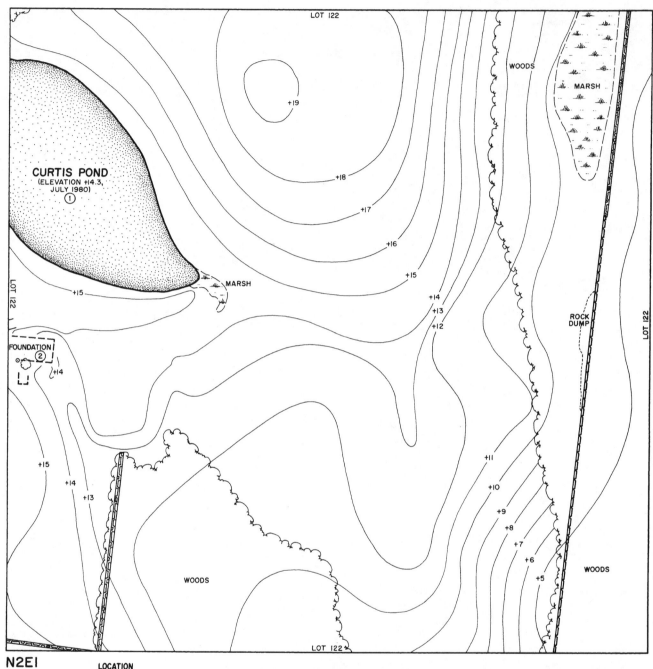

LOT 122

CURTIS POND
(ELEVATION +14.3,
JULY 1980)
①

+19

+18

+17

+16

+15

+14
+13
+12

MARSH

WOODS

MARSH

ROCK
DUMP

LOT 122

LOT 122

+15

FOUNDATION
②

+14

+15

+14

+13

+11

+10

+9

+8

+7

+6

+5

WOODS

WOODS

LOT 122

N2E1

LOCATION

MAGNETIC NORTH

TRUE NORTH

15½°

CANTERBURY SHAKER VILLAGE

0 5 10 15 20 25   50 METERS

CONTOUR INTERVAL 1 METER

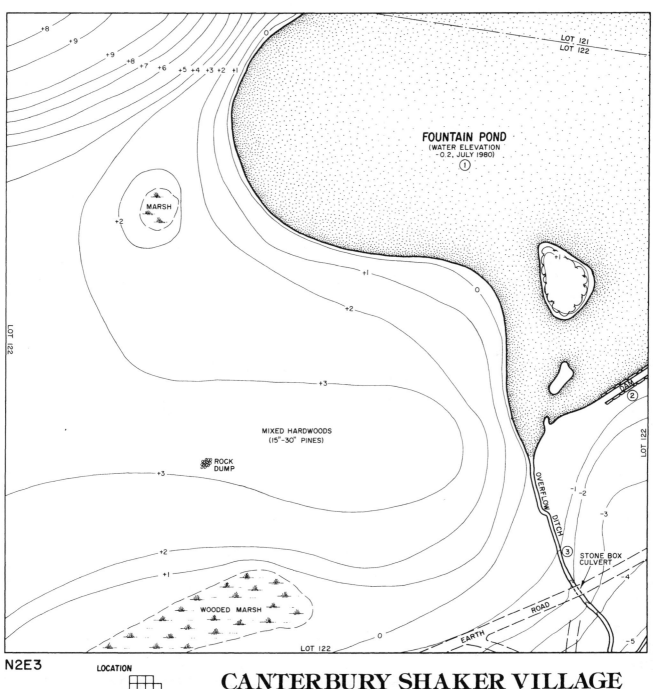

FOUNTAIN POND
(WATER ELEVATION
-0.2, JULY 1980)

MARSH

MIXED HARDWOODS
(15"-30" PINES)

ROCK
DUMP

WOODED MARSH

STONE BOX
CULVERT

N2E3

LOCATION

CANTERBURY SHAKER VILLAGE

0 5 10 15 20 25   50 METERS

CONTOUR INTERVAL 1 METER

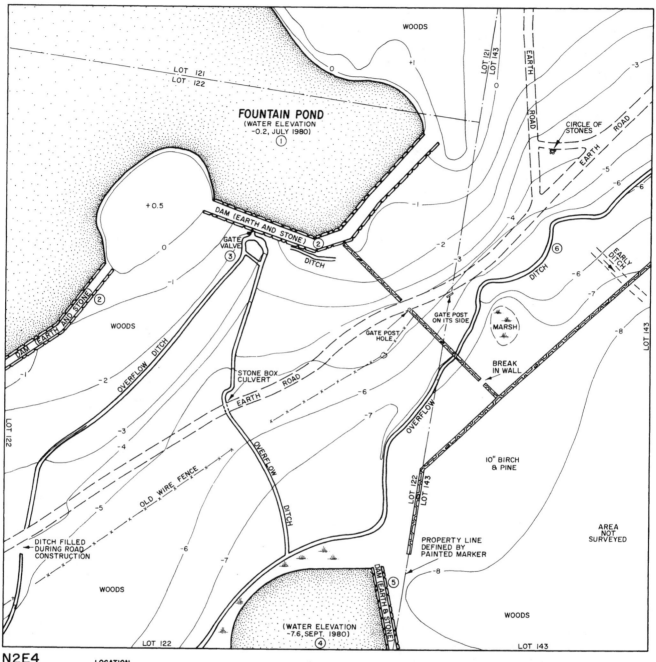

FOUNTAIN POND
(WATER ELEVATION
-0.2, JULY 1980)
①

LOT 121
LOT 122

WOODS

CIRCLE OF
STONES

LOT 121
LOT 143

EARTH ROAD

EARTH ROAD

+0.5

DAM (EARTH AND STONE)
②

GATE
VALVE
③

DITCH

⑥

DITCH

EARLY
DITCH

DAM (EARTH AND STONE)
②

WOODS

GATE POST
ON ITS SIDE

MARSH

LOT 143

OVERFLOW DITCH

GATE POST
HOLE

BREAK
IN WALL

LOT 122

STONE BOX
CULVERT

EARTH ROAD

OVERFLOW DITCH

OVERFLOW

10" BIRCH
& PINE

LOT 122
LOT 143

OLD WIRE FENCE

AREA
NOT
SURVEYED

DITCH FILLED
DURING ROAD
CONSTRUCTION

PROPERTY LINE
DEFINED BY
PAINTED MARKER

WOODS

WOODS

DAM (EARTH & STONE)

⑤

(WATER ELEVATION
-7.6, SEPT. 1980)
④

LOT 122

LOT 143

N2E4

LOCATION

MAGNETIC NORTH
TRUE NORTH
15½°

CANTERBURY SHAKER VILLAGE

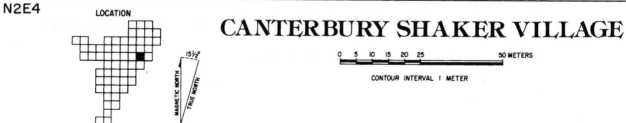

0 5 10 15 20 25   50 METERS

CONTOUR INTERVAL 1 METER

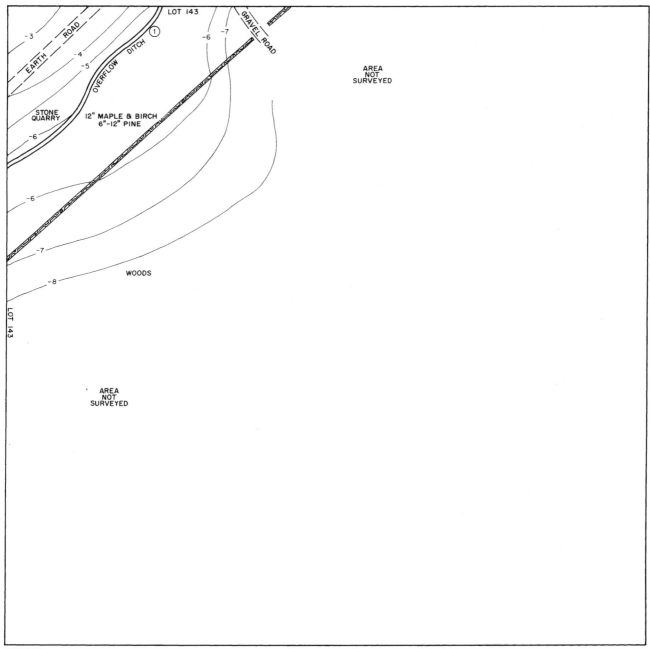

LOT 143

EARTH ROAD

-3
-4
-5

OVERFLOW DITCH (1)

-6
-7

GRAVEL ROAD

AREA
NOT
SURVEYED

STONE
QUARRY

12" MAPLE & BIRCH
6"-12" PINE

-6

-6

-7

WOODS

-8

LOT 143

AREA
NOT
SURVEYED

N2E5

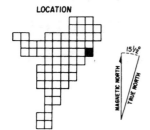

LOCATION

15½°

MAGNETIC NORTH

TRUE NORTH

CANTERBURY SHAKER VILLAGE

0 5 10 15 20 25   50 METERS

CONTOUR INTERVAL 1 METER

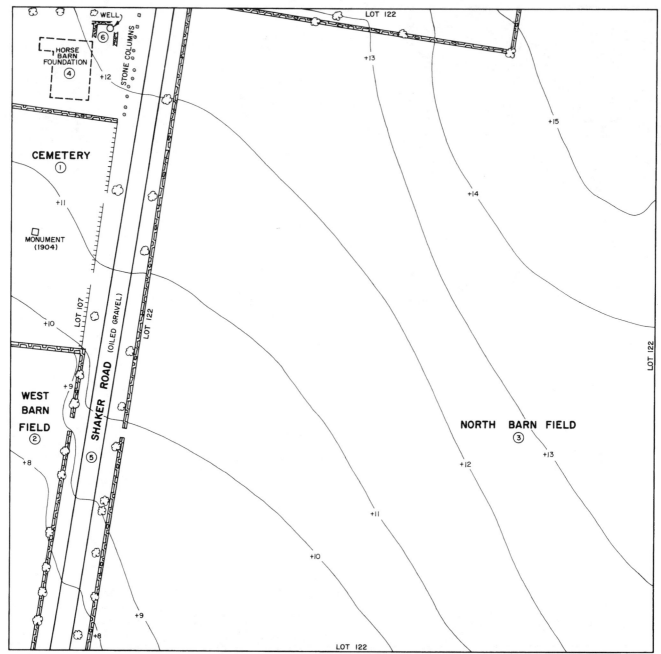

LOT 122

+13

+15

+14

WELL
⑥

STONE COLUMNS

HORSE
BARN
FOUNDATION
④

+12

LOT 122

CEMETERY
①

+11

MONUMENT
(1904)

LOT 107

+10

LOT 122

SHAKER ROAD (OILED GRAVEL)

WEST
BARN
FIELD
②

+9

⑤

+8

NORTH BARN FIELD
③

+12   +13

+11

+10

LOT 122

+9

+8

LOT 122

NIEO

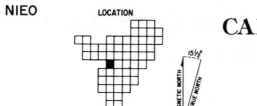

LOCATION

15½°

MAGNETIC NORTH

TRUE NORTH

CANTERBURY SHAKER VILLAGE

0   5   10   15   20   25   50 METERS

CONTOUR INTERVAL 1 METER

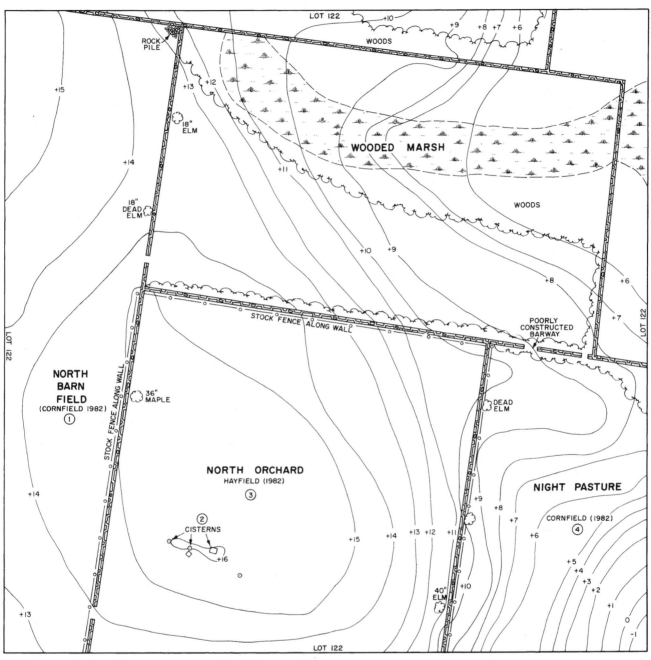

LOT 122

WOODS

WOODED MARSH

WOODS

+15

+13 +12

18" ELM

+14

18" DEAD ELM

+11

+10 +9

+8

+6

+7

POORLY CONSTRUCTED BARWAY

STOCK FENCE ALONG WALL

NORTH BARN FIELD
(CORNFIELD 1982)
①

36" MAPLE

DEAD ELM

NORTH ORCHARD
HAYFIELD (1982)
③

NIGHT PASTURE
CORNFIELD (1982)
④

+14

②
CISTERNS

+16

+15 +14 +13 +12 +11

+9 +8

+7

+6

+5
+4
+3
+2
+1

+13

40" ELM

+10

+9

0

-1

LOT 122

NIEI

LOCATION

MAGNETIC NORTH TRUE NORTH 15½°

CANTERBURY SHAKER VILLAGE

0 5 10 15 20 25   50 METERS

CONTOUR INTERVAL 1 METER

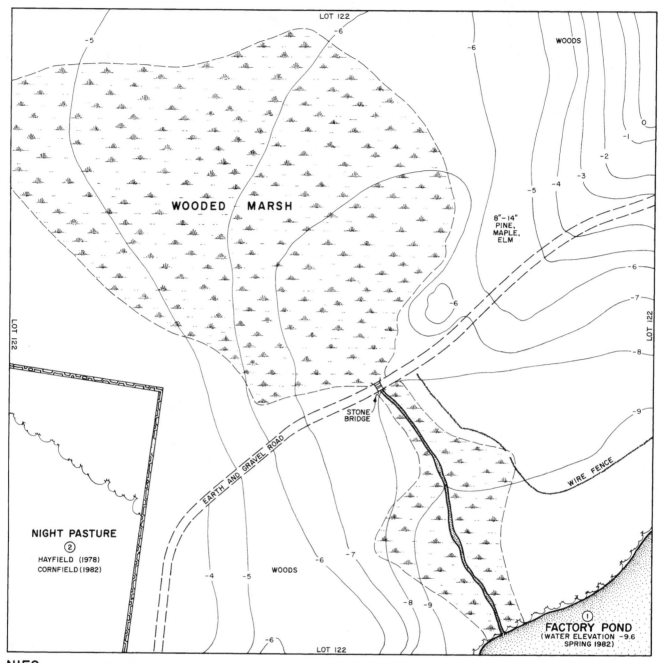

LOT 122

WOODS

WOODED MARSH

8"–14"
PINE,
MAPLE,
ELM

LOT 122

LOT 122

STONE
BRIDGE

WIRE FENCE

NIGHT PASTURE
②
HAYFIELD (1978)
CORNFIELD (1982)

EARTH AND GRAVEL ROAD

WOODS

FACTORY POND
①
(WATER ELEVATION -9.6
SPRING 1982)

LOT 122

NIE2

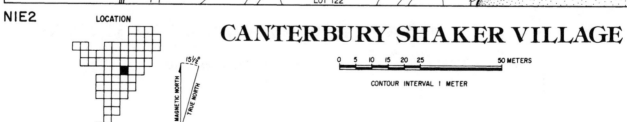

LOCATION

MAGNETIC NORTH
TRUE NORTH
15½°

CANTERBURY SHAKER VILLAGE

0 5 10 15 20 25   50 METERS

CONTOUR INTERVAL 1 METER

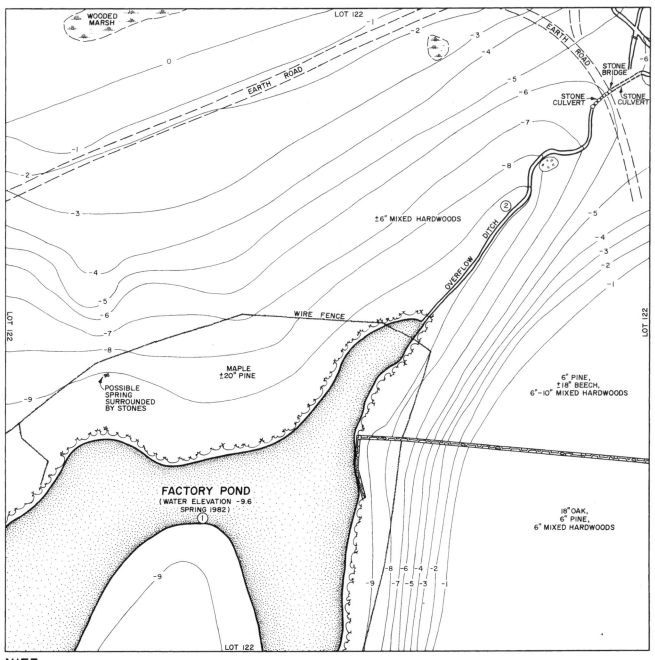

WOODED
MARSH

LOT 122

EARTH ROAD

EARTH ROAD

STONE
BRIDGE

STONE
CULVERT

STONE
CULVERT

±6" MIXED HARDWOODS

OVERFLOW DITCH

WIRE FENCE

MAPLE
±20" PINE

6" PINE,
±18" BEECH,
6"-10" MIXED HARDWOODS

POSSIBLE
SPRING
SURROUNDED
BY STONES

FACTORY POND
(WATER ELEVATION -9.6
SPRING 1982)

18" OAK,
6" PINE,
6" MIXED HARDWOODS

LOT 122

LOT 122

NIE3

LOCATION

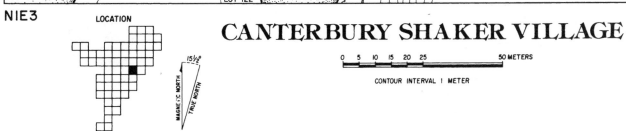

MAGNETIC NORTH

TRUE NORTH

15½°

CANTERBURY SHAKER VILLAGE

0 5 10 15 20 25   50 METERS

CONTOUR INTERVAL 1 METER

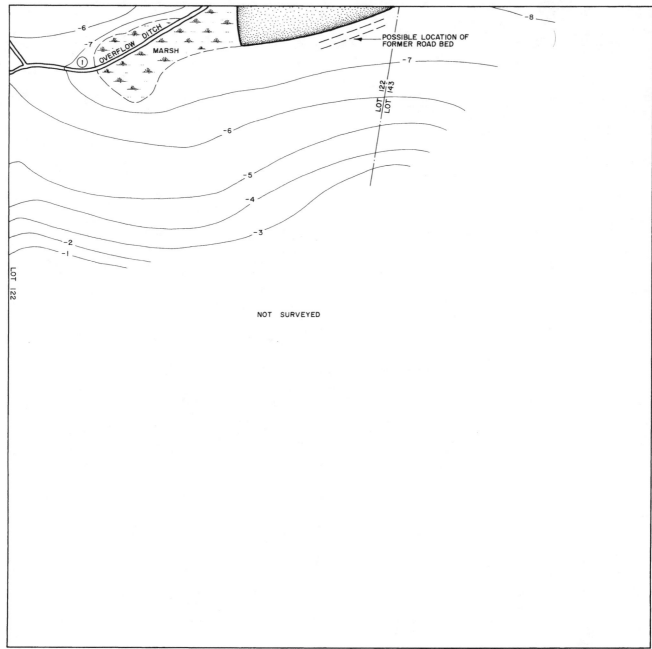

NIE4

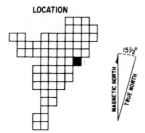

CANTERBURY SHAKER VILLAGE

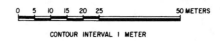

CONTOUR INTERVAL 1 METER

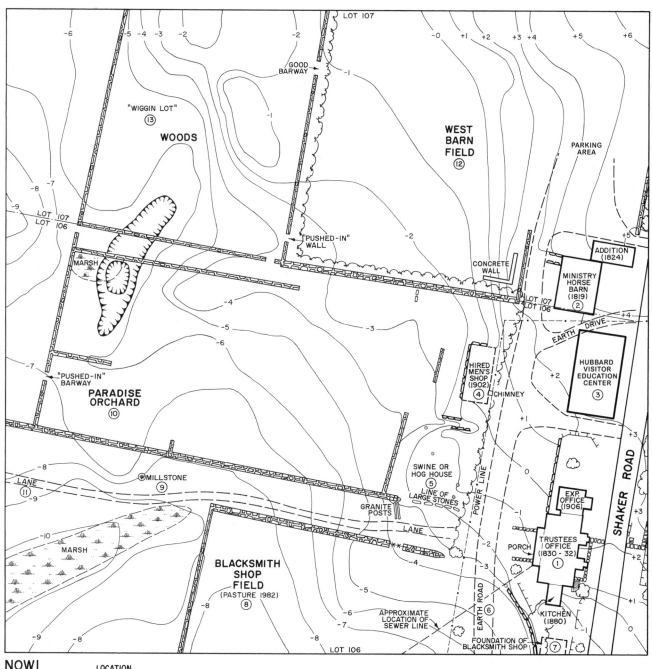

LOT 107

GOOD
BARWAY

"WIGGIN LOT"
⑬

WOODS

WEST
BARN
FIELD
⑫

PARKING
AREA

LOT 107
LOT 106

MARSH

"PUSHED-IN"
WALL

ADDITION
(1824)

CONCRETE
WALL

MINISTRY
HORSE
BARN
(1819)
②

LOT 107
LOT 106

EARTH DRIVE

HUBBARD
VISITOR
EDUCATION
CENTER
③

"PUSHED-IN"
BARWAY

HIRED
MEN'S
SHOP
(1902)
④

CHIMNEY

PARADISE
ORCHARD
⑩

SWINE OR
HOG HOUSE
⑤

POWER LINE

SHAKER ROAD

MILLSTONE
⑨

LANE
⑪

LINE OF
LARGE STONES

EXP.
OFFICE
(1906)

GRANITE
POSTS

LANE

PORCH

TRUSTEES
OFFICE
(1830-32)
①

MARSH

BLACKSMITH
SHOP
FIELD
(PASTURE 1982)
⑧

EARTH ROAD
⑥

APPROXIMATE
LOCATION OF
SEWER LINE

KITCHEN
(1880)

FOUNDATION OF
BLACKSMITH SHOP
⑦

LOT 106

NOWI

LOCATION

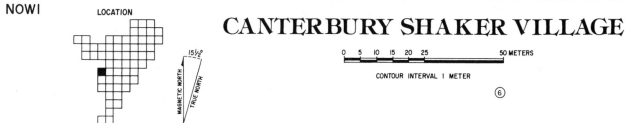

CANTERBURY SHAKER VILLAGE

MAGNETIC NORTH
TRUE NORTH
15½°

0 5 10 15 20 25   50 METERS

CONTOUR INTERVAL 1 METER

⑥

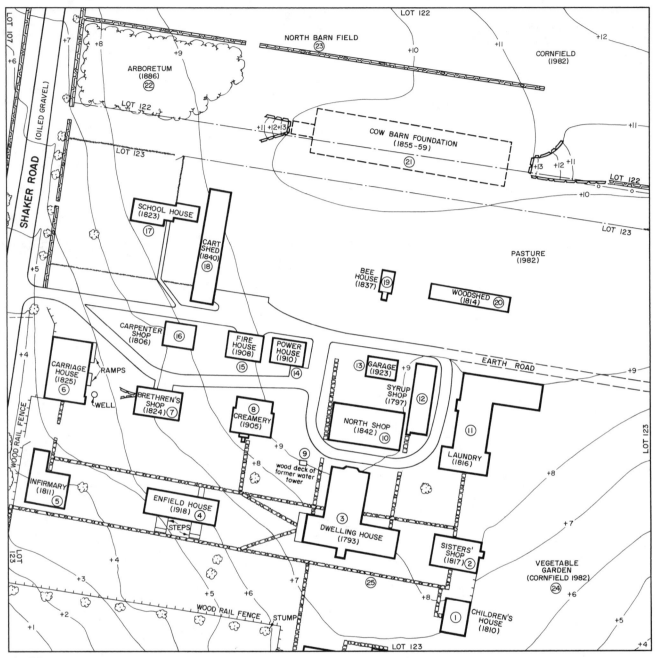

LOT 122

NORTH BARN FIELD (23)

CORNFIELD (1982)

ARBORETUM (1886) (22)

LOT 122

LOT 123

COW BARN FOUNDATION (1855-59) (21)

LOT 122

LOT 123

SHAKER ROAD (OILED GRAVEL)

LOT 107

SCHOOL HOUSE (1823) (17)

CART SHED (1840) (18)

PASTURE (1982)

BEE HOUSE (1837) (19)

WOODSHED (1814) (20)

CARPENTER SHOP (1806) (16)

FIRE HOUSE (1908) (15)

POWER HOUSE (1910) (14)

GARAGE (1923) (13)

EARTH ROAD

CARRIAGE HOUSE (1825) (6)

RAMPS

WELL

BRETHREN'S SHOP (1824) (7)

CREAMERY (1905) (8)

SYRUP SHOP (1797) (12)

NORTH SHOP (1842) (10)

(11)

LAUNDRY (1816)

WOOD RAIL FENCE

wood deck of former water tower (9)

INFIRMARY (1811) (5)

ENFIELD HOUSE (1918) (4)

STEPS

DWELLING HOUSE (1793) (3)

SISTERS' SHOP (1817) (2)

VEGETABLE GARDEN (CORNFIELD 1982) (24)

LOT 123

(25)

WOOD RAIL FENCE

STUMP

CHILDREN'S HOUSE (1810) (1)

LOT 123

NOEO

LOCATION

MAGNETIC NORTH TRUE NORTH 15½°

CANTERBURY SHAKER VILLAGE

0 5 10 15 20 25   50 METERS

CONTOUR INTERVAL 1 METER

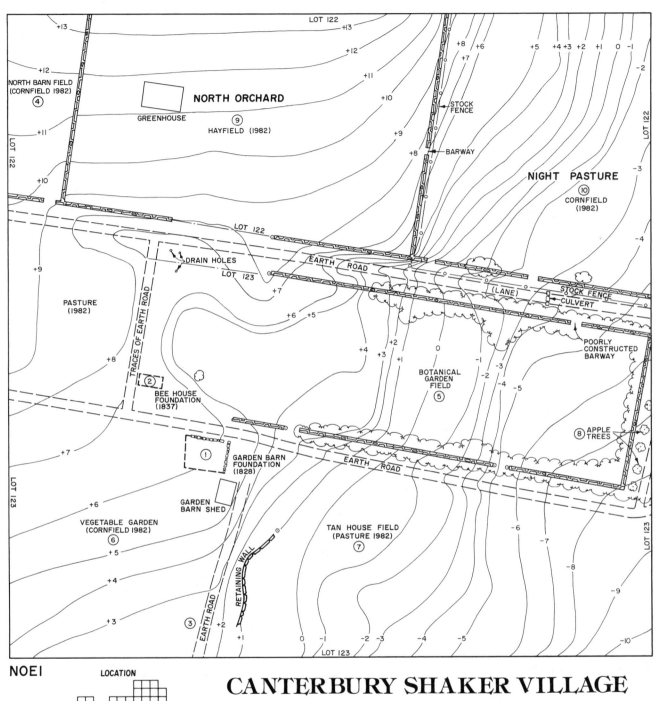

NOEI

LOCATION

CANTERBURY SHAKER VILLAGE

0 5 10 15 20 25   50 METERS

CONTOUR INTERVAL 1 METER

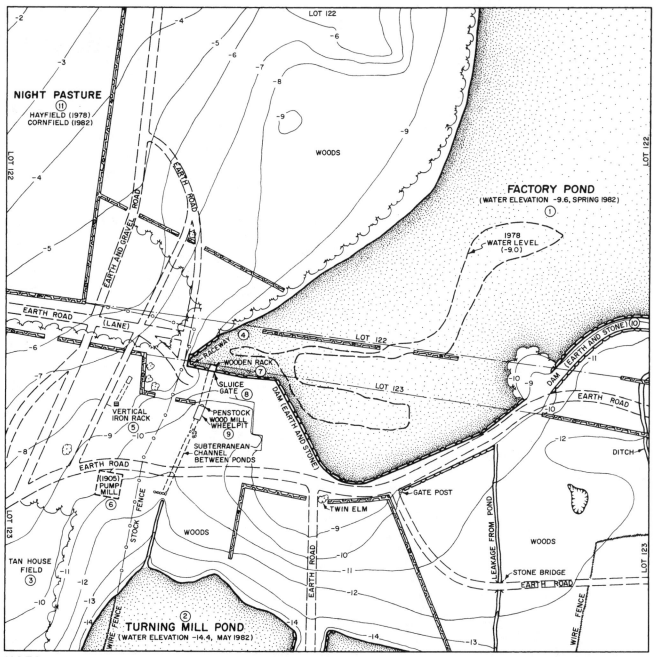

NIGHT PASTURE
⑪
HAYFIELD (1978)
CORNFIELD (1982)

LOT 122

WOODS

FACTORY POND
(WATER ELEVATION -9.6, SPRING 1982)
①

1978
WATER LEVEL
(-9.0)

LOT 122

EARTH ROAD

(LANE)

RACEWAY
④

WOODEN RACK
⑦

SLUICE
GATE
⑧

VERTICAL
IRON RACK
⑤

PENSTOCK
WOOD MILL
WHEELPIT
⑨

LOT 122

LOT 123

DAM (EARTH AND STONE) ⑩

EARTH ROAD

DITCH

SUBTERRANEAN
CHANNEL
BETWEEN PONDS

EARTH ROAD

(1905)
PUMP
MILL
⑥

GATE POST

TWIN ELM

LEAKAGE FROM POND

WOODS

WOODS

TAN HOUSE
FIELD
③

STONE BRIDGE
EARTH ROAD

LOT 123

TURNING MILL POND
②
(WATER ELEVATION -14.4, MAY 1982)

WIRE FENCE

LOT 123

STOCK FENCE

WIRE FENCE

NOE2

CANTERBURY SHAKER VILLAGE

0 5 10 15 20 25   50 METERS

CONTOUR INTERVAL 1 METER

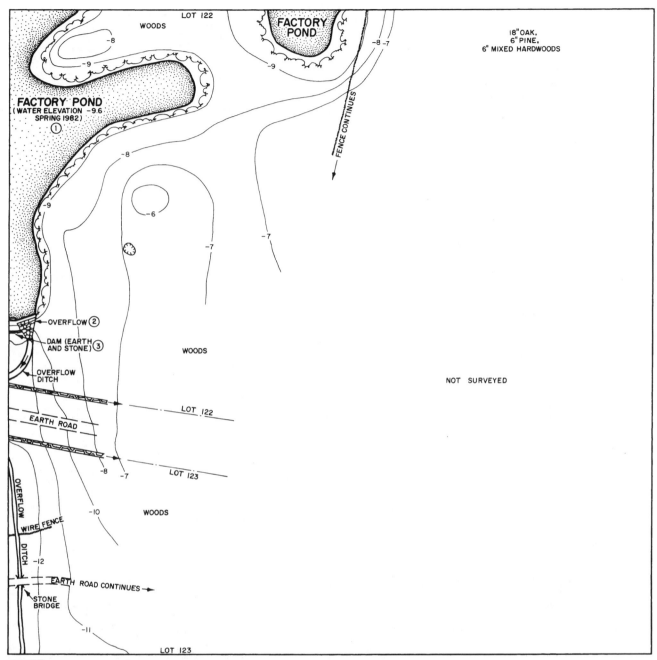

Factory Pond
(Water Elevation -9.6
Spring 1982)
①

WOODS

LOT 122

FACTORY
POND

18" OAK,
6" PINE,
6" MIXED HARDWOODS

FENCE CONTINUES

← OVERFLOW ②

DAM (EARTH
AND STONE) ③

OVERFLOW
DITCH

WOODS

NOT SURVEYED

LOT 122

EARTH ROAD

LOT 123

OVERFLOW

WIRE FENCE

DITCH

WOODS

EARTH ROAD CONTINUES →

STONE
BRIDGE

LOT 123

NOE3

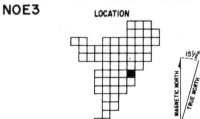

LOCATION

MAGNETIC NORTH
TRUE NORTH
15½°

CANTERBURY SHAKER VILLAGE

0 5 10 15 20 25   50 METERS

CONTOUR INTERVAL 1 METER

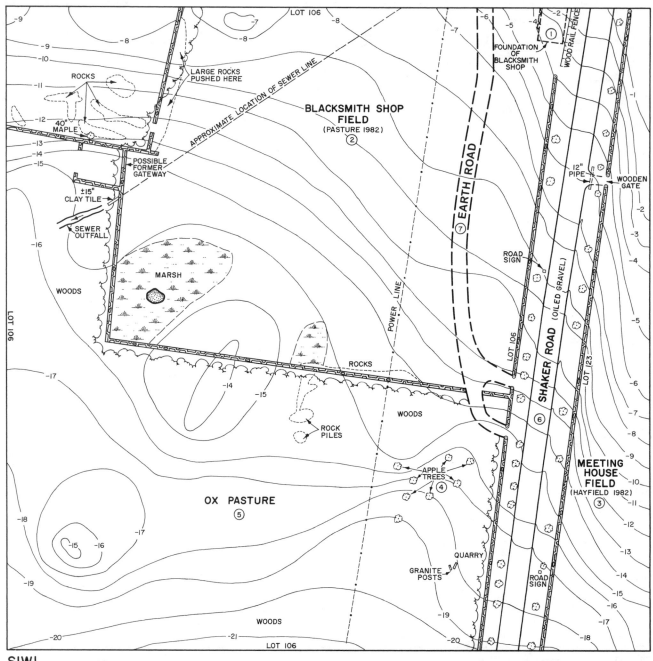

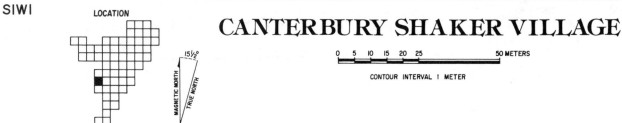

SIWI

CANTERBURY SHAKER VILLAGE

LOCATION

15½°

MAGNETIC NORTH

TRUE NORTH

0 5 10 15 20 25   50 METERS

CONTOUR INTERVAL 1 METER

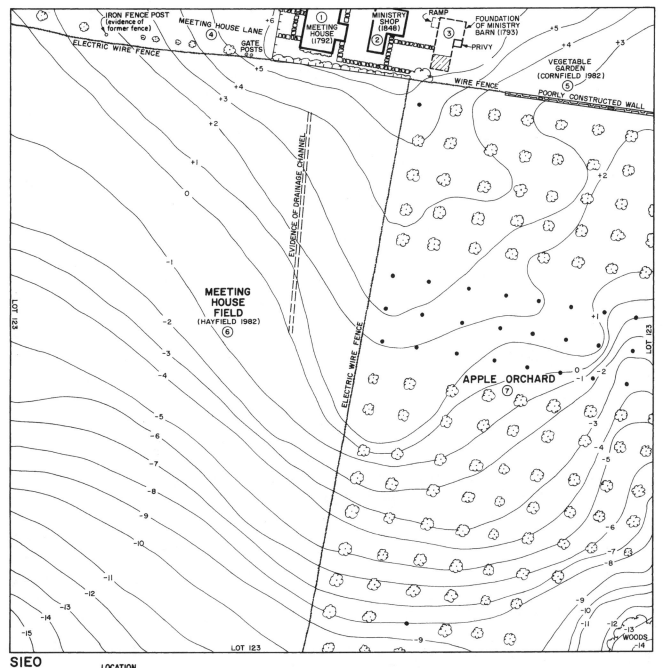

SIEO

LOCATION

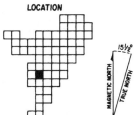

MAGNETIC NORTH
TRUE NORTH
15½°

CANTERBURY SHAKER VILLAGE

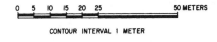

0 5 10 15 20 25   50 METERS

CONTOUR INTERVAL 1 METER

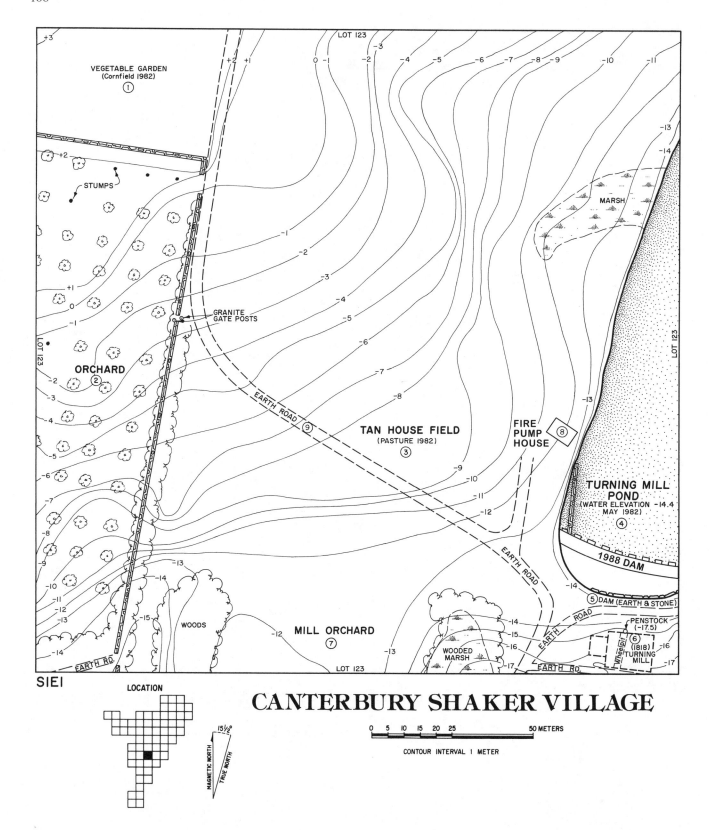

SIEI

LOCATION

MAGNETIC NORTH
TRUE NORTH
15½°

CANTERBURY SHAKER VILLAGE

0 5 10 15 20 25   50 METERS

CONTOUR INTERVAL 1 METER

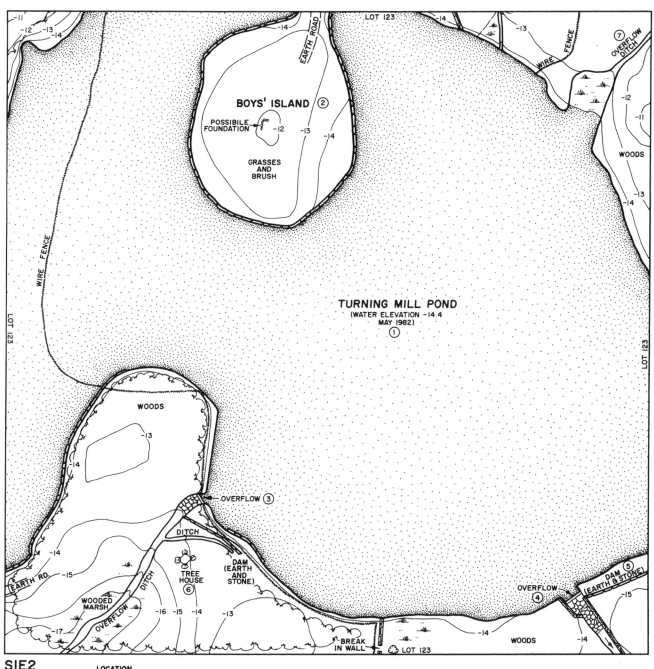

SIE2

LOCATION

CANTERBURY SHAKER VILLAGE

0 5 10 15 20 25   50 METERS

CONTOUR INTERVAL 1 METER

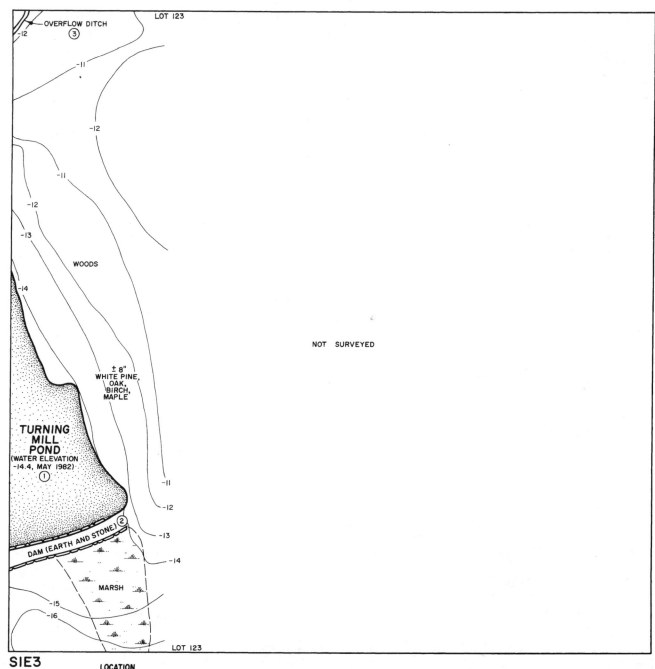

LOT 123

OVERFLOW DITCH ③

-12

-11

-12

-11

-12

-13

WOODS

-14

± 8"
WHITE PINE,
OAK,
BIRCH,
MAPLE

NOT SURVEYED

TURNING
MILL
POND
(WATER ELEVATION
-14.4, MAY 1982)
①

-11

-12

② -13

DAM (EARTH AND STONE)

-14

MARSH

-15

-16

LOT 123

SIE3

LOCATION

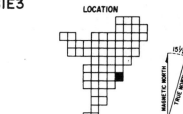

MAGNETIC NORTH   15½°   TRUE NORTH

CANTERBURY SHAKER VILLAGE

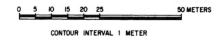

0 5 10 15 20 25   50 METERS

CONTOUR INTERVAL 1 METER

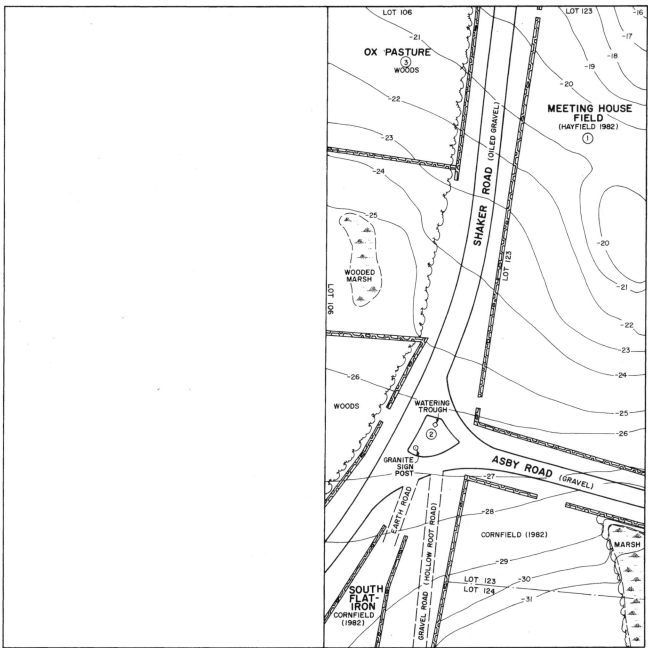

LOT 106

OX PASTURE
③
WOODS

—21

—22

—23

—24

—25

WOODED
MARSH

LOT 106

—26

WOODS

WATERING
TROUGH

②

GRANITE
SIGN
POST

LOT 123

—16

—17

—18

—19

—20

SHAKER ROAD (OILED GRAVEL)

MEETING HOUSE
FIELD
(HAYFIELD 1982)
①

—20

—21

—22

—23

—24

—25

—26

LOT 123

ASBY ROAD (GRAVEL)

—27

EARTH ROAD

GRAVEL ROAD (HOLLOW ROOT ROAD)

—28

CORNFIELD (1982)

MARSH

—29

SOUTH
FLAT-
IRON
CORNFIELD
(1982)

LOT 123
LOT 124

—30

—31

S2WI

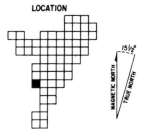

LOCATION

15½°

MAGNETIC NORTH

TRUE NORTH

CANTERBURY SHAKER VILLAGE

0   5   10   15   20   25   50 METERS

CONTOUR INTERVAL 1 METER

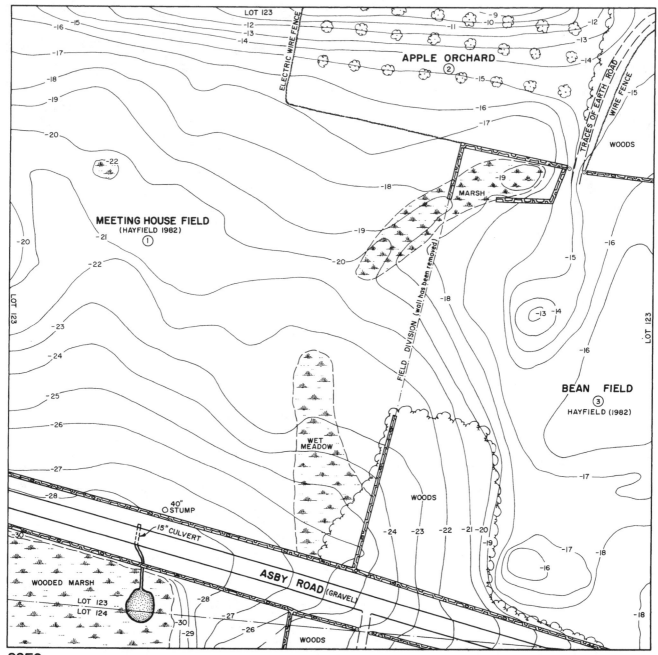

LOT 123

APPLE ORCHARD ②

ELECTRIC WIRE FENCE

TRACES OF EARTH ROAD

WIRE FENCE

WOODS

MARSH

MEETING HOUSE FIELD
(HAYFIELD 1982) ①

FIELD DIVISION (wall has been removed)

LOT 123

LOT 123

BEAN FIELD ③
HAYFIELD (1982)

WET MEADOW

WOODS

40" STUMP

15" CULVERT

WOODED MARSH
LOT 123
LOT 124

ASBY ROAD (GRAVEL)

WOODS

S2E0

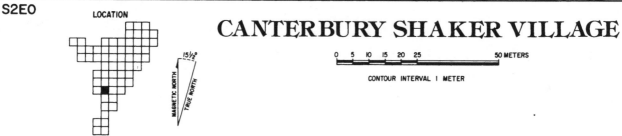

LOCATION

MAGNETIC NORTH
TRUE NORTH
15½°

CANTERBURY SHAKER VILLAGE

0 5 10 15 20 25   50 METERS

CONTOUR INTERVAL 1 METER

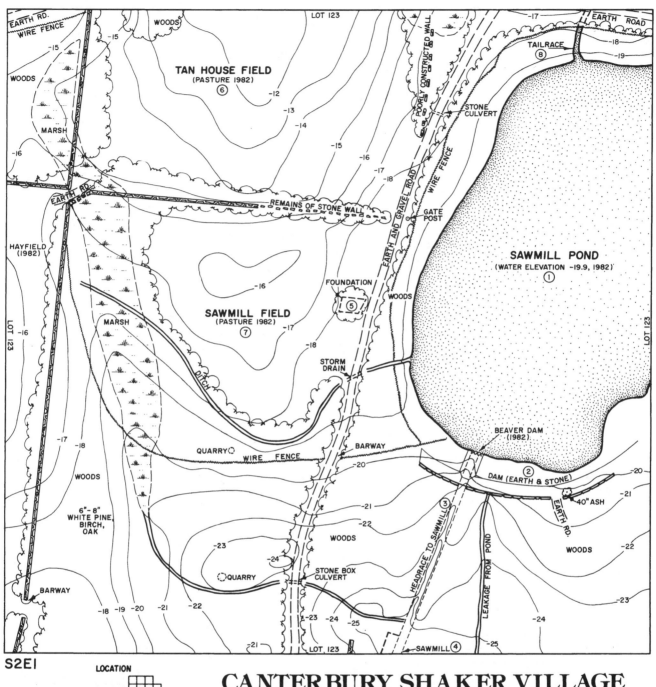

S2EI

LOCATION

MAGNETIC NORTH 15½° TRUE NORTH

CANTERBURY SHAKER VILLAGE

0 5 10 15 20 25   50 METERS

CONTOUR INTERVAL 1 METER

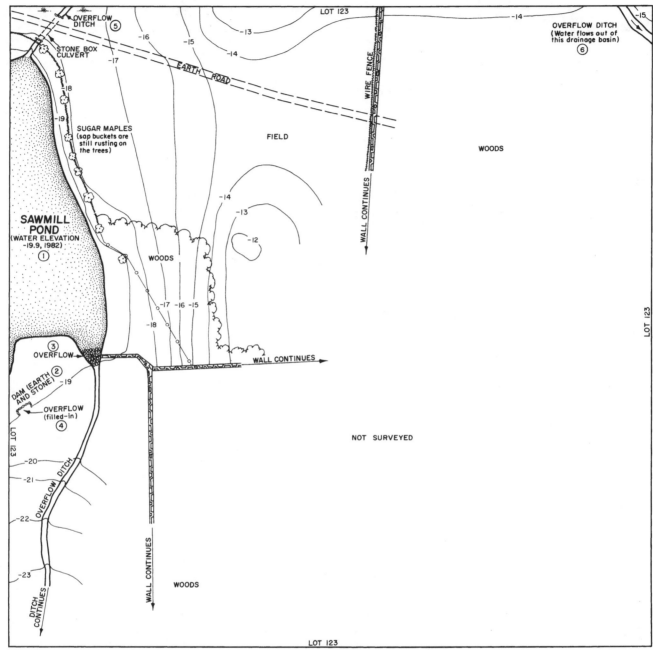

OVERFLOW
DITCH ⑤

STONE BOX
CULVERT

LOT 123

-14

OVERFLOW DITCH
(Water flows out of
this drainage basin)
⑥

-16

-15

-13

-14

EARTH ROAD

-17

WIRE FENCE

-18

FIELD

WOODS

-19

SUGAR MAPLES
(sap buckets are
still rusting on
the trees)

WALL CONTINUES

SAWMILL
POND
(WATER ELEVATION
-19.9, 1982)
①

-14

-13

-12

WOODS

WOODS

-17 -16 -15

-18

③
OVERFLOW

WALL CONTINUES

LOT 123

DAM (EARTH
AND STONE) ②

-19

OVERFLOW
(filled-in)
④

NOT SURVEYED

LOT 123

-20

OVERFLOW DITCH

-21

-22

WALL CONTINUES

-23

WOODS

DITCH
CONTINUES

LOT 123

S2E2

LOCATION

15½°

MAGNETIC NORTH

TRUE NORTH

CANTERBURY SHAKER VILLAGE

0 5 10 15 20 25   50 METERS

CONTOUR INTERVAL 1 METER

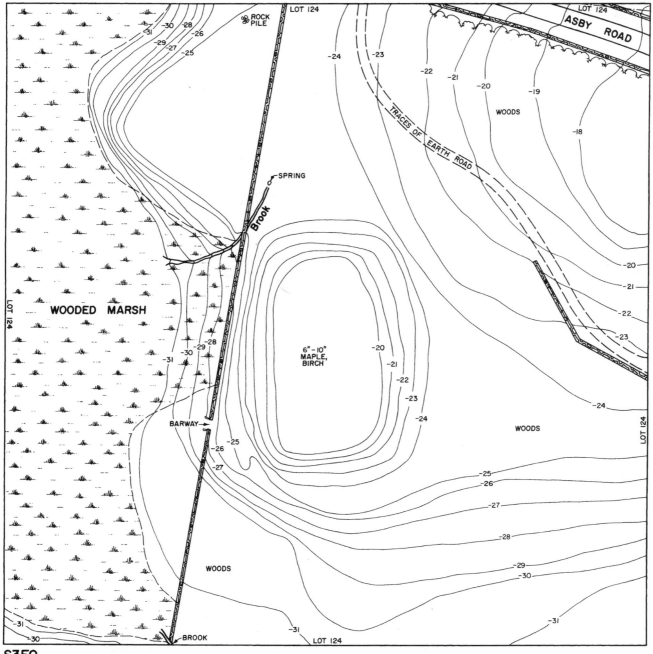

LOT 124

ASBY ROAD

ROCK PILE

-30 -28
-31 -26
-29 -27
-25

SPRING

-24 -23

-22
-21
-20
-19
-18

WOODS

TRACES OF EARTH ROAD

Brook

WOODED MARSH

LOT 124

-28
-30 -29
-31

6"-10"
MAPLE,
BIRCH

-20
-21
-22
-23
-24

-20

-21

-22

-23

-24

WOODS

LOT 124

BARWAY

-25
-26
-27

-25
-26
-27

-28

-29
-30

WOODS

-31

-31

BROOK

LOT 124

S3EO

LOCATION

MAGNETIC NORTH
TRUE NORTH
15½°

CANTERBURY SHAKER VILLAGE

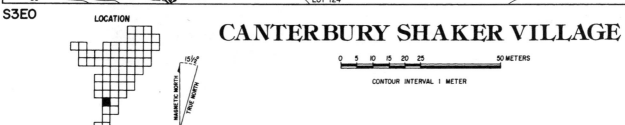

0 5 10 15 20 25   50 METERS

CONTOUR INTERVAL 1 METER

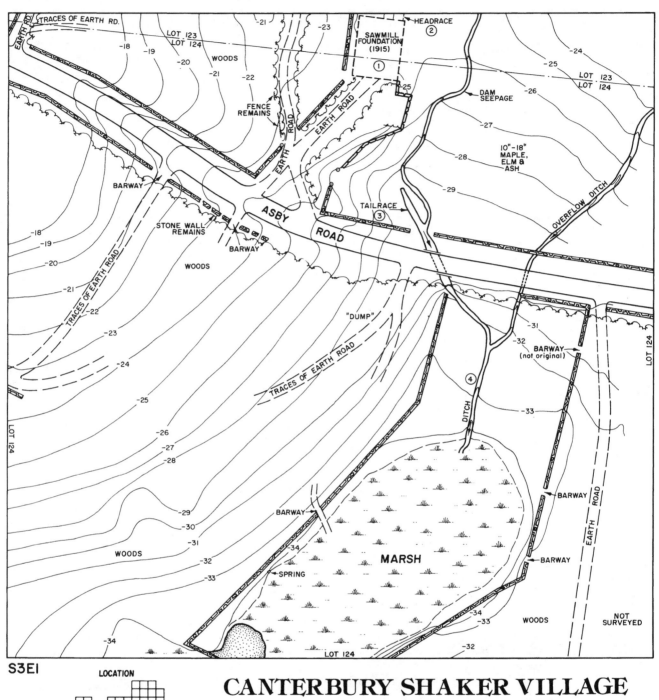

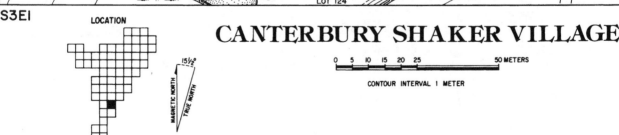

S3EI

CANTERBURY SHAKER VILLAGE

LOCATION

0 5 10 15 20 25   50 METERS

CONTOUR INTERVAL 1 METER

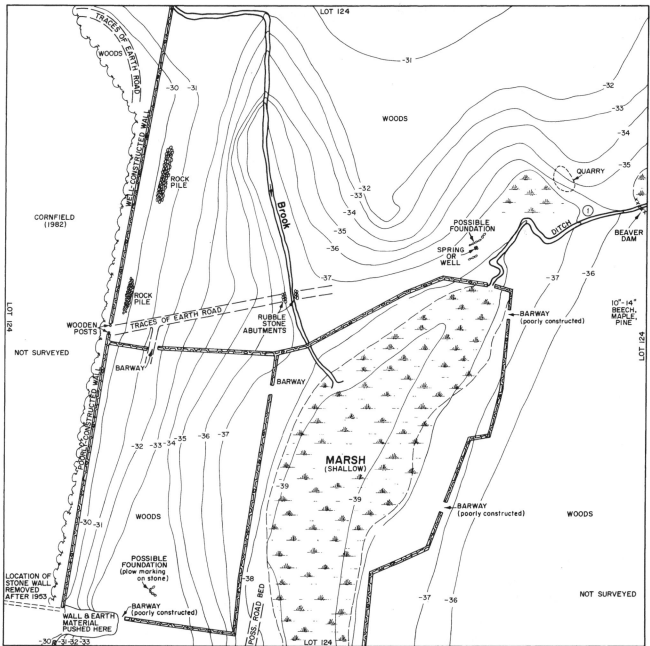

LOT 124

TRACES OF EARTH ROAD

WOODS

WELL-CONSTRUCTED WALL

-30 -31

ROCK PILE

CORNFIELD (1982)

LOT 124

ROCK PILE

WOODEN POSTS

TRACES OF EARTH ROAD

NOT SURVEYED

POORLY CONSTRUCTED WALL

BARWAY

LOCATION OF STONE WALL REMOVED AFTER 1953

WALL & EARTH MATERIAL PUSHED HERE

-30 -31 -32 -33

Brook

-32
-33

-34

-35

-36

-37

RUBBLE STONE ABUTMENTS

BARWAY

-32 -33 -34 -35 -36 -37

WOODS

POSSIBLE FOUNDATION (plow marking on stone)

BARWAY (poorly constructed)

-30 -31

POSS. ROAD BED

-38

LOT 124

WOODS

-31

-32

-33

-34

-35

QUARRY

POSSIBLE FOUNDATION

SPRING OR WELL

DITCH

BEAVER DAM

-37 -36

BARWAY (poorly constructed)

10"-14" BEECH, MAPLE, PINE

LOT 124

MARSH (SHALLOW)

-39

-39

BARWAY (poorly constructed)

WOODS

NOT SURVEYED

-37 -36

S4E0

LOCATION

MAGNETIC NORTH   TRUE NORTH   15½°

CANTERBURY SHAKER VILLAGE

0 5 10 15 20 25   50 METERS

CONTOUR INTERVAL 1 METER

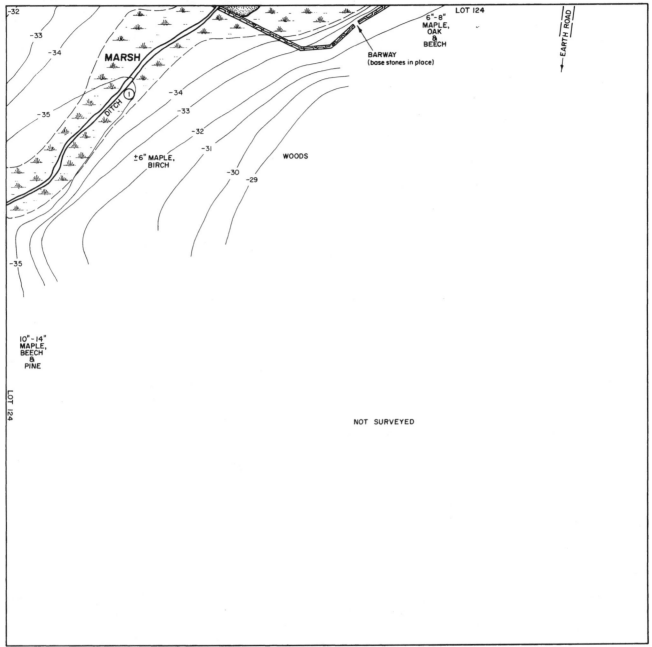

-32
-33
-34
MARSH
DITCH ①
-35

-34
-33
-32
-31
-30 -29

±6" MAPLE,
BIRCH

WOODS

LOT 124

6"-8"
MAPLE,
OAK
&
BEECH

BARWAY
(base stones in place)

EARTH ROAD

-35

10"-14"
MAPLE,
BEECH
&
PINE

LOT 124

NOT SURVEYED

S4EI

LOCATION

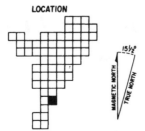

15½°

MAGNETIC NORTH
TRUE NORTH

CANTERBURY SHAKER VILLAGE

0 5 10 15 20 25 50 METERS

CONTOUR INTERVAL 1 METER

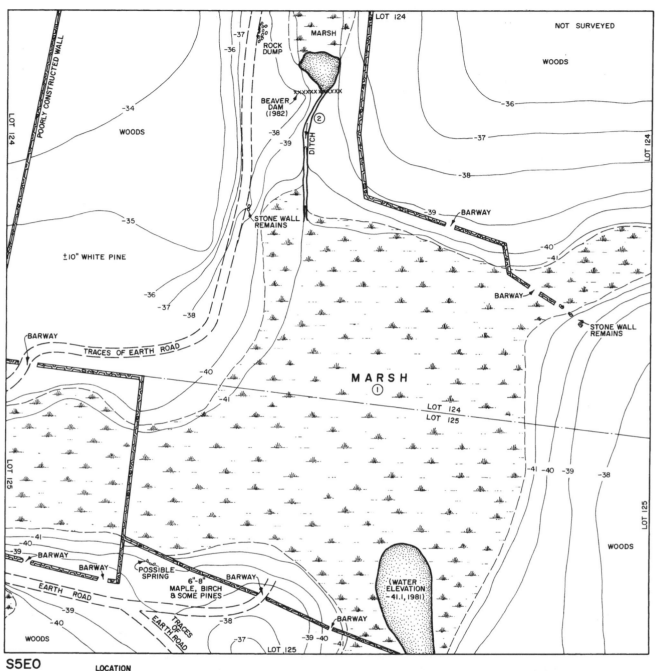

CANTERBURY SHAKER VILLAGE

S5E0

LOCATION

MAGNETIC NORTH
TRUE NORTH
15½°

0 5 10 15 20 25   50 METERS

CONTOUR INTERVAL 1 METER

180

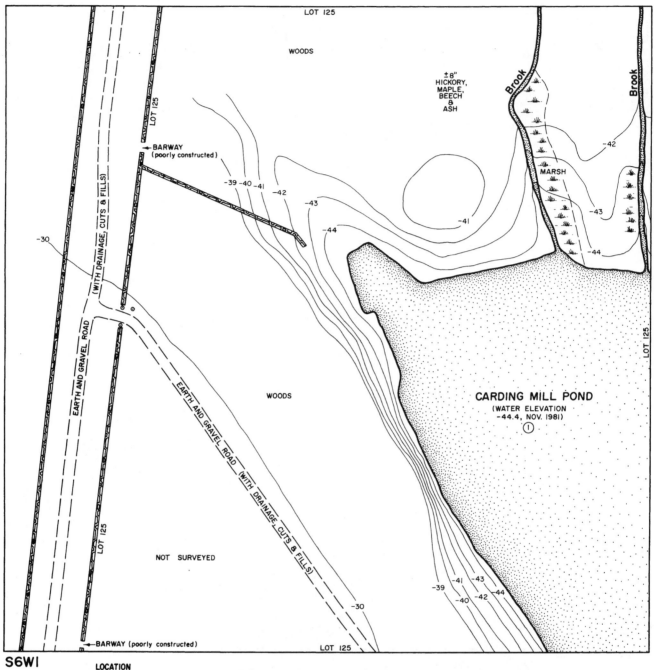

LOT 125

WOODS

±8"
HICKORY,
MAPLE,
BEECH
&
ASH

Brook

Brook

-42

BARWAY
(poorly constructed)

-39 -40 -41
-42
-43
-44

MARSH

-43

-44

-41

-30

WOODS

CARDING MILL POND
(WATER ELEVATION
-44.4, NOV. 1981)
①

NOT SURVEYED

-39 -41 -43
-40 -42 -44

-30

BARWAY (poorly constructed)

LOT 125

S6WI

LOCATION

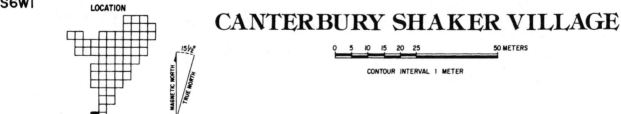

MAGNETIC NORTH
TRUE NORTH
15½°

CANTERBURY SHAKER VILLAGE

0 5 10 15 20 25   50 METERS

CONTOUR INTERVAL 1 METER

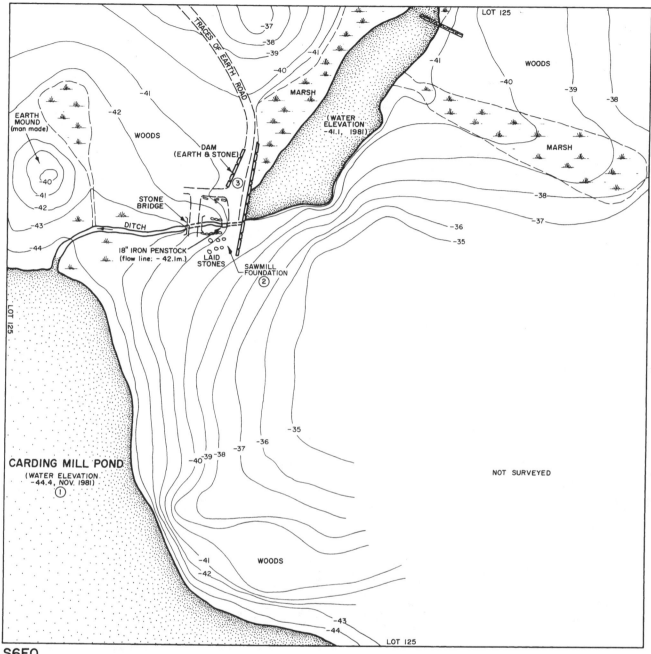

LOT 125

−37
−38
−39
−41
−40

TRACES OF EARTH ROAD

WOODS

MARSH

(WATER
ELEVATION
−41.1, 1981)

−41

−41

−40

−39

−38

WOODS

MARSH

−38

−37

−41

−42

EARTH
MOUND
(man made)

WOODS

−40

−41

−42

−43

−44

DAM
(EARTH & STONE)

③

STONE
BRIDGE

DITCH

18" IRON PENSTOCK
(flow line: −42.1m.)

LAID
STONES

SAWMILL
FOUNDATION
②

−36
−35

LOT 125

NOT SURVEYED

−35

CARDING MILL POND
(WATER ELEVATION
−44.4, NOV. 1981)
①

−37
−36

−40 −39 −38

−41
−42

WOODS

−43
−44

LOT 125

S6E0

LOCATION

MAGNETIC NORTH   TRUE NORTH   15½°

CANTERBURY SHAKER VILLAGE

0 5 10 15 20 25   50 METERS

CONTOUR INTERVAL 1 METER

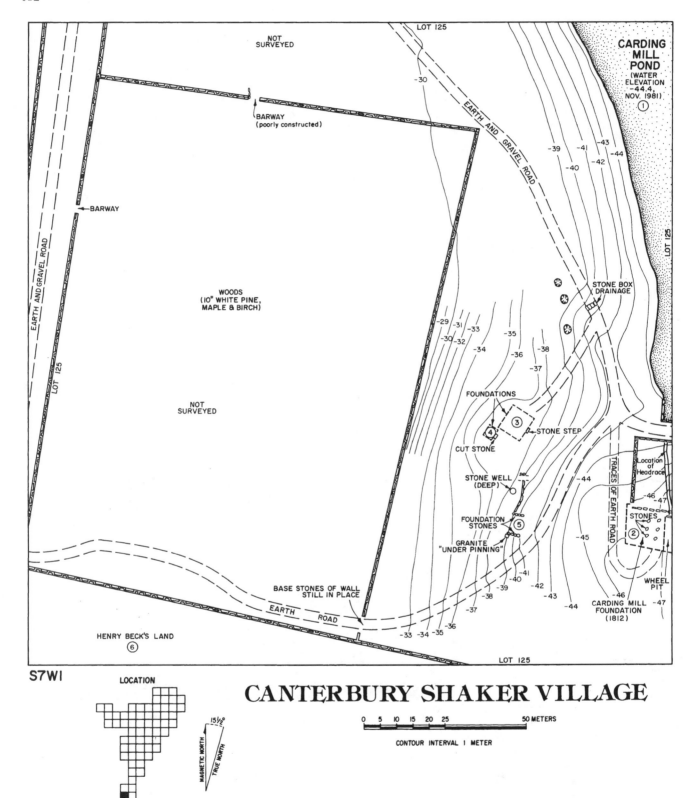

NOT
SURVEYED

LOT 125

CARDING
MILL
POND
(WATER
ELEVATION
-44.4,
NOV. 1981)
①

-30

BARWAY
(poorly constructed)

-39 -41 -43
-40 -42 -44

BARWAY

EARTH AND GRAVEL ROAD

WOODS
(10" WHITE PINE,
MAPLE & BIRCH)

STONE BOX
DRAINAGE

-29 -31 -33
-30 -32   -35
-34   -36   -38
-37

NOT
SURVEYED

LOT 125

FOUNDATIONS

③
④
CUT STONE

STONE STEP

Location
of
Headrace

STONE WELL
(DEEP)

-44

TRACES OF EARTH ROAD

STONES

②

FOUNDATION
STONES
⑤

GRANITE
"UNDER PINNING"

-45

WHEEL
PIT

-46 -47

CARDING MILL
FOUNDATION
(1812)

-41
-40   -42
-39   -43
-38   -44
-37
-36

BASE STONES OF WALL
STILL IN PLACE

EARTH   ROAD

-33 -34 -35

HENRY BECK'S LAND
⑥

LOT 125

S7WI

LOCATION

15½°

MAGNETIC NORTH
TRUE NORTH

CANTERBURY SHAKER VILLAGE

0 5 10 15 20 25   50 METERS

CONTOUR INTERVAL 1 METER

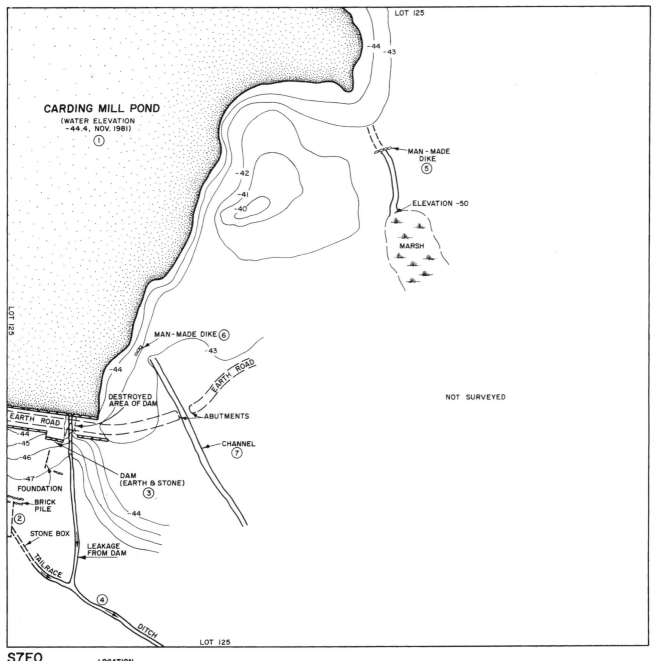

LOT 125

CARDING MILL POND
(WATER ELEVATION
-44.4, NOV. 1981)
①

-44
-43

-42
-41
-40

MAN-MADE
DIKE
⑤

ELEVATION -50

MARSH

MAN-MADE DIKE ⑥

-43

EARTH ROAD

-44

DESTROYED
AREA OF DAM

NOT SURVEYED

ABUTMENTS

EARTH ROAD

CHANNEL
⑦

-44
-45
-46

-47
FOUNDATION

DAM
(EARTH & STONE)
③

BRICK
PILE

②

STONE BOX

-44

LEAKAGE
FROM DAM

TAILRACE

④

DITCH

LOT 125

LOT 125

S7EO

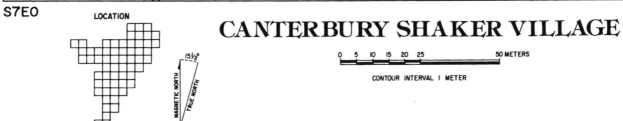

LOCATION

MAGNETIC NORTH   TRUE NORTH
15½°

CANTERBURY SHAKER VILLAGE

0 5 10 15 20 25   50 METERS

CONTOUR INTERVAL 1 METER

Further Reading

Primary Sources

Blinn, Henry C. "Church Record, 1784–1879." MS 764, Collections of Canterbury Shaker Village, Canterbury, N.H., n.d.

———. "A Historical Record of the Society of Believers in Canterbury, N.H., from the Time of its Organization in 1792 till the year one thousand eight hundred and forty eight." MS 763, Collections of Canterbury Shaker Village, Canterbury, N.H., n.d.

Briggs, Nicholas A. "Forty Years a Shaker." *The Granite Monthly* 52 (December 1920): 463–474; 53 (January, February, March 1921): 19–32, 56–65, 113–121.

Clark, Edith. "Notes of Brother Irving Greenwood's History of the Canterbury Buildings." Collections of Canterbury Shaker Village, Canterbury, N.H., n.d.

Evans, Jessie, et al. "Family Journal or Current Events, Compiled and Transcribed By Jessie Evans, et al., from 1901 to . . . Church Family, East Canterbury, N.H." MS 34, Collections of Canterbury Shaker Village, Canterbury, N.H., 1901–1931.

Evans, Sister Jessie. *The Story of Shakerism by One Who Knows.* East Canterbury, N.H.: Canterbury Shakers, 1907.

Frost, Marguerite. "Notebook of Buildings." Collections of Canterbury Shaker Village, Canterbury, N.H., n.d.

———. *The Shaker Story.* Canterbury, N.H.: Canterbury Shakers, n.d.

Greenwood, Irving. "Notebook of Information on Machinery, Buildings, Equipment, Property, etc." MS 28, Collections of Canterbury Shaker Village, Canterbury, N.H., n.d.

Hill, Isaac. "The Shakers." *The Farmer's Monthly Visitor* 2, no. 8 (August 31, 1840): 113–118.

"Historical Record of the Church Family, East Canterbury, N.H. Compiled by the Brethren for Special Reference. 1890–1930." MS 33, Collections of Canterbury Shaker Village, Canterbury, N.H., n.d.

Lindsay, Bertha. "Transcript of Tape Cassette No. 1." Collections of Canterbury Shaker Village, Canterbury, N.H., 1978.

Whitcher, John. "A Brief History or Record of the Commencement & Progress of the United Society of Believers, at Canterbury. County of Merrimack. And. State of New Hampshire." MS 21, Collections of Canterbury Shaker Village, Canterbury, N.H., n.d.

Winkley, Francis, and anonymous contributors. "Journal, Canterbury, N.H., 1784–1845." MS 25, Collections of Canterbury Shaker Village, Canterbury, N.H.

Secondary Sources

Andrews, Edward Deming. *The Community Industries of the Shakers.* Albany, N.Y.: New York State Museum Handbook, no. 15, 1933.

———. *The People Called Shakers: A Search for the Perfect Society.* New York: Oxford University Press, 1954; reprint, New York: Dover Publications, 1963.

Andrews, Edward Deming, and Faith Andrews. *Religion in Wood: A Book of Shaker Furniture.* Bloomington: Indiana University Press, 1966.

Barry, Ellen. "Shaking up Shaker Myths at N.H.'s Canterbury Village." *Boston Sunday Globe*, April 23, 2000: B1, B3.

Borges, Richard C. "The Canterbury Shakers: A Demographic Study." Durham: The University of New Hampshire, Ph.D. dissertation, 1988.

Boucher, Roland R. "The Shakers in New Hampshire." Durham: The University of New Hampshire, M.A. thesis, 1947.

Brewer, Priscilla J. *Shaker Communities, Shaker Lives.* Hanover, N.H.: University Press of New England, 1986.

Campion, Nardi Reeder. *Mother Ann Lee: Morning Star of the Shakers.* Hanover, N.H.: University Press of New England, 1990.

Chagnon, Napoleon. *Yanomamo: The Fierce People.* Fourth Edition. New York: Holt, Rinehart & Winston, 1992.

Clark, Tim. "Shattering the Shaker Image." *Yankee* (May 1980): 80–85, 130–135, 138–139, 141.

Collins, Jim. "Shakers Awakening." *Yankee* (May 1999): 68–78, 124, 126.

Cranmer, Leon. "The Shaker Community at Sabbathday Lake." Paper presented at the Annual Meeting of the Society for Historical Archaeology, Quebec City, Quebec, 2000.

Emlen, Robert P. *Shaker Village Views: Illustrated Maps and Landscape Drawings by Shaker Artists of the Nineteenth Century.* Hanover, N.H.: University Press of New England, 1987.

Falk, Robert J. "Investigations at the Hancock Shaker Woolen Factory, Hancock, Massachusetts." MS paper, Rensselaer Polytechnic Institute, Troy, N.Y., 1985.

Harper, Karen. *Shaker Run.* Don Mills, Ontario: Mira Books, 2001.

Hubbard, Phyl. Letter to the editors. *Discover* 21, no. 7 (2000): 15.

Janzen, Donald E. *The Shaker Mills on Shawnee Run: Historical Archaeology at Shakertown at Pleasant Hill.* Harrodsburg, Ky.: Pleasant Hill Press, 1981.

Jung, S. Paul, Jr. *John Taber and John Taber Jr.: Two New England Clay Tobacco Pipemakers.* Bel Air, Md.: Privately published, 1996.

Keatley, Jeffrey Owen. "The Search for the Shaker Slaughterhouse: Excavations at Hancock Shaker Village, Hancock, Massachusetts, 1984." MS paper, Rensselaer Polytechnic Institute, Troy, N.Y., 1986.

Leone, Mark P. "The Relationship between Artifacts and the Public in Outdoor History Museums." *Annals of the New York Academy of Sciences* 376 (1981): 301–313.

Light, John D. "The Archeological Investigation of Blacksmith Shops." *IA, The Journal of the Society for Industrial Archeology* 10, no. 1 (1984): 55–68.

Light, John D., and Henry Unglik. *A Frontier Fur Trade Blacksmith Shop, 1796–1812.* Studies in Archaeology, Architecture, and History. Ottawa: Parks Canada, 1984.

Lindsay, Eldress Bertha. *Seasoned with Grace: My Generation of Shaker Cooking.* Edited by Mary Rose Boswell. Woodstock, Vt.: The Countryman Press, 1987.

Lyford, James Otis. *History of the Town of Canterbury, New Hampshire, 1727–1912.* Reprint, Canterbury, N.H.: The Rumford Press, 1973.

McBride, Kim A. "Holy Sinai's Plain: Rediscovery and Restoration of an Outdoor Worship Area at the Pleasant Hill, Kentucky, Shaker Village." Paper presented at the Annual Meeting of the Society for Historical Archaeology, Quebec City, Quebec, 2000.

Melcher, Marguerite F. *The Shaker Adventure.* Old Chatham, N.Y.: The Shaker Museum, 1986.

Neal, Julia. *By Their Fruits: The Story of Shakerism in South Union, Kentucky.* Chapel Hill: The University of North Carolina Press, 1947.

Nordhoff, Charles. *The Communistic Societies of the United States from Personal Observations.* New York: Harper & Brothers, Publishers, 1875; reprint, New York: Dover Publications, 1966.

O'Brien, Marcy. "A Simple Wish." *Yankee* (May 2001): 80–85, 124, 126.

Powell, Eric. "Shakers Behaving Badly." *Discover* 21, no. 5 (2000): 20.

Robinson, Charles Edson. *The Shakers and Their Homes.* Canterbury, N.H.: Shaker Village, 1893; reprint: Somersworth, N.H.: New Hampshire Publishing Company, 1976.

Sprigg, June. *By Shaker Hands.* Hanover, N.H.: University Press of New England, 1975, 1990.

———. *Simple Gifts: A Memoir of a Shaker Village.* New York: Alfred A. Knopf, 1998.

Starbuck, David R. *Canterbury Shaker Village: An Historical Survey, Volume 2.* Durham: University of New Hampshire, 1981.

———. "The Shaker Concept of Household." *Man in the Northeast* 28 (1984): 73–86.

———. "The Shaker Mills in Canterbury, New Hampshire." *IA, The Journal of the Society for Industrial Archeology* 12, no. 1 (1986): 11–38.

———. "Documenting the Canterbury Shakers." *Historical New Hampshire* 43, no. 1 (1988): 1–20.

———. "Canterbury Shaker Village: Archeology and Landscape." *The New Hampshire Archeologist* 31, no. 1 (1990): 1–163.

———. "Those Ingenious Shakers!" *Archaeology* 43, no. 4 (1990): 40–47.

———. "Recent Excavations at Canterbury Shaker Village." *The New Hampshire Archeologist* 37, no. 1 (1997): 9–27.

———. "New Perspectives on Shaker Life." *Expedition* 40, no. 3 (1998): 3–16.

———. "Latter-Day Shakers." *Archaeology* 52, no. 1 (1999): 28–29.

———. Letter to the editors. *Discover* 21, no. 7 (2000): 15.

———. "Waiting for the Second Coming: The Canterbury Shakers, an Archaeological Perspective on Blacksmithing and Pipe Smoking." *Northeast Historical Archaeology* 29 (2000): 83–106.

Starbuck, David R., and Margaret Supplee Smith, eds. *Historical Survey of Canterbury Shaker Village.* Boston: Boston University, 1979.

Starbuck, David R., and Scott T. Swank. *A Shaker Family Album: Photographs from the Collection of Canterbury Shaker Village.* Hanover, N.H.: University Press of New England, 1998.

Stein, Stephen J. *The Shaker Experience in America: A History of the United Society of Believers*. New Haven, Conn.: Yale University Press, 1992.

Swank, Scott T. *Shaker Life, Art, and Architecture*. New York: Abbeville Press, 1999.

Vaillancourt, Dana R. "Archaeological Excavations at the North Family Dwelling House Site, Hancock Shaker Village, Town of Hancock, Berkshire County, Massachusetts." MS paper, Rensselaer Polytechnic Institute, Troy, N.Y., 1983.

White, Anna, and Leila S. Taylor. *Shakerism: Its Meaning and Message*. Columbus, Ohio: Press of Fred J. Heer, 1904.

Whitson, Robley Edward. *The Shakers: Two Centuries of Spiritual Reflection*. New York: Paulist Press, 1983.

Wiegand, Ernest A. "The Archaeology of Decline and Abandonment at the North Family Site, Mount Lebanon Shaker Village, New Lebanon, New York." Paper presented at the Annual Meeting of the Society for Historical Archaeology, Kingston, Jamaica, 1992.

———. "Conformity or Deviance: Shaker and Non-Shaker Behavior at Mount Lebanon Shaker Village." Paper presented at the Annual Meeting of the Society for Historical Archaeology, Quebec City, Quebec, 2000.

Weintraub, Boris. "New Window on Shaker Life." *National Geographic* 196, no. 2 (1999): Geographica.

Wolkomir, Richard, and Joyce Wolkomir. "Living a Tradition." *Smithsonian* 32, no. 1 (2001): 98–108.

Zitzler, Paula A. "Waterpower at Hancock Shaker Village: A Study in Industrial Archaeology." MS paper, Rensselaer Polytechnic Institute, Troy, N.Y., 1985.

Index

Alcohol: 16, 45–46, 48, 61, 63, 64, 66, 85; beer or ginger beer, 9–10, 46, 48, 51, 52, 58, 59, 62, 64–65, 67; whiskey, 9, 10, 51, 52, 58, 59, 62, 64–65, 67; wine, 10, 46, 52, 55, 61, 64–66, 67, 83, 86, 107
Andrews, Edward and Faith, 15, 46
Arboretum, 112
Asby Road, 118, 120
Auchmoody, Jack, vii, 3
Automobiles, 46, 47, 85, 109, 110

Barns: Church Family cow barn, viii, 9–10, 19, 49, 52, 64–66, 102, 112, 113; Church Family garden barn, 9, 49, 50–51, 53, 113; Church Family ministry barn, 116; Church Family ministry horse barn, 104; Hancock Shaker Village round barn, 6; North Family cow barn, 94; North Family horse barn, 93; Second Family horse barn, 102, 103
Beck, Henry, 121
Bee house, Church Family, 49, 50–51, 53, 113
Beer. See Alcohol
Blacksmith shop: Church Family, viii, 10, 68, 71, 76–84, 105; North Family, 94; Second Family, 9, 68–75, 77, 82, 83, 84
Blacksmith shop field, 105
Blinn, Elder Henry, 19, 20, 34, 41, 43, 49, 55, 66, 70, 71, 76, 78, 93, 94, 96, 97, 98, 99, 100, 101, 102, 105, 106, 110, 111, 112, 114, 116, 119, 121
Borges, Richard, vii, 7
Bottles, 6, 9, 51, 52, 53, 55, 56, 59, 61, 62, 64, 65, 66, 67, 78, 83
Boys' Island, 117
Brethren's shop: Church Family, 76, 105; North Family, 94; Second Family, 101
Bricks, 19, 53, 54, 56, 77, 93, 97, 98, 100, 101, 103, 105
Bridges, 22, 24, 28, 92
Bruce, Elder Arthur, ix, 20, 21, 24, 46

Cameras, 46
Canning jars, 51, 63

Carding Mill Pond, 24–26, 28, 33, 42–43, 120–121
Carpenter shop, Church Family, 110–111
Carriage house, Church Family, 107
Carriage shed, Church Family, 104
Cart shed, Church Family, 49, 111
Cattle, x, 6, 16, 17, 41, 118
Cemetery, 102
Ceramics: creamware, 52, 82, 84, 93; delft or tin-glazed earthenware, 52, 57, 58, 64; pearlware, 52, 82, 84, 93; porcelain, 52, 59, 80; redware, 51, 52, 59, 75, 78, 82, 84, 93; Rockingham decoration, 52, 57, 58; stoneware, 10, 52, 56, 58, 59, 64, 65, 66, 75, 82, 84; transfer print decoration, 64, 82; whiteware, 6, 10, 51, 52, 55, 58, 59, 60, 64, 75, 78, 84, 93; yellowware, 55, 58, 59
Chagnon, Napoleon, 4
Chauncey, Israel, 16
Children's house, Church Family, 105, 110
Cider, 10, 45, 83, 101, 103, 107
Cisterns, 39, 93, 103
Clark, Sister Edith, iv, 77
Coe, Michael, 5
Combs, 57
Cooley, Ebenezer, 16
Corbett, Thomas, 113
Cows. See Cattle
Cranmer, Leon, 5
Creamery, Church Family, 104, 108

Dams, 6, 22–44, 91–93, 95, 97–99, 101–102, 113, 115–118, 120–121
Dentures, 10, 52, 66
Dolls, 6, 52
Dorothy Shaker Cloak, 20
Drying house, Church Family, 49
Dumps, 5, 6, 7, 9, 10, 20, 45–67, 68, 73, 75, 78–84, 85, 87, 91, 112
Durgin, Eldress Dorothy, 20
Dwelling house: Church Family, ix, 4, 7, 17, 18, 58, 106, 108, 111; Hancock Shaker Vil-

lage, 6; North Family, 98; Second Family, 100; West Family, 94

East Pond, 22, 24, 38, 92–93
Electricity, 25, 40, 109–110, 115, 117
Enfield House, Church Family, 101, 106, 107
Enfield (N.H.) Shaker Village, ix, 107

Factory Pond, 24–25, 28–29, 32, 38–39, 43–44, 97, 103, 113–115, 117
False teeth. See Dentures
Fancywork, 9, 17
Father Matthew, 59
Feast Ground. See Holy Ground
Firehouse, Church Family, 110
Fort St. Joseph Blacksmith Shop, 68
Fountain Pond, 24, 31, 35, 38, 99, 101–102
Freewill Baptist, 17, 20
Frost, Sister Marguerite, iv, 15

Ginger beer. See Alcohol
Gravestones. See Tombstones
Greenwood, Brother Irving, x, 20, 21, 35, 43, 44, 46, 48, 49, 76, 92, 94, 95, 96, 97, 103, 112, 113

Hack, Shery, vii, 64
Hancock Shaker Village, 5, 6, 14
Hawthorne, Nathaniel, ix
Headrace, 118–119
Hill, Isaac, 22, 24, 35, 38, 39, 40, 41, 42, 53, 94, 95, 100, 102, 104, 114, 117, 118, 120, 121
Hired men, 20, 48, 49, 53, 54, 61, 64, 67, 85, 104, 110, 121
Hired men's shop, Church Family, 48, 54, 57, 64, 104, 105
Historic American Buildings Survey (HABS), 7
"Hog Heaven," viii, 9, 52, 53–64, 87, 104
Hog house. See "Hog Heaven"
Holy Ground, 96–97
Horse mill, Church Family, 53, 104
Horse stand. See Carriage shed

Horses, 46, 85, 104, 105, 116, 118
Hubbard Visitor Education Center, 103, 104, 105
Hudson, Sister Ethel, vii, x, 4, 7, 45, 102, 106

Ice Mill Pond. *See* Factory Pond
Icehouse, 25, 39, 103, 115
Infirmary: Church Family, 17, 61, 76, 107; North Family, 94
Ingall's Dam, 117–118
Intermodal Surface Transportation Enhancement Act (ISTEA), 9

Janzen, Donald, 5
Johnson, Moses, ix, 17, 115

Keatley, Jeffrey Owen, 6

Laundry: Church Family, 17, 105, 108–109; North Family, 94, 98; Second Family, 99, 100
Lead Ministry, ix, x, 14, 20, 21, 103
Lee, Mother Ann, ix, 3, 13, 20, 46, 86
Leone, Mark, 5
Light, John, 68
Lindsay, Eldress Bertha, vii, x, 4, 7, 15, 21, 46, 66, 68, 77, 95, 97, 98, 103, 104, 105, 113, 115, 116, 117, 118
"Long Ditch," 8, 22, 24, 28, 31, 42, 44, 92, 113
Lyford Pond, 22, 24, 29, 92

McBride, Kim, 5
McClintock, John, 42, 119
Meadow Brook, 25, 36, 97, 98
Meadow Pond, 97, 98, 99, 105
Meetinghouse, Church Family, 7, 17, 18, 86, 115–116
Meeting House Field, 115, 116
Meeting House Lane, 92, 116
Millennial Laws, ix, 45, 55, 75, 85, 87, 104
Mills: carding mill, 6, 22, 25, 42, 105, 120, 121; clothiers' mill, 25, 39, 103, 114; fulling mill, 25, 38, 103, 115; gristmill, 22, 25, 34, 41, 53, 105, 118; pump mill, 25, 39, 40, 41, 103, 113, 114; sawmill, 6, 22, 25, 29, 31, 34, 35, 36, 41, 42, 43, 44, 53, 95, 97, 105, 117, 118, 120; threshing mill, 25, 38, 39, 103, 114–115; turning mill, 22, 25, 29, 31, 34, 35, 36, 39, 40, 53, 95, 115, 117, 120; wood mill, 25, 28, 29, 34, 38, 39, 43, 44, 95, 103, 114–115
Ministry shop, Church Family, 116
Mother Ann. *See* Lee, Mother Ann
Motorboats, 46
Mount Lebanon. *See* New Lebanon Shaker Village
Music, iv, 15, 20, 106

New Gloucester. *See* Sabbathday Lake Shaker Village

New Lebanon Shaker Village, ix, 5, 46, 74, 106, 115, 121
New Pond, 24, 29, 92
Niskeyuna. *See* Watervliet Shaker Village
North Barn Field, 49, 102, 103
North Family Pond, 8, 24–25, 28, 31, 34–35, 92, 95
North Shop, Church Family, 108

Orchards, 7, 16, 17, 20, 39, 91, 94, 95, 96, 99, 100, 103, 105, 113, 115, 116, 117
Overflows. *See* Spillways
Ox pasture, 115, 118
Ox shed, 76, 77, 82

Parent Ministry. *See* Lead Ministry
Parker, Brother David, ix, 103
Patent medicine, 17, 51, 53, 56, 61, 62, 63, 64, 83
Penn, Theodore, 38
Penstock, 25, 28, 29, 35, 38, 39, 42, 95, 114, 115, 117, 118, 120
Perfume, 9, 10, 51, 52, 62, 64, 66, 67
"Pickle Establishment," North Family, 94
Pigs, 6, 45, 53, 55, 56, 63, 85, 93, 104
"Pleasant Grove." *See* Holy Ground
Pleasant Hill Shaker Village, 5
"Point Comfort," 46
Porcelain. *See* Ceramics
Pork. *See* Pigs
Pottery. *See* Ceramics
Powerhouse, Church Family, 109–110
Privy, 56, 116
Pump house, Church Family, 117

Radios, 48
Rukeyser, Louis, 7

Sabbathday Lake Shaker Village, x, 5, 14
Sacred Roll, ix
Sanborn, Israel, ix
Saratoga Congress Water, 52, 62, 63
Sarle, Sister Cora Helena, 109
Sawmill Field, 120
Sawmill Pond, 24, 25, 30, 32, 34, 40–44, 117–120
Saxophones, ii, iv
Schoolhouse, Church Family, 7, 10, 17, 111
Seed industry, ix, 6, 17, 49, 69, 105, 107, 112, 113
Shaker Manifesto, ix, 20
Shaker Road, 102, 104, 115, 118
Shakertown. *See* Pleasant Hill Shaker Village
Shoes, 53, 54, 56, 57, 63, 77, 80
Sisters' shop: Church Family, 105–106; North Family, 94, 98–99; Second Family, 70, 100
Slaughterhouse: Church Family, 53; Hancock Shaker Village, 5, 6
Sluice gate, 28, 29, 39, 114
Smith, Roland, viii, 56

Soapstone, 57, 78, 83, 84
Soule, Eldress Gertrude, vii, x, 4, 7, 21, 45, 86, 104
Spillways, 25–28, 30, 35–37, 39, 40, 42, 43, 92, 95, 97, 98, 115, 117–118, 120, 121
Steel garage, Church Family, 109
Stein, Stephen, 46
Stevens, Levi, 43
Swank, Scott T., vii, 48
Syrup shop, Church Family, 63, 108, 109

Taber, John, 74
Tailraces, 25, 44, 120
Tan House Field, 113
Tannery, Church Family, 25, 38, 113
Temperance, 59
Teotihuacan Mapping Project, 91
Tibbets Brook, 92
Tombstones, 84, 102
Tobacco, 9, 16, 45, 46, 68, 74–75, 82, 85, 100
Tobacco pipes, 9, 10, 11, 46, 52, 55, 72–75, 78, 82, 83–84, 93, 97, 99
Trash racks, 25, 28, 29, 39, 41, 113, 114
Trustees' office: Church Family, 3–4, 14, 17, 19, 20, 53, 54, 56, 76, 102, 103, 104, 105, 113, 115; North Family, 98; Second Family, 100–101, 106
Tucker, Micajah, 118
Turbines, 6, 22, 29, 38–39, 41, 114–115, 117, 119, 120
Turning Mill Pond, 23–27, 30, 32, 34, 39–40, 42, 44, 113, 115–120

Unglik, Henry, 68

Van Hazinga, Emily, vii, 7
Vegetable garden, Church Family, 112–113, 116

Wall Street Week in Review, 7
Wardley, James and Jane, ix, 13
Watering trough, Church Family, 118
Watervliet Shaker Village, ix, 3, 13, 46, 74
Waterwheel, 25, 40, 43, 44, 114, 117, 118, 121
Wells, 53, 93, 94, 98, 102, 104, 108, 121
Wells, Mildred, 40
West Barn Field, 102
Wheel pit, 25, 28, 29, 35, 38, 40, 42, 44, 95, 114, 115, 116, 117, 120, 121
Whiskey. *See* Alcohol
Whitcher, Benjamin, ix, 16, 109, 115
Whittaker, Father James, ix
Wiegand, Ernest, 5
Wiggin, Chase, ix, 105
Wilson, Elder Delmer, x, 14
Wilson, Linda Ray, 3
Wine. *See* Alcohol
Winkley, Brother Francis, 41, 92, 93, 109, 113, 116, 118, 120
Wood shed, Church Family, 111, 115